Prentice Hall

GRAMMAR HANDBOOK

Grade 10

PEARSON

Upper Saddle River, New Jersey
Boston, Massachusetts
Chandler, Arizona
Glenview, Illinois

Prentice Hall Grammar Handbook Consulting Author

We wish to thank Jeff Anderson who guided the pedagogical approach to grammar instruction utilized in this handbook.

Grateful acknowledgment is made to the following for copyrighted material:

Longman Publishing Group, A Division of Pearson Education, Inc.

"Writing in a Second Language" from *Writing: A Guide for College and Beyond (2nd Edition)* by Lester Faigley. Copyright © 2010 by Pearson Education, Inc.

Edna St. Vincent Millay Society

"Conscientious Objector" by Edna St. Vincent Millay. From *Collected Poems,* HarperCollins. Copyright © 1934, 1962 by Edna St. Vincent Millay and Norma Millay Ellis. All rights reserved.

Note: Every effort has been made to locate the copyright owner of material reproduced in this component. Omissions brought to our attention will be corrected in subsequent editions.

Credits

Cover

Photos provided by istockphoto.com

Illustrations

Martin Haake

Photographs

All interior photos provided by Shutterstock, Inc.

ISBN-13: 978-0-13-363843-1
ISBN-10: 0-13-363843-X
6 7 8 9 10 V054 15 14 13 12

GRAMMAR

USAGE

CONTENTS

MECHANICS

CONTENTS

Numbered tags like this **EL1** are used on instruction pages of the
Grammar Handbook to indicate where to find a related tip in the
English Learner's Resource.

CHAPTER 1

THE PARTS *of* SPEECH

Use each part of speech to its best advantage to help you craft clear sentences.

WRITE GUY *Jeff Anderson, M.Ed.*

WHAT DO YOU NOTICE?

Track down parts of speech as you zoom in on these sentences from "Swimming to Antarctica: Tales of a Long-Distance Swimmer" by Lynne Cox.

MENTOR TEXT

> He and all the crew were watching me intently, their faces filled with tension and concern.
> I put my head down, and something suddenly clicked.

Now, ask yourself the following questions:

- Which nouns are concrete, and which are abstract?
- Which part of speech are the words *intently* and *suddenly*, and what words do they modify?

The concrete nouns, which can be perceived using one of the senses, are *crew*, *faces*, and *head*. *Tension* and *concern* are the abstract nouns; they name concepts that cannot be directly perceived with the senses. The words *intently* and *suddenly* are adverbs. *Intently* modifies the verb *were watching*, and *suddenly* modifies *clicked*.

Grammar for Writers When writers master how to use parts of speech, they have tools for crafting excellent writing. Increase your writing tools by learning why each part of speech is important.

I'd like to see your list of abstract nouns.

Is it okay that the paper it's on is *concrete*?

1

1.1 Nouns and Pronouns

Nouns and pronouns make it possible for people to label everything around them.

Nouns

The word *noun* comes from the Latin word *nomen*, which means "name."

> **A noun is the part of speech that names a person, place, thing, or idea.**

Nouns that name a *person* or *place* are easy to identify.

PERSON	Uncle Mike, neighbor, girls, Bob, swimmer, Ms. Yang, Captain Smith
PLACE	library, Dallas, garden, city, kitchen, James River, canyon, Oklahoma

The category *thing* includes visible things, ideas, actions, conditions, and qualities.

VISIBLE THINGS	chair, pencil, school, duck, daffodil, fort
IDEAS	independence, democracy, militarism, capitalism, recession, freedom
ACTIONS	work, research, exploration, competition, exercise, labor
CONDITIONS	sadness, illness, excitement, joy, health, happiness
QUALITIES	kindness, patience, ability, compassion, intelligence, drive

Concrete and Abstract Nouns

Nouns can also be grouped as *concrete* or *abstract*. A **concrete noun** names something you can see, touch, taste, hear, or smell. An **abstract noun** names something you cannot perceive through any of your five senses.

CONCRETE NOUNS	person, cannon, road, city, music
ABSTRACT NOUNS	hope, improvement, independence, desperation, cooperation

See Practice 1.1A

Collective Nouns

A **collective noun** names a *group* of people or things. A collective noun looks singular, but its meaning may be singular or plural, depending on how it is used in a sentence.

COLLECTIVE NOUNS			
army	choir	troop	faculty
cast	class	crew	legislature

Do not confuse collective nouns—nouns that name a collection of people or things acting as a unit—with plural nouns.

Compound Nouns

A **compound noun** is a noun made up of two or more words acting as a single unit. Compound nouns may be written as separate words, hyphenated words, or combined words.

COMPOUND NOUNS	
Separate	life preserver coffee table bird dog
Hyphenated	sergeant-at-arms self-rule daughter-in-law
Combined	battlefield dreamland porthole

Check a dictionary if you are not sure how to write a compound noun.

Common and Proper Nouns

Any noun may be categorized as either *common* or *proper*.
A **common noun** names any one of a class of people, places,
or things. A **proper noun** names a specific person, place, or thing.
Proper nouns are capitalized, but common nouns are not.
(See Chapter 10 for rules of capitalization.)

COMMON NOUNS	building, writer, nation, month, leader, place, book, war
PROPER NOUNS	Jones, Virginia, *Leaves of Grass,* Revolutionary War, White House, Mark Twain, France, June

A noun of direct address—the name of a person to whom you
are directly speaking—is always a proper noun, as is a family
title before a name. In the examples below, common nouns are
highlighted in yellow, and proper nouns are highlighted in orange.

COMMON NOUNS	My **dad** is a **doctor**.
	Our **teacher** is never late for class.
	My favorite person is my **aunt**.
DIRECT ADDRESS	Please, **Grandma**, tell us about your trip.
	Dad, can you drop me off?
	Alex, please bring your pasta dish when you come to the party.
FAMILY TITLE	**Aunt Anne** is visiting from **England**.
	Grandma doesn't really cook, but she bakes great muffins.
	My favorite person is **Aunt Krissy**.

See Practice 1.1B

PRACTICE 1.1A ▶ **Identifying and Labeling Nouns as Concrete or Abstract**

Read each sentence. Then, write the nouns in each sentence, and label them *concrete* or *abstract*.

EXAMPLE   Stacy overcame her fears.

ANSWER   *Stacy* — concrete
fears — abstract

1. The climbers' main concern was time.
2. Noah was hoping for a major promotion.
3. Thomas often thought about his adolescence.
4. My neighbor shows much compassion for his dog.
5. The sprinter has natural talent and agility.
6. Did the owner expand his business?
7. Success is something that drives Neil.
8. A positive outlook is something that separates Ameera from most people.
9. The fisherman came back with nothing to show for his effort.
10. I gave Terry my advice: search the Internet.

PRACTICE 1.1B ▶ **Recognizing Kinds of Nouns (Collective, Compound, Proper)**

Read each sentence. Then, write whether the underlined nouns are *collective*, *compound*, or *proper*. Answer in the order the words appear.

EXAMPLE   Did you lend your <u>suitcase</u> to <u>Louise</u>?

ANSWER   *compound, proper*

11. Next semester, our <u>class</u> will be traveling to <u>Utah</u>.
12. Toward the end of the close game, it appeared our <u>team</u> would be the winners.
13. My <u>brother-in-law</u> is moving out of the state.
14. The chef has opened a <u>takeout</u> restaurant called <u>Good Eatin'</u>.
15. The <u>caravan</u> can accommodate many passengers.
16. My cousin, <u>Santos</u>, is a senior at the high school.
17. This book is a biography about a man who spoke for the poor <u>minority</u>.
18. I hope my uncle will visit our <u>family</u> this weekend.
19. We visited a <u>battlefield</u> in <u>Virginia</u> last summer.
20. During this time of year, you can get pecans from <u>Texas</u>.

SPEAKING APPLICATION

With a partner, take turns describing a scene from a movie that you create. The scene must contain three abstract nouns and three concrete nouns. Your partner should listen for and name the specific nouns.

WRITING APPLICATION

Using sentence 11 as your first sentence, write a brief fictional paragraph describing the trip. Be sure to include common, collective, compound, and proper nouns.

Pronouns

Pronouns help writers and speakers avoid awkward repetition of nouns.

RULE

1.1.2

> **Pronouns** are words that stand for nouns or for words that take the place of nouns.

Antecedents of Pronouns Pronouns get their meaning from the words they stand for. These words are called **antecedents.**

RULE

1.1.3

> **Antecedents** are nouns or words that take the place of nouns to which pronouns refer.

The arrows point from pronouns to their antecedents.

EXAMPLES   **Heather** said **she** lost **her** ring at the concert.

When the **Halperns** moved, **they** gave **their** dog to me.

Attending the state seminar is tiring, but **it** is fun!

Antecedents do not always appear before their pronouns, however. Sometimes an antecedent follows its pronoun.

EXAMPLE   Because of **its** food, **Houston** , Texas, is my favorite city.

There are several kinds of pronouns. Most of them have specific antecedents, but a few do not.

See Practice 1.1C

Personal Pronouns The most common pronouns are the **personal pronouns.**

> **Personal pronouns** refer to the person speaking (first person), the person spoken to (second person), or the person, place, or thing spoken about (third person).

1.1.4 RULE

PERSONAL PRONOUNS		
	SINGULAR	PLURAL
First Person	I, me my, mine	we, us our, ours
Second Person	you your, yours	you your, yours
Third Person	he, him, his she, her, hers it, its	they, them their, theirs

In the first example below, the antecedent of the personal pronoun is the person speaking. In the second, the antecedent of the personal pronoun is the person being spoken to. In the last example, the antecedent of the personal pronoun is the thing spoken about.

FIRST
PERSON **My** name is not Heather.

SECOND
PERSON When **you** left, **you** forgot **your** phone.

THIRD
PERSON The quilt is old, but **its** colors are still bright.

Reflexive and Intensive Pronouns These two types of pronouns look the same, but they function differently in sentences.

> A **reflexive pronoun** ends in *-self* or *-selves* and indicates that someone or something in the sentence acts for or on itself. A reflexive pronoun is essential to the meaning of a sentence. An **intensive pronoun** ends in *-self* or *-selves* and simply adds emphasis to a noun or pronoun in the sentence.

1.1.5 RULE

REFLEXIVE AND INTENSIVE PRONOUNS		
	SINGULAR	PLURAL
First Person	myself	ourselves
Second Person	yourself	yourselves
Third Person	himself, herself, itself	themselves

REFLEXIVE   The family prepared **themselves** for the upcoming
vacation.

INTENSIVE   George McDoogle **himself** wrote an account of
the conspiracy.

See Practice 1.1D

Reciprocal Pronouns **Reciprocal pronouns** show a mutual action
or relationship.

RULE 1.1.6

> The **reciprocal pronouns** *each other* and *one another*
> refer to a plural antecedent. They express a mutual action or
> relationship.

EXAMPLES   The two children sprayed water all over **each other** .
The children shared water balloons with
one another .

See Practice 1.1E

Demonstrative Pronouns **Demonstrative pronouns** are used to
point out one or more nouns.

RULE 1.1.7

> A **demonstrative pronoun** directs attention to a specific
> person, place, or thing.

There are four demonstrative pronouns.

DEMONSTRATIVE PRONOUNS	
SINGULAR	PLURAL
this, that	these, those

Demonstrative pronouns may come before or after their antecedents.

BEFORE   **That** is the **house** I would like to live in.

AFTER   I hope to visit **Anita** and **Sonia**. **Those** are my first choices.

One of the demonstrative pronouns, *that*, can also be used as a relative pronoun.

Relative Pronouns

Relative pronouns are used to relate one idea in a sentence to another. There are five relative pronouns.

> A **relative pronoun** introduces an adjective clause and connects it to the word that the clause modifies.

1.1.8 RULE

RELATIVE PRONOUNS				
that	which	who	whom	whose

EXAMPLES   We read a **play** **that** contained an account of the couple's story.

The **couple** **who** had written it described their conflicts.

The **storm**, **which** they knew would be strong, was fast approaching.

See Practice 1.1F

Read each sentence. Then, identify the pronoun and its antecedent in each sentence. If the sentence has no antecedent, write *none*.

EXAMPLE   Steve fell and hurt his foot.

ANSWER   *his, Steve*

1. He is nervous about the tryouts.
2. Taylor went to the putting green to practice his skills.
3. Meena had her van towed to the garage.
4. Mark couldn't understand the math problem until Harry wrote it on the board.
5. I will be happy to pay for lunch.
6. My brother, sometimes, loses his keys.
7. She should ask a teacher for help with the science assignment.
8. Tyra loves advanced science because she gets to dissect frogs.
9. To make an attractive border of roses, plant them close together.
10. After Jeremy painted the portrait, it was hung in the hallway.

Read each sentence. Then, write the pronoun(s) in each sentence and identify it as *personal*, *reflexive*, or *intensive*.

EXAMPLE   Do muffins have fruit inside them?

ANSWER   *them* — personal

11. My favorite talk show changed its host.
12. A number of my classmates read their essays aloud themselves.
13. He made sure the room was locked himself.
14. Between you and me, I am not sure we are going to make it on time.
15. Colleen and she will be math partners.
16. The waiting children amused themselves by drawing on the chalkboard.
17. The sun itself provides energy.
18. We told ourselves that we were going to win the race.
19. My driving all the way across the country worries my family.
20. The lawyer's clients are they.

SPEAKING APPLICATION

Take turns with a partner. Describe a fun situation you have had with a friend. Use pronouns referring to yourselves whenever possible. Your partner should identify the pronouns and their antecedents.

WRITING APPLICATION

Write a brief paragraph describing a visit to a doctor's office. Use at least one reflexive, intensive, and personal pronoun in your paragraph.

PRACTICE 1.1E > **Identifying Reciprocal Pronouns**

Read each sentence. Then, write the reciprocal pronoun in each sentence.

EXAMPLE   The groomsmen toasted one another.

ANSWER   *one another*

1. They talk to one another about pop culture.
2. The two articles definitely contradict each other.
3. Pam and Howard are completely devoted to each other.
4. We certainly missed each other while on vacation.
5. They all said hello to one another.
6. They met each other at the library.
7. Tyrone, Michael, and Keith help one another with their studies.
8. They made plans to visit one another's families during their break.
9. Lance and Gloria did each other's chores.
10. The candidates had mutual respect for each other after the debate.

PRACTICE 1.1F > **Recognizing Demonstrative and Relative Pronouns**

Read each sentence. Then, label the underlined pronoun *demonstrative* or *relative*.

EXAMPLE   The book, <u>which</u> was written by a lawyer, was fascinating.

ANSWER   *relative*

11. <u>That</u> was a filling dinner!
12. Last week, my uncle, <u>who</u> is a doctor, saved a patient's life.
13. <u>This</u> and many other questions can be answered by checking online.
14. Tommy is the guy <u>whose</u> answer is correct.
15. The highway <u>that</u> I take to school is under construction.
16. Malia is the baby <u>whom</u> everyone loves to hold.
17. Might <u>these</u> be the earliest films ever recorded?
18. <u>That</u> might be the strangest dress in the show.
19. Of all the shoes on the rack, <u>these</u> appear to be the best-selling pair.
20. Jason's helmet, <u>which</u> is brand new, is guaranteed not to break.

SPEAKING APPLICATION

Take turns with a partner. Describe an enjoyable weekend you have had. Show that you understand reciprocal pronouns by using some in your response. Your partner should listen for and identify the reciprocal pronouns that you use.

WRITING APPLICATION

Write a brief paragraph, describing the room you are in or the items in it. Include two demonstrative and two relative pronouns in your paragraph.

Interrogative Pronouns

Interrogative pronouns are used to ask questions.

> An **interrogative pronoun** is used to begin a question.

The five interrogative pronouns are *what*, *which*, *who*, *whom*, and *whose*. Sometimes the antecedent of an interrogative pronoun is not known.

EXAMPLE   **Who** picked up the puppy?

See Practice 1.1G

Indefinite Pronouns

Indefinite pronouns sometimes lack specific antecedents.

> An **indefinite pronoun** refers to a person, place, or thing that may or may not be specifically named.

INDEFINITE PRONOUNS				
SINGULAR			PLURAL	BOTH
another	everyone	nothing	both	all
anybody	everything	one	few	any
anyone	little	other	many	more
anything	much	somebody	others	most
each	neither	someone	several	none
either	nobody	something		some
everybody	no one			

Indefinite pronouns sometimes have specific antecedents.

NO SPECIFIC
ANTECEDENT   **Everyone** has visited New York City.

SPECIFIC
ANTECEDENTS   **Most** of the **students** read.

Indefinite pronouns can also function as adjectives.

ADJECTIVE   **Few** teams are as famous as this one.

See Practice 1.1H

PRACTICE 1.1G Recognizing Interrogative Pronouns

Read each sentence. Then, write the correct interrogative pronoun needed for each sentence.

EXAMPLE ＿＿ is your favorite movie?

ANSWER *What*

1. ＿＿ of the houses do you like the best?
2. ＿＿ voice can be heard in the background?
3. ＿＿ gave you the application form to this job?
4. Behind ＿＿ of the walls do you hear the scratching?
5. ＿＿ are you doing after the year is over?
6. Of all the people in the room, ＿＿ can lead you in the right direction?
7. ＿＿ do you think it will take to win the contest?
8. ＿＿ did you think was the best speech?
9. ＿＿ has heard of such horrible behavior?
10. With ＿＿ are you going to the beach?

PRACTICE 1.1H Identifying Indefinite Pronouns

Read each sentence. Then, write the indefinite pronoun in each sentence.

EXAMPLE None of us realized what happened.

ANSWER *None*

11. Everyone in the stands was cheering loudly.
12. Someone had already collected all the tickets.
13. Though there were plenty of people, none of the guests had much to say.
14. Few of the senators would admit that anything had happened.
15. No one could deny that something specific should be accomplished.
16. Several of my teachers advised me that much remained to be done.
17. Many of my friends have opinions about everything.
18. Does either of the teams seem better than the other?
19. Few people live in areas where there is no electricity.
20. Did you get everything for the party?

SPEAKING APPLICATION

With a partner, take turns interviewing each other as if on a talk show. Use interrogative pronouns in all of your questions.

WRITING APPLICATION

Rewrite sentences 11, 12, and 17, replacing all the nouns and indefinite pronouns. Make sure that the sentences still make sense.

1.2 Verbs

Every complete sentence must have at least one **verb**, which may consist of as many as four words.

 1.2.1

A **verb** is a word or group of words that expresses time while showing an action, a condition, or the fact that something exists.

Action Verbs and Linking Verbs

Action verbs express action. They are used to tell what someone or something does, did, or will do. **Linking verbs** express a condition or show that something exists.

 1.2.2

An **action verb** tells what action someone or something is performing.

ACTION
VERBS

Tara **learned** about summer sports.

The television **blared** the broadcast of the new show.

We **chose** two artists from Texas.

I **remember** the film about the Alamo.

The action expressed by a verb does not have to be visible. Words expressing mental activities—such as *learn, think,* or *decide*—are also considered action verbs.

The person or thing that performs the action is called the *subject* of the verb. In the examples above, *Tara, television, we,* and *I* are the subjects of *learned, blared, chose,* and *remember.*

> A **linking verb** is a verb that connects its subject with a noun, pronoun, or adjective that identifies or describes the subject.

LINKING
VERBS

The man **is** a famous actor.

The stage floor **seems** polished.

EL6

The verb *be* is the most common linking verb.

THE FORMS OF *BE*			
am	am being	can be	have been
are	are being	could be	has been
is	is being	may be	had been
was	was being	might be	could have been
were	were being	must be	may have been
		shall be	might have been
		should be	shall have been
		will be	should have been
		would be	will have been
			would have been

Most often, the forms of *be* that function as linking verbs express the condition of the subject. Occasionally, however, they may merely express existence, usually by showing, with other words, where the subject is located.

EXAMPLE   The player **is** on the field.

Other Linking Verbs A few other verbs can also serve as linking verbs.

OTHER LINKING VERBS		
appear	look	sound
become	remain	stay
feel	seem	taste
grow	smell	turn

EXAMPLES

The cut grass **smelled** fresh and clean.

The fans **sound** excited.

The bus driver **stayed** alert.

The conditions on board **remained** dangerous.

The students **grew** nervous.

Some of these verbs may also act as action—not linking—verbs. To determine whether the word is functioning as an action verb or as a linking verb, insert *am*, *are*, or *is* in place of the verb. If the substitute makes sense while connecting two words, then the original verb is a linking verb.

LINKING VERB   The air **felt** warm. (The air **is** warm.)

ACTION VERB   The surfers **felt** the wave crash.

LINKING VERB   The mangos **taste** sweet. (The mangos **are** sweet.)

ACTION VERB   I **taste** the mango.

See Practice 1.2A
See Practice 1.2B

PRACTICE 1.2A > Identifying Action and Linking Verbs

Read each sentence. Then, write the action verb in each sentence.

EXAMPLE   They talked about life on Mars.

ANSWER   *talked*

1. The gardener mowed the thick green lawn.
2. The carpenter sawed the pine boards.
3. The waitress looked at the soggy mess.
4. Ana picked the strawberries in the garden.
5. The frog jumped from one lily pad to another.

Read each sentence. Then, write the linking verb(s) in each sentence.

EXAMPLE   Safety should be your first concern.

ANSWER   *should be*

6. Elaine is often late for appointments.
7. That will be a sufficient amount of time.
8. That strawberry tasted sweet.
9. George W. Bush was the forty-third president.
10. That stranger looks suspicious.

PRACTICE 1.2B > Distinguishing Between Action and Linking Verbs

Read each sentence. Then, write the verb in each sentence and label it *action* or *linking*.

EXAMPLE   The puppy looks hungry.

ANSWER   *looks* — linking

11. In their garden, they grow tomatoes.
12. Do you feel sick?
13. Our furniture looks new.
14. The boy on horseback sounded the alarm.
15. Pedro tapped the piano keys.
16. Your idea sounds very interesting.
17. She grew fond of her new sister.
18. The car looks unsafe for the road.
19. Taste this salad dressing.
20. The coach praised the players for their effort.

SPEAKING APPLICATION

Take turns with a partner. Tell about a game you played with friends recently. Your partner should listen for and name three action verbs.

WRITING APPLICATION

Use *look, feel,* and *taste* in original sentences. First, use the words as action verbs. Then, use the words as linking verbs.

Transitive and Intransitive Verbs

All verbs are either **transitive** or **intransitive,** depending on whether or not they transfer action to another word in a sentence.

A transitive verb directs action toward someone or something named in the same sentence. An **intransitive verb** does not direct action toward anyone or anything named in the same sentence.

The word toward which a transitive verb directs its action is called the *object* of the verb. Intransitive verbs never have objects. You can determine whether a verb has an object by asking *whom* or *what* after the verb.

TRANSITIVE   Cara **read** the book.

(Read what? book)

We **ate** the veggie burger.

(Ate what? veggie burger)

INTRANSITIVE   The choir **practiced** on the stage.

(Practiced what? [no answer])

The teacher **answered** quickly.

(Answered what? [no answer])

Because linking verbs do not express action, they are always intransitive. Most action verbs can be either transitive or intransitive, depending on the sentence. However, some action verbs can only be transitive, and others can only be intransitive.

TRANSITIVE   I **wrote** a letter from Israel.

INTRANSITIVE   The students **wrote** quickly.

See Practice 1.2C

ALWAYS TRANSITIVE	The Bobcats **rival** the Panthers.
ALWAYS INTRANSITIVE	He **winced** at the sound of the horn.

EL5

Verb Phrases

A verb that has more than one word is a **verb phrase.**

> A **verb phrase** consists of a main verb and one or more helping verbs.

1.2.6 RULE

Helping verbs are often called auxiliary verbs. One or more helping verbs may precede the main verb in a verb phrase.

VERB PHRASES

I **will be taking** a tour of the city.

I **should have been watching** the weather report.

All the forms of *be* listed in this chapter can be used as helping verbs. The following verbs can also be helping verbs.

OTHER HELPING VERBS			
do	have	shall	can
does	has	should	could
did	had	will	may
		would	might
			must

A verb phrase is often interrupted by other words in a sentence.

INTERRUPTED VERB PHRASES

I **will** definitely **be taking** a tour of the city next winter.

Should I **take** a tour of the city next winter?

See Practice 1.2D

PRACTICE 1.2C ▷ **Distinguishing Between Transitive and Intransitive Verbs**

Read each sentence. Then, write the action verb in each sentence, and label it *intransitive* or *transitive*.

EXAMPLE   The harpist plucked the shortest string.

ANSWER   *plucked* — transitive

1. The car moved into the parking space easily.
2. The shop sells beautiful floral centerpieces.
3. Please put those cabbages on the counter.
4. The plane finally arrived after a three-hour delay.
5. The bird cage swung from a golden chain.
6. He shuddered with fright during the scary movie.
7. The dog wagged his tail happily.
8. We made lemonade for the picnic.
9. Steak and potatoes sizzled in the pan.
10. The waves crashed upon the shore.

PRACTICE 1.2D ▷ **Recognizing Verb Phrases**

Read each sentence. Then, write the verb phrase in each sentence.

EXAMPLE   Contact lenses are becoming popular.

ANSWER   *are becoming*

11. The sun will have set by seven o'clock.
12. A dolphin was swimming in the water.
13. My car will be fixed at the service station.
14. The woodcutter has been sawing all day.
15. Paul has acted strangely today.
16. Abigail did tell me about the party.
17. He does ride the bus to school each day.
18. Choi could have offered us his help.
19. Rehearsal should have lasted another hour.
20. I have seen better performances.

SPEAKING APPLICATION

Take turns with a partner. Tell about an important event that has occurred in your life. Your partner should identify both the intransitive and transitive verbs in your sentences.

WRITING APPLICATION

Rewrite sentences 14 and 20, keeping the subject but changing the verb phrases.

1.3 Adjectives and Adverbs

Adjectives and **adverbs** are the two parts of speech known as *modifiers*—that is, they slightly change the meaning of other words by adding description or making them more precise.

Adjectives

An **adjective** clarifies the meaning of a noun or pronoun by providing information about its appearance, location, and so on.

> An **adjective** is a word used to describe a noun or pronoun or to give it a more specific meaning.

1.3.1 RULE

An adjective answers one of four questions about a noun or pronoun: *What kind? Which one? How many? How much?*

EXAMPLES   **oak** tree (What kind of tree?)

that house (Which house?)

12 roses (How many roses?)

extensive snowfall (How much snow?)

When an adjective modifies a noun, it usually precedes the noun. Occasionally, the adjective may follow the noun.

EXAMPLES   The realtor was **tactful** about my concerns.

I considered the realtor **tactful**.

An adjective that modifies a pronoun usually follows it. Sometimes, however, the adjective precedes the pronoun as it does in the example on the next page.

AFTER	They were **excited** when they heard the news.

BEFORE	**Excited** about the upcoming vacation, they began to pack.

More than one adjective may modify a single noun or pronoun.

EXAMPLE	We hired a **competent, enthusiastic** coach.

Articles Three common adjectives—*a, an*, and *the*—are known as **articles.** *A* and *an* are called **indefinite articles** because they refer to any one of a class of nouns. *The* refers to a specific noun and, therefore, is called the **definite article.**

INDEFINITE EXAMPLES	DEFINITE EXAMPLES
a daisy	the stem
an orchid	the mask

Remember that *an* is used before a vowel sound; *a* is used before a consonant sound.

EXAMPLES	**a** one-car family (*w* sound)
	a unicorn (*y* sound)
	an honest president (no *h* sound)

See Practice 1.3A

Nouns Used as Adjectives Words that are usually nouns sometimes act as adjectives. In this case, the noun answers the questions *What kind?* or *Which one?* about another noun.

NOUNS USED AS ADJECTIVES	
flower	flower garden
lawn	lawn mower

See Practice 1.3B

Proper Adjectives Adjectives can also be proper. **Proper adjectives** are proper nouns used as adjectives or adjectives formed from proper nouns. They usually begin with capital letters.

PROPER NOUNS	PROPER ADJECTIVES
Monday	Monday morning
San Francisco	San Francisco streets
Europe	European roses
Rome	Roman hyacinth

Compound Adjectives Adjectives can be compound. Most are hyphenated; others are combined or are separate words.

HYPHENATED | **rain-forest** plants

water-soluble pigments

COMBINED | **airborne** pollen

evergreen shrubs

See Practice 1.3C | SEPARATE | **North American** rhododendrons

Pronouns Used as Adjectives Certain pronouns can also function as adjectives. The seven personal pronouns, known as either **possessive adjectives** or **possessive pronouns,** do double duty in a sentence. They act as pronouns because they have antecedents. They also act as adjectives because they modify nouns by answering *Which one?* The other pronouns become adjectives instead of pronouns when they stand before nouns and answer the question *Which one?*

> **A pronoun is used as an adjective if it modifies a noun.**

1.3.2 RULE

Possessive pronouns, demonstrative pronouns, interrogative pronouns, and indefinite pronouns can all function as adjectives when they modify nouns.

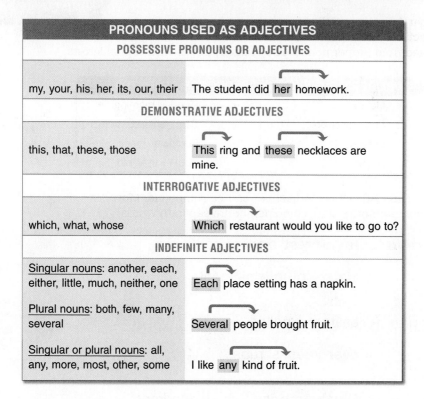

PRONOUNS USED AS ADJECTIVES	
POSSESSIVE PRONOUNS OR ADJECTIVES	
my, your, his, her, its, our, their	The student did her homework.
DEMONSTRATIVE ADJECTIVES	
this, that, these, those	This ring and these necklaces are mine.
INTERROGATIVE ADJECTIVES	
which, what, whose	Which restaurant would you like to go to?
INDEFINITE ADJECTIVES	
<u>Singular nouns</u>: another, each, either, little, much, neither, one	Each place setting has a napkin.
<u>Plural nouns</u>: both, few, many, several	Several people brought fruit.
<u>Singular or plural nouns</u>: all, any, more, most, other, some	I like any kind of fruit.

Verb Forms Used as Adjectives Verb forms used as adjectives usually end in -*ing* or -*ed* and are called **participles.**

EXAMPLE   I threw out the **rotting** fruit.

Nouns, pronouns, and verb forms function as adjectives only when they modify other nouns or pronouns. The following examples show how their function in a sentence can change.

	REGULAR FUNCTION	AS AN ADJECTIVE
Noun	The driveway was very slippery.	I slid on the driveway surface.
Pronoun	This was a joyful event.	This event was joyful.
Verb	The snow finally melted!	The melted snow made a puddle.

See Practice 1.3D

PRACTICE 1.3A ▷ Recognizing Adjectives and Articles

Read each sentence. Then, write the adjective in each sentence.

EXAMPLE   The lonesome howl came from the woods.

ANSWER   *lonesome*

1. There was a major accident on the highway.
2. You have an important medical appointment.
3. There wasn't enough money to pay the bill.
4. A dozen eggs will be enough to make bread.
5. The railing was silvery in the dim shadows.

Read each sentence. Then, write the article(s) in each sentence.

EXAMPLE   The rainy weather turned pleasant.

ANSWER   *The*

6. The timid driver was afraid to drive on the roads.
7. A purple eggplant and a red tomato are in the bowl.
8. An old fence surrounded the vast estate.
9. The bird in the cage is a parrot.
10. The room had dull walls and a dingy rug.

PRACTICE 1.3B ▷ Identifying Nouns Used as Adjectives

Read each sentence. Then, write the noun that is used as an adjective in each sentence and the noun that it modifies.

EXAMPLE   Our class is visiting the state capital next week.

ANSWER   *state, capital*

11. We use the good dishes for our holiday meals.
12. Grandma made a peach cobbler.
13. Fernando glanced at the storm clouds.
14. She wished she had worn her leather gloves.
15. She waited at the bus stop.
16. Eve remembered the card that came with her birthday present.
17. My dad hung the curtain rod yesterday.
18. The television station was having a contest.
19. My office chair was broken.
20. Alan showed me how to fix my bicycle chain.

SPEAKING APPLICATION

Take turns with a partner. Tell about your favorite meal. Use different kinds of adjectives. Your partner should name the adjectives and say if they tell what kind or how many.

WRITING APPLICATION

Write three sentences that contain nouns used as adjectives. Then, exchange papers with a partner and underline the nouns used as adjectives.

| PRACTICE 1.3C | **Recognizing Proper and Compound Adjectives** |

Read each sentence. Then, write the adjective(s) in each sentence, and label each adjective as either *proper* or *compound*.

EXAMPLE   Olivia doesn't like the July heat.

ANSWER   *July* — proper

1. Spencer would like to be an airplane pilot.
2. Celtic music can be heard on the radio.
3. The family enjoys eating in Chinese restaurants.
4. She read another bedtime story to her sister.
5. The concert was held in a downtown park.
6. I know the star of that British science-fiction movie.
7. He tried the Turkish saltwater taffy.
8. The foolishness of their actions was self-evident.
9. We bought a Victorian table for the bedroom.
10. He wore a waterproof Icelandic parka.

| PRACTICE 1.3D | **Recognizing Pronouns and Verbs Used as Adjectives** |

Read each sentence. Then, write the pronoun or verb used as an adjective in each sentence and the noun that it modifies.

EXAMPLE   Dad replaced the shattered windowpane.

ANSWER   *shattered, windowpane*

11. Their baby kept us awake.
12. We moved the fallen branch from the driveway.
13. The freezing rain was the cause of the icy roads.
14. Many students enjoy doing math work.
15. He flipped the sizzling pancake.
16. The departing passengers checked in at the gate.
17. The milk was spilled by the hurrying waiter.
18. The meeting room will be ready on Tuesday.
19. My solar car is powered by the sun's energy.
20. Each contestant hoped to win the grand prize.

SPEAKING APPLICATION

With a partner, name four adjectives that are proper and compound. Then, take turns using each of them in a sentence.

WRITING APPLICATION

Replace the pronouns or verbs used as adjectives in sentences in Practice 1.3D with other pronouns or verbs.

Adverbs

Adverbs, like adjectives, describe other words or make other words more specific.

> **An adverb is a word that modifies a verb, an adjective, or another adverb.**

When an adverb modifies a verb, it will answer any of the following questions: *Where? When? In what way? To what extent?*

An adverb answers only one question when modifying an adjective or another adverb: *To what extent?* Because it specifies the degree or intensity of the modified adjective or adverb, such an adverb is often called an **intensifier.**

The position of an adverb in relation to the word it modifies can vary in a sentence. If the adverb modifies a verb, it may precede or follow it or even interrupt a verb phrase. Normally, adverbs modifying adjectives and adverbs will immediately precede the words they modify.

ADVERBS MODIFYING VERBS	
Where?	**When?**
The vegetables grew outside.	She never cleaned the garden.
The vegetables were planted there.	Later, we toured the gardens.
The rabbit ran away.	The sun shines daily on the garden.
In what way?	**To what extent?**
He efficiently sold the vegetables.	The music was still playing loudly.
She graciously weeded the garden.	He always played the best.
Annie left quickly after the meeting.	Be sure to clean completely before leaving.

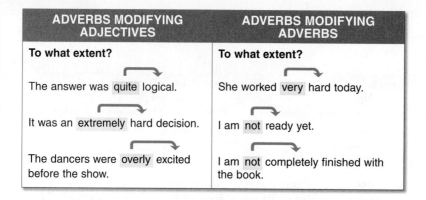

ADVERBS MODIFYING ADJECTIVES	ADVERBS MODIFYING ADVERBS
To what extent?	**To what extent?**
The answer was quite logical.	She worked very hard today.
It was an extremely hard decision.	I am not ready yet.
The dancers were overly excited before the show.	I am not completely finished with the book.

Adverbs as Parts of Verbs Some verbs require an adverb to complete their meaning. Adverbs used this way are considered part of the verb. An adverb functioning as part of a verb does not answer the usual questions for adverbs.

EXAMPLES   The car **backed up** into the other car.

Please **point out** which flower you like best.

Carolyn had to **run out** at lunch to get

a salad.

See Practice 1.3E

Nouns Functioning as Adverbs
Several nouns can function as adverbs that answer the questions *Where?* or *When?* Some of these words are *home, yesterday, today, tomorrow, mornings, afternoons, evenings, nights, week, month,* and *year.*

NOUNS USED AS ADVERBS	
NOUNS	**AS ADVERBS**
Mornings are always rushed.	I run mornings.
My afternoon looks busy.	I work afternoons.
Yesterday was a rainy day.	Peter finished his book yesterday.

Adverb or Adjective?

Adverbs usually have different forms from adjectives and thus are easily identified. Many adverbs are formed by the addition of *-ly* to an adjective.

ADJECTIVES   The teacher looked **proud** .

Jeff ran through the **open** door.

ADVERBS   The teacher looked at her students **proudly** .

The committee discussed the issue **openly** .

Some adjectives, however, also end in *-ly*. Therefore, you cannot assume that every word ending in *-ly* is an adverb.

ADJECTIVES   a **daily** schedule

an **early** lunch

a **ghostly** noise

hilly terrain

Some adjectives and adverbs share the same form. You can determine the part of speech of such words by checking their function in the sentence. An adverb will modify a verb, adjective, or adverb; an adjective will modify a noun or pronoun.

ADVERB   The class ran **late** .

ADJECTIVE   We enjoy playing **late** in the summer.

ADVERB   The girl walked **straight** through the tunnel.

See Practice 1.3F   ADJECTIVE   The road was **straight** .

PRACTICE 1.3E Recognizing Adverbs

Read each sentence. Then, write the adverb or adverbs in each sentence.

EXAMPLE   Ted just recently learned to sail.

ANSWER   *just, recently*

1. Sasha typed quite rapidly.

2. The actors gave a surprisingly good performance.

3. My mom's job suits her very well.

4. He readily accepted the offer.

5. Our hard work and practice made it a truly close contest.

6. Dad leaves for work fairly early.

7. The clothes dried rapidly in the sun.

8. Kevin's secret project is very nearly finished.

9. The workers have almost totally rebuilt the home.

10. Alfredo is an exceptionally talented artist.

PRACTICE 1.3F Identifying Adverbs and the Words They Modify

Read each sentence. Then, write the adverb in each sentence and the word it modifies.

EXAMPLE   We are walking home.

ANSWER   *home, walking*

11. The first session of summer camp starts tomorrow.

12. Because she had to leave, Juanita took the test early.

13. We watched to see who would finish first in the contest.

14. Our new neighbors arrived yesterday from Florida.

15. I ran fast and tried to warn the others.

16. Dad asked me to quickly shut the windows.

17. Because of the snow, we left later than our friends.

18. My dad works nights at the factory.

19. The teacher reminded us that we have only one chance to pass the test.

20. Ping worked hard to finish his project and meet the deadline.

SPEAKING APPLICATION

Take turns with a partner. Tell about something that you enjoy doing. Your partner should name adverbs that you use to describe where, when, in what way, and to what extent you do the activity.

WRITING APPLICATION

Use sentences 13, 16, and 17 as models to write three sentences of your own. Replace the adverbs with other adverbs. Make sure that the sentences still make sense.

1.4 Prepositions, Conjunctions, and Interjections

Prepositions and conjunctions function in sentences as connectors. **Prepositions** express relationships between words or ideas, whereas **conjunctions** join words, groups of words, or even entire sentences. **Interjections** function by themselves and are independent of other words in a sentence.

Prepositions and Prepositional Phrases

Prepositions make it possible to show relationships between words. The relationships may involve, for example, location, direction, time, cause, or possession. A preposition may consist of one word or multiple words. (See the chart on the next page.)

> **A preposition** relates the noun or pronoun that appears with it to another word in the sentence.

RULE 1.4.1

Notice how the prepositions below, highlighted in pink, relate to the words highlighted in yellow.

LOCATION   Vegetables **are grown** **around** the **world** .

TIME   Some stories **last** **for** **generations** .

CAUSE   Joe is **late** **because of** of the **weather** .

> **A prepositional phrase** is a group of words that includes a preposition and a noun or pronoun.

RULE 1.4.2

The noun or pronoun with a preposition is called the **object of the preposition.** Objects may have one or more modifiers. A prepositional phrase may also have more than one object. In the example below, the objects of the prepositions are highlighted in blue, and the prepositions are in pink.

EXAMPLE   Jack and Kara registered **for** **classes** **on** **Friday** .

PREPOSITIONS			
aboard	before	in front of	over
about	behind	in place of	owing to
above	below	in regard to	past
according to	beneath	inside	prior to
across	beside	in spite of	regarding
across from	besides	instead of	round
after	between	into	since
against	beyond	in view of	through
ahead of	but	like	throughout
along	by	near	till
alongside	by means of	nearby	to
along with	concerning	next to	together with
amid	considering	of	toward
among	despite	off	under
apart from	down	on	underneath
around	during	on account of	until
aside from	except	onto	unto
as of	for	on top of	up
as	from	opposite	upon
atop	in	out	with
barring	in addition to	out of	within
because of	in back of	outside	without

See Practice 1.4A

Preposition or Adverb?

Many words may be used either as prepositions or adverbs. Words that can function in either role include *around, before, behind, down, in, off, on, out, over,* and *up.* If an object accompanies the word, the word is used as a preposition.

PREPOSITION   The novel developed **around** a detailed outline.

ADVERB   My plot originally went **around and around**.

See Practice 1.4B

**Identifying Prepositions and
Prepositional Phrases**

Read each sentence. Then, write the
prepositional phrase(s) in each sentence and
underline the preposition(s).

EXAMPLE   I took the kids to the park on Elm
Street.

ANSWER   *to the park; on Elm Street*

1. According to this poster, the block party
starts at noon.

2. There is an empty locker for you next to mine.

3. The teacher announced a contest between
the two classes.

4. We need three cups of blueberries for the pie.

5. A city with a warm climate will be perfect
for us.

6. Nita likes to ride in the front of the plane.

7. The children peered through the glass door.

8. Our neighbor down the street has a
trampoline in his yard.

9. We jumped into the lake with our inflatable
raft.

10. The raccoon was hiding underneath the
porch.

**Distinguishing Between
Prepositions and Adverbs**

Read each sentence. Then, label each underlined
word as a *preposition* or an *adverb*.

EXAMPLE   The house has a basement storage
area and an attic <u>above</u>.

ANSWER   *adverb*

11. Before we went inside, we took our boots <u>off</u>.

12. My mom enjoys moving furniture <u>around</u>.

13. We saw fish swimming just <u>below</u> the
surface of the water.

14. Let's put our bikes <u>inside</u> the garage tonight.

15. To finish making the batter, mix the nuts
evenly <u>throughout</u>.

16. The reporter did not realize that the interview
was <u>off</u> the record.

17. Please do not write anything on the lines
<u>below</u> the shaded box.

18. Dad had to move the barbeque <u>inside</u> when it
started to rain.

19. We built a fence <u>around</u> the yard.

20. The children ride their bikes <u>throughout</u> the
neighborhood.

SPEAKING APPLICATION

With a partner, take turns describing the
locations of objects in the room. Your partner
should listen for and identify the prepositional
phrases that you use and the preposition in
each phrase.

WRITING APPLICATION

Write a sentence using the word *behind* as
a preposition. Then, write a sentence using
behind as an adverb.

Conjunctions

There are three main kinds of conjunctions: **coordinating, correlative,** and **subordinating.** Sometimes a type of adverb, the **conjunctive adverb,** is also considered a conjunction.

> A **conjunction** is a word used to connect other words or groups of words.

Coordinating Conjunctions The seven coordinating conjunctions are used to connect similar parts of speech or groups of words of equal grammatical weight.

COORDINATING CONJUNCTIONS						
and	but	for	nor	or	so	yet

EXAMPLES   My mother **and** father ran the club.

Maria left early, **so** I left with her.

Correlative Conjunctions The five paired correlative conjunctions join elements of equal grammatical weight.

CORRELATIVE CONJUNCTIONS		
both . . . and	either . . . or	neither . . . nor
not only . . . but also	whether . . . or	

EXAMPLES   She saw **both** whales **and** sharks.

Neither Ricky **nor** Dan came to the meeting.

I don't know **whether** to read the book **or** see the movie.

Subordinating Conjunctions Subordinating conjunctions join two complete ideas by making one of the ideas subordinate to, or dependent upon, the other.

SUBORDINATING CONJUNCTIONS			
after	because	lest	till
although	before	now that	unless
as	even if	provided	until
as if	even though	since	when
as long as	how	so that	whenever
as much as	if	than	where
as soon as	inasmuch as	that	wherever
as though	in order that	though	while

The subordinate idea in a sentence always begins with a subordinating conjunction and makes up what is known as a subordinate clause. A subordinate clause may either follow or precede the main idea in a sentence.

EXAMPLES   We protect the rain forest **because** it is important to the environment.

As soon as the firefighters arrived, they began to put the fire out.

Conjunctive Adverbs Conjunctive adverbs act as transitions between complete ideas by indicating comparisons, contrasts, results, and other relationships. The chart below lists the most common conjunctive adverbs.

CONJUNCTIVE ADVERBS		
accordingly	finally	nevertheless
again	furthermore	otherwise
also	however	then
besides	indeed	therefore
consequently	moreover	thus

Prepositions, Conjunctions, and Interjections   **35**

Punctuation With Conjunctive Adverbs Punctuation is usually required both before and after conjunctive adverbs.

EXAMPLES   The committee was very successful. **Therefore**, they continued to plan with great detail.

Ricky played several sports very well; **however**, his favorite was hockey.

I forgot my ticket; **therefore**, I could not get in.   See Practice 1.4C

Interjections

Interjections express emotion. Unlike most words, they have no grammatical connection to other words in a sentence.

1.4.4

> An **interjection** is a word that expresses feeling or emotion and functions independently of a sentence.

Interjections can express a variety of sentiments, such as happiness, fear, anger, pain, surprise, sorrow, exhaustion, or hesitation.

SOME COMMON INTERJECTIONS				
ah	dear	hey	ouch	well
aha	goodness	hurray	psst	whew
alas	gracious	oh	tsk	wow

EXAMPLES   **Ouch**! That curling iron is very hot.

Wow! That is well done!

Oh! I don't know.

Whew! I thought I'd lost you in the huge shopping mall.   See Practice 1.4D

PRACTICE 1.4C > Identifying Different Conjunctions

Read each sentence. Then, write the conjunction in each sentence and label it as *coordinating, correlative, subordinating,* or *conjunctive adverb.*

EXAMPLE   The movie was not only boring but also long.

ANSWER   *not only ... but also* — correlative

1. We finished cooking dinner before our neighbors arrived.

2. The assignment was difficult yet interesting.

3. The player fell; therefore, the game was stopped briefly.

4. I need both a map and a title to complete my report.

5. Harry bounced a basketball while he waited for the bus.

6. Our new coach is tougher than our old one was.

7. Neither Shawna nor Luke knew the answer.

8. The weather was warm but pleasant on Sunday.

9. The referee was fair; indeed, every call was accurate.

10. We poured water on the fire until it was completely out.

PRACTICE 1.4D > Supplying Interjections

Read each sentence. Then, write an interjection that shows the feeling expressed in the sentence.

EXAMPLE   _____, I can't find my coat!

ANSWER   *Oh no*

11. _____! I hurt my arm!

12. _____, the stain did not come out.

13. _____! Did you see that shooting star?

14. _____, I saw you at the game last night.

15. _____, that elephant is huge!

16. _____! I'm afraid of heights.

17. _____, I can't believe I lost again!

18. _____, what will I do now?

19. _____! We won!

20. _____! I need to take a break!

SPEAKING APPLICATION

Take turns with a partner. Tell about something that you did with a friend. Your partner should name conjunctions that you use and tell what kind of conjunction each one is.

WRITING APPLICATION

Write three sentences using interjections.

1.5 Words as Different Parts of Speech

Words are flexible, often serving as one part of speech in one sentence and as another part of speech in another.

Identifying Parts of Speech

To *function* means "to serve in a particular capacity." The function of a word may change from one sentence to another.

RULE 1.5.1

The way a word is used in a sentence determines its part of speech.

The word *well* has different meaning in the following sentences.

As a Noun	Our well was full.
As a Verb	After arguing with Christopher, tears welled in Amy's eyes.
As an Adjective	Mark did not feel well today.

Nouns, Pronouns, and Verbs A **noun** names a person, place, or thing. A **pronoun** stands for a noun. A **verb** shows action, condition, or existence.

The chart below reviews the definition of each part of speech.

PARTS OF SPEECH	QUESTIONS TO ASK YOURSELF	EXAMPLES
Noun	Does the word name a person, place, or thing?	Our trip to New York City excited George.
Pronoun	Does the word stand for a noun?	They shared some with her.

PARTS OF SPEECH	QUESTIONS TO ASK YOURSELF	EXAMPLES
Verb	Does the word tell what someone or something did? Does the word link one word with another word that identifies or describes it? Does the word show that something exists?	We played soccer. That man was the coach. The coach appeared frazzled. The other team is here.

See Practice 1.5A

The Other Parts of Speech An **adjective** modifies a noun or pronoun. An **adverb** modifies a verb, an adjective, or another adverb. A **preposition** relates a noun or pronoun that appears with it to another word. A **conjunction** connects words or groups of words. An **interjection** expresses emotion.

PARTS OF SPEECH	QUESTIONS TO ASK YOURSELF	EXAMPLES
Adjective	Does the word tell *what kind, which one, how many, or how much?*	Those three oranges have an unusual flavor.
Adverb	Does the word tell *where, when, in what way,* or *to what extent?*	Run home. Come now. Speak very quietly. I am thoroughly exhausted.
Preposition	Is the word part of a phrase that includes a noun or pronoun?	Near our house, the bonfire was in full swing.
Conjunction	Does the word connect other words in the sentence or connect clauses?	Both Mom and I will go because they need more help; besides, we will have fun.
Interjection	Does the word express feeling or emotion and function independently of the sentence?	Hey, I want that! Wow! That's great!

See Practice 1.5B

PRACTICE 1.5A > Identifying Nouns, Pronouns, and Verbs

Read each sentence. Then, label the underlined word in each sentence as a *noun*, *pronoun*, or *verb*.

EXAMPLE   Jeri is the best writer in <u>our</u> class.

ANSWER   *pronoun*

1. I glanced at my <u>watch</u> every five minutes.
2. We will <u>watch</u> the game on TV at eight o'clock.
3. The neighbors are planting a tree in <u>their</u> yard.
4. Belle asked the teacher for <u>her</u> opinion.
5. My mom and dad are both very good <u>cooks</u>.
6. Mom <u>cooks</u> Indian food on the weekends.
7. Ed is coming, and <u>he</u> is wearing a suit and tie!
8. My doctor keeps a <u>record</u> of all my visits.
9. My brother <u>records</u> the songs that he writes.
10. <u>You</u> never know what the future will bring.

PRACTICE 1.5B > Recognizing All the Parts of Speech

Read each sentence. Then, write which part of speech the underlined word is in each sentence.

EXAMPLE   No one <u>but</u> Dad can help me with this.

ANSWER   *preposition*

11. Chris speaks Spanish, <u>but</u> I don't.
12. Let's go outside <u>because</u> the weather is so nice.
13. <u>Hey</u>, what are you doing in the kitchen?
14. I walked home in the rain yesterday, and I've been sick ever <u>since</u>.
15. Mom took me to the <u>late</u> movie.
16. We <u>arrived</u> late for the start of the game.
17. <u>After</u> the snowstorm, we built a snowman.
18. A band played after the <u>mayor</u> made her speech.
19. I received an <u>early</u> phone call from my friend.
20. Have <u>you</u> chosen a college yet?

SPEAKING APPLICATION

Take turns with a partner. Tell about something that you did earlier today. Your partner should identify the nouns, pronouns, and verbs that you use.

WRITING APPLICATION

Write the part of speech of each word in sentence 18.

BASIC SENTENCE PARTS

Create memorable sentences by pairing interesting subjects and verbs and by using complements for elaboration.

WRITE GUY *Jeff Anderson, M.Ed.*

WHAT DO YOU NOTICE?

Spot different sentence parts as you zoom in on these sentences from the essay "The Spider and the Wasp" by Alexander Petrunkevitch.

MENTOR TEXT

> The female produces but a few eggs, one at a time at intervals of two or three days. For each egg the mother must provide one adult tarantula, alive but paralyzed.

Now, ask yourself the following questions:

- What is the verb, and what is the direct object in the first sentence?
- What is the verb, and what is the direct object in the second sentence?

In the first sentence, *produces* is the verb; the direct object is *eggs* because it receives the action of the verb. A direct object is a complement that completes the meaning of an action verb. In the second sentence, the verb is *must provide*, and the direct object is *tarantula*.

Grammar for Writers Writers can use direct objects to bring verbs to life. Try adding interesting and surprising direct objects to your sentences!

Ask some direct objects! They're experts in receiving.

Do you think it's better to give or to receive?

2.1 Subjects and Predicates

A **sentence** is a group of words that expresses a complete unit of thought. *The cereal in the bowl* is not a complete unit of thought because you probably wonder what the writer wanted to say about the cereal. *The cereal in the bowl is soggy,* however, does express a complete unit of thought.

EL9

> A **sentence** is a group of words that has two main parts: a complete subject and a complete predicate. Together, these parts express a complete thought or paint a complete picture.

The **complete subject** contains a noun, pronoun, or group of words acting as a noun, plus its modifiers. These words tell *who* or *what* the sentence is about. The **complete predicate** consists of the verb or verb phrase, plus its modifiers. These words tell what the complete subject is or does.

COMPLETE SUBJECTS	COMPLETE PREDICATES
Snakes	slither.
A bell-clanging streetcar	moved through the turn.
Wood or cellulose	makes a delicious meal for a termite.
The candidate's approach to fiscal problems	impressed the voters attending the rally.

Sometimes, part of the predicate precedes the complete subject.

EXAMPLES   **At noon** , **the hive of bees**
           complete   complete subject
           made honey .
             predicate

           Today   **my cooking class**
           complete   complete subject
           visited a sushi restaurant .
             predicate

See Practice 2.1A

Simple Subjects and Predicates

The most essential parts of a sentence are the **simple subject** and the **simple predicate.** These words tell you the basics of what you need to know about the topic of the sentence. All of the other words in the sentence give you information about the simple subject and simple predicate.

> The **simple subject** is the essential noun, pronoun, or group of words that acts as a noun in a complete subject. The **simple predicate** is the essential verb or verb phrase in a complete predicate.

2.1.2 RULE

Note: When sentences are discussed in this chapter, the term *subject* will refer to a simple subject, and the term *verb* will refer to a simple predicate.

SUBJECTS	VERBS
Small puppies	fit nicely into the box.
Many comedy films	have used stuntmen to hilarious effects.
Bottles of fresh water	were sitting on the table.
A colorful quilt	covered the bed.
The writer's home	explained a lot about his personality.
Studies of wolves	have certainly revealed much about their behavior.

See Practice 2.1B

In the last example, the simple subject is *studies,* not *wolves; wolves* is the object of the preposition *of.* Objects of prepositions never function as simple subjects. In this same example, the simple predicate is a verb phrase. In addition, the word *certainly* is not part of the simple predicate because it does not provide essential information.

PRACTICE 2.1A ▷ **Recognizing Complete Subjects and Predicates**

Read each sentence. Then, underline the complete subject and double underline the complete predicate.

EXAMPLE   The jacket with the hood belongs to me.

ANSWER   *The jacket with the hood belongs to me.*

1. Trucks are not permitted on this road.

2. Jean did not have time to stop for lunch.

3. This class demands a lot of reading.

4. Those dark clouds in the sky make me fear an approaching storm.

5. The chef prepared a special meal for us.

6. The first school in our town was a one-room cabin.

7. The library downtown is adding two new floors.

8. Children like to play at the park in the summer.

9. Horseback riding is offered at the camp.

10. We immediately accepted their offer of help.

PRACTICE 2.1B ▷ **Identifying Simple Subjects and Predicates**

Read each sentence. The complete subject is underlined. The rest of the sentence is the complete predicate. Write the simple subject and simple predicate in each sentence.

EXAMPLE   An ostrich is a large bird.

ANSWER   *ostrich, is*

11. A hat with a wide brim is essential for sun protection.

12. My cousins go to Mexico every year for three weeks.

13. People all around the world enjoy jazz music.

14. In the winter, we skate on the frozen lake.

15. Most birds stay in this area for only part of the year.

16. The basketball team expects to win first place this year.

17. Many autumn leaves turn shades of red and yellow.

18. The mother lion taught her cubs to hunt.

19. A dozen or so bees buzzed around our heads.

20. Ants march in a line back to their nest.

SPEAKING APPLICATION

Take turns with a partner. Tell about something interesting that happened to you. Your partner should tell the complete subject and complete predicate in each of your sentences.

WRITING APPLICATION

Write a paragraph about a favorite place. In each sentence, underline the simple subject and double underline the simple predicate.

Fragments

A **fragment** is a group of words that does not contain either a complete subject or a complete predicate, or both. Fragments are usually not used in formal writing. You can correct a fragment by adding the parts needed to complete the thought.

> A **fragment** is a group of words that lacks a subject or a predicate, or both. It does not express a complete unit of thought.

RULE 2.1.3

FRAGMENTS	COMPLETE SENTENCES
the basket of muffins (complete predicate missing)	The basket of muffins was very good. (complete predicate added)
thrive in the woods (complete subject missing)	Bears thrive in the woods. (complete subject added)
from the tree (complete subject and predicate missing)	Bees from the tree swarmed into the house. (subject and complete predicate added)

In conversations, fragments usually do not present a problem because tone of voice, gestures, and facial expressions can add the missing information. A reader, however, cannot ask a writer for clarification.

Fragments are sometimes acceptable in writing that represents speech, such as the dialogue in a play or short story. Fragments are also sometimes acceptable in elliptical sentences.

> An **elliptical sentence** is one in which the missing word or words can be easily understood.

RULE 2.1.4

EXAMPLES   Until tomorrow.

Why such a happy face?

Please be early!

Locating Subjects and Verbs

To avoid writing a fragment, look for the subject and verb in a sentence. To find the subject, ask, "Which word tells *what* or *who* this sentence is about?" Once you have the answer (the subject), then ask, "What does the subject do?" or "What is being done to the subject?" This will help you locate the verb.

In some sentences, it's easier to find the verb first. In this case, ask, "Which word states the action or condition in this sentence?" This question should help you locate the verb. Then ask, "*Who* or *what* is involved in the action of the verb?" The resulting word or words will be the subject.

EXAMPLE   Kittens often run in the grass.

To find the subject first, ask, "Which word or words tell what or whom this sentence is about?"

ANSWER   Kittens (*Kittens* is the subject.)

Then ask, "What do kittens do?"

ANSWER   run (*Run* is the verb.)

To find the verb first, ask, "Which word or words state the action or condition in the sentence?"

ANSWER   run (*Run* states the action, so it is the verb.)

Then ask, "Who or what runs?"

ANSWER   Kittens (*Kittens* is the subject.)

To easily locate the subject and verb, mentally cross out any adjectives, adverbs, and prepositional phrases you see. These words add information, but they are usually less important than the simple subject and verb.

EXAMPLE   ~~School~~ **attendance** **should grow**
           simple subject   verb phrase
           ~~rapidly in the next ten years.~~

Sentences With More Than One Subject or Verb

Some sentences contain a **compound subject** or a **compound verb,** or a subject or verb with more than one part.

RULE 2.1.5

> A **compound subject** consists of two or more subjects. These subjects may be joined by a conjunction such as *and* or *or*.

EXAMPLES   The **campers** and **hikers** rappelled against the wall with rope.

Kittens, bunnies, and **puppies** are always running around the yard.

Neither the **puppy** nor the **owner** looked tired.

RULE 2.1.6

> A **compound verb** consists of two or more verbs. These verbs may be joined by a conjunction such as *and, but, or,* or *nor.*

EXAMPLES   I neither **saw** the video nor **heard** the song.

Mike **left** work and **ran** to the benefit.

She **complained** and **whined** all day.

Some sentences contain both a compound subject and a compound verb.

EXAMPLES   My **sister** and **mother** **swatted** at the bees but **hit** the glasses on the table instead.

The **lion** and **hyena** eyed each other, **circled** warily, and then **advanced** toward each other.

See Practice 2.1C
See Practice 2.1D

PRACTICE 2.1C Locating Subjects and Verbs

Read each sentence. Then, write the subject and the verb in each sentence. Underline the subject.

EXAMPLE   Each of my teammates signed the card.

ANSWER   *Each*, *signed*

1. Many of the children had become restless.
2. Trish and I enjoyed the parade in spite of the large crowd.
3. The sponsors of the show and the audience were thrilled with its content.
4. The scent of night-blooming flowers filled the garden and wafted over the walls.
5. All of the members of the team get a chance to play.
6. You guaranteed that this car would run.
7. A few of our neighbors moved away for the winter.
8. A number of farms and homes were flooded by the rains.
9. Who leads the planning committee?
10. The teacher has not graded our tests or read our essays yet.

PRACTICE 2.1D Fixing Sentence Errors

Read each fragment. Then, use each fragment in a sentence.

EXAMPLE   will drive us to the store

ANSWER   *Dad will drive us to the store.*

11. clapped, cheered, and laughed
12. while she was running for the bus
13. occasional blasts from a car horn
14. fresh bear tracks
15. where palm trees sway in the breeze
16. often windy or stormy
17. sneaking, stalking, and hunting
18. which made me remember that Mom was waiting
19. must have been lost by a fan
20. whomever she chooses

SPEAKING APPLICATION

Take turns with a partner. Tell about your favorite possessions. Your partner should name the subject and verb in each of your sentences.

WRITING APPLICATION

Write your own fragment. Then, use the fragment to write three different sentences.

2.2 Hard-to-Find Subjects

While most sentences have subjects that are easy to find, some present a challenge.

Subjects in Declarative Sentences Beginning With *Here* or *There*

When the word *here* or *there* begins a declarative sentence, it is often mistaken for the subject.

> **Here** and **there** are never the subject of a sentence.

RULE

2.2.1

Here and *there* are usually adverbs that modify the verb by pointing out *where* something is located. However, *there* may occasionally begin a sentence simply as an introductory word.

In some sentences beginning with *here* or *there*, the subject appears before the verb. However, many sentences beginning with *here* or *there* are **inverted.** In an inverted sentence, the subject follows the verb. If you rearrange such a sentence in subject–verb order, you can identify the subject more easily.

INVERTED   There **are** the **planes**. (verb–subject order)

REARRANGED   The **planes are** there. (subject–verb order)

SENTENCES BEGINNING WITH *HERE* OR *THERE*	SENTENCES REARRANGED IN SUBJECT–VERB ORDER
There are the apartment buildings.	The apartment buildings are there.
Here is the ticket for your movie.	The ticket for your movie is here.
There is money in my wallet.	Money is in my wallet there.

> **In some declarative sentences, the subject is placed after the verb in order to give the subject greater emphasis.**

RULE

2.2.2

Because most sentences are written in subject–verb order, changing that order makes readers stop and think. Inverted sentences often begin with prepositional phrases.

SENTENCES INVERTED FOR EMPHASIS	SENTENCES REARRANGED IN SUBJECT–VERB ORDER
Toward the waiting plane rushed the morning travelers.	The morning travelers rushed toward the waiting plane.
Around the next stop careened the speeding bus.	The speeding bus careened around the next stop.

Subjects in Interrogative Sentences

Some interrogative sentences use subject–verb order. Often, however, the word order of an interrogative sentence is verb–subject.

EXAMPLES
Which **store** **has** the best prices?
(subject–verb order)

When **are** **we** going?
(verb–subject order)

> **In interrogative sentences, the subject often follows the verb.**

An inverted interrogative sentence can begin with an action verb, a helping verb, or one of the following words: *how, what, when, where, which, who, whose,* or *why.* Some interrogative sentences divide the helping verb from the main verb. To help locate the subject, mentally rearrange the sentence into subject–verb order.

INTERROGATIVE SENTENCES	REARRANGED IN SUBJECT–VERB ORDER
Is the Bronx Zoo open this morning?	The Bronx Zoo is open this morning.
Do they own that car?	They do own that car.
Where will the concert be held?	The concert will be held where?

Subjects in Imperative Sentences

EL9

The subject of an imperative sentence is usually implied rather than specifically stated.

> In imperative sentences, the subject is understood to be *you*.

2.2.4 RULE

IMPERATIVE SENTENCES	SENTENCES WITH *YOU* ADDED
First, visit the Magic Kingdom.	First, [you] visit the Magic Kingdom.
After the tour, come back to the hotel.	After the tour, [you] come back to the hotel.
Tara, show me the itinerary.	Tara, [you] show me the itinerary.

In the last example, the name of the person being addressed, *Tara*, is not the subject of the imperative sentence. Instead, the subject is still understood to be *you*.

Subjects in Exclamatory Sentences

In some **exclamatory sentences,** the subject appears before the verb. In others, the verb appears first. To find the subject, rearrange the sentence in subject–verb order.

> In exclamatory sentences, the subject often appears after the verb, or it may be understood.

2.2.5 RULE

EXAMPLES   What **does she know**!
(**She does know** what.)

Leave now!
(Subject understood: **[You]** leave now!)

In other exclamatory sentences, both the subject and verb may be unstated.

EXAMPLES   Smoke! ([**You watch** out for the] smoke!)

See Practice 2.2A
See Practice 2.2B

Bees! ([**I see**] bees!)

PRACTICE 2.2A ▷ **Identifying Hard-to-Find Subjects**

Read each sentence. Then, write the subject of each sentence.

EXAMPLE   Here is your stepbrother!

ANSWER   *stepbrother*

1. Through the doors of the store rushed the eager customers.
2. How will you ever get it all done?
3. Somewhere between bland and hot lies the perfect salsa.
4. There are two accidents on the freeway.
5. Just beyond the pier frolicked several dolphins.
6. Here are your library books.
7. There is the faulty wire.
8. There she was, with no ticket.
9. Here are some ideas for your artwork.
10. There are many possible reasons for the traffic jam.

PRACTICE 2.2B ▷ **Locating Hard-to-Find Verbs**

Read each sentence. Then, write the verb in each sentence.

EXAMPLE   Look for the man I told you about.

ANSWER   *Look*

11. Can you believe the size of that car?
12. Why would you think such a thing!
13. I see lightning!
14. Before math class, show me your history project.
15. Leave the school grounds, please.
16. Was that a mountain lion?
17. Hey, put that down!
18. Where is your coat?
19. Will you show me where the gym is?
20. Go outside and play.

SPEAKING APPLICATION

Take turns with a partner. Say sentences that describe someone doing something. Your partner should invert the order of the words in your sentences and then name the subjects.

WRITING APPLICATION

Write three exclamatory sentences. Underline the subject and double underline the verb in each sentence.

2.3 Complements

Some sentences are complete with just a subject and a verb or with a subject, verb, and modifiers: *The crowd cheered.* Other sentences need more information to be complete.

The meaning of many sentences, however, depends on additional words that add information to the subject and verb. For example, although *The satellite continually sends* has a subject and verb, it is an incomplete sentence. To complete the meaning of the predicate—in this case, to tell *what* a satellite sends—a writer must add a **complement.**

> A **complement** is a word or group of words that completes the meaning of the predicate of a sentence.

2.3.1 RULE

There are five kinds of complements in English: **direct objects, indirect objects, object complements, predicate nominatives,** and **predicate adjectives.** The first three occur in sentences that have transitive verbs. The last two are often called **subject complements.** Subject complements are found only with linking verbs. (See Chapter 1 for more information about action and linking verbs.)

Direct Objects

Direct objects are the most common of the five types of complements. They complete the meaning of action verbs by telling *who* or *what* receives the action.

> A **direct object** is a noun, pronoun, or group of words acting as a noun that receives the action of a transitive verb.

2.3.2 RULE

EXAMPLES **I visited** the **Museum of Natural History**.
direct object

Rain and **melting snow flooded** the **gutters**.
direct object

Direct Objects and Action Verbs The direct object answers the question *Whom?* or *What?* about the action verb. If you cannot answer the question *Whom?* or *What?* the verb may be intransitive, and there is no direct object in the sentence.

EXAMPLES

Hawks **can see** from high in the sky.
(Ask, "Hawks can see *what*?" No answer; the verb is intransitive.)

The satellite **spun** above Earth.
(Ask, "The satellite spun *what*?" No answer; the verb is intransitive.)

In some inverted questions, the direct object may appear before the verb. To find the direct object easily, rearrange inverted questions in subject–verb order.

INVERTED
QUESTION

Which **movies** **did** **they** **see**?
            direct object

REARRANGED
IN SUBJECT–
VERB ORDER

They **did see** which **movies**?
                              direct object

Some sentences have more than one direct object, known as a **compound direct object.** If a sentence contains a compound direct object, asking *Whom?* or *What?* after the action verb will yield two or more answers.

EXAMPLES

The bikers **wore** **helmets** and
                        direct object
kneepads.
  direct object

The band **has played** at **stadiums** and
                              direct object
arenas all over the United States.
  direct object

In the last example, *United States* is the object of the preposition *over*. The object of a preposition is never a direct object.

Indirect Objects

Indirect objects appear only in sentences that contain transitive verbs and direct objects. Indirect objects are common with such verbs as *ask, bring, buy, give, lend, make, show, teach, tell,* and *write.* Some sentences may contain a compound indirect object.

> An **indirect object** is a noun or pronoun that appears with a direct object. It often names the person or thing that something is given to or done for.

2.3.4
RULE

EXAMPLES

NASA gave the **engineers** a course
                        indirect object
correction .
direct object

I showed my **sister** and **brother** the movie
                        compound indirect object
poster .
direct object

To locate an indirect object, make sure the sentence contains a direct object. Then, ask one of these questions after the verb and direct object: *To* or *for whom?* or *To* or *for what?*

EXAMPLES

The **teacher taught** our **class poetry** .
(The teacher taught poetry *to whom*? ANSWER: our class)

We made our **dog** a **sweater** .
(Made a sweater *for what*? ANSWER: our dog)

An indirect object almost always appears between the verb and the direct object. In a sentence with subject–verb order, the indirect object never follows the direct object, nor will it ever be the object of the preposition *to* or *for.*

EXAMPLES

Mike sent the **story** to **me** .
                        direct   *object of*
                        object   *preposition*

Mike sent me the **story** .
                        indirect   *direct*
                        object   *object*

Mike gave Rick an **overview** of the book.
                        indirect object   *direct object*

See Practice 2.3A

Object Complements

While an indirect object almost always comes *before* a direct object, an **object complement** almost always *follows* a direct object. The object complement completes the meaning of the direct object.

> An **object complement** is an adjective or noun that appears with a direct object and describes or renames it.

A sentence that contains an object complement may seem to have two direct objects. However, object complements occur only with such verbs as *appoint, call, consider, declare, elect, judge, label, make, name, select,* and *think.* The words *to be* are often understood before an object complement.

EXAMPLES   The **organizers** of the auction **declared** **it**
direct
object
successful.
object complement

The **principal** **identified** **him** **valedictorian**
direct   object complement
of the class.   object

I **consider** **Felix** a persuasive **writer** and
direct object   object complement
graceful **speaker**.
object complement

Subject Complements

Linking verbs require **subject complements** to complete their meaning.

> A **subject complement** is a noun, pronoun, or adjective that appears with a linking verb and gives more information about the subject.

There are two kinds of subject complements: **predicate nominatives** and **predicate adjectives**.

Predicate Nominatives

The **predicate nominative** refers to the same person, place, or thing as the subject of the sentence.

> A **predicate nominative** is a noun or pronoun that appears with a linking verb and renames, identifies, or explains the subject. Some sentences may contain a compound predicate nominative.

2.3.7 RULE

EXAMPLES **Michael Jones** **is** an **agent** with the FBI.
  predicate nominative

The **winner** **will be** **I**.
  predicate nominative

Tara Halpern **was** a **doctor** and a former **surgeon**.
  compound predicate nominative

Predicate Adjectives

A **predicate adjective** is an adjective that appears with a linking verb. It describes the subject in much the same way that an adjective modifies a noun or pronoun. Some sentences may contain a compound predicate adjective.

> A **predicate adjective** is an adjective that appears with a linking verb and describes the subject of the sentence.

2.3.8 RULE

EXAMPLES Your **reasoning** **seems** **illogical**.
  predicate adjective

The **runner** **was** **fast**.
  predicate adjective

The **thunder** **sounded** **loud** and **frightening**.
  compound predicate adjective

The **uniforms** **are** **tan** and **black**.
  compound predicate adjective

See Practice 2.3B

PRACTICE 2.3A ⟩ Identifying Direct and Indirect Objects

Read each sentence. Then, write and label the *direct object* in each sentence. If there is an indirect object in a sentence, write and label it, too.

EXAMPLE   My parents gave me my own room.

ANSWER   *room* — direct object

me — indirect object

1. I take the trash out every Tuesday.
2. Dad bought Taylor and me science fiction books.
3. The coach named Josh the captain of the team.
4. That singer has recorded two albums in one year.
5. The tour group took a train to the village.
6. The store is offering students a chance to win a computer.
7. We can ask that officer for directions.
8. Did you show your parents your report card?
9. The store gave me a refund.
10. We asked the lifeguard if it was safe to swim.

PRACTICE 2.3B ⟩ Locating Object and Subject Complements

Read each sentence. Then, write the complement and label it as an *object complement* or a *subject complement*.

EXAMPLE   The play's ending left us sad.

ANSWER   *sad* — object complement

11. A man's best friend is his dog.
12. After the storm, we all felt relieved.
13. The fireworks made the evening very festive.
14. We just elected Steve president.
15. Eli became confident during his time away.
16. That movie became an instant hit.
17. The castle's gardens are as beautiful now as ever.
18. The fire chief declared the building unsafe.
19. The constant rain kept us all cranky for days.
20. We decided to call our cockatoo Vinca.

SPEAKING APPLICATION

Take turns telling a partner about a family event. Your partner should name the direct object and indirect object, if any, in each of your sentences.

WRITING APPLICATION

Use sentences 11 and 12 as models to write sentences of your own. Underline and label the complement in each sentence.

CHAPTER 3

PHRASES *and* CLAUSES

Use phrases and clauses to add interesting detail and description to your sentences.

WRITE GUY *Jeff Anderson, M.Ed.*

WHAT DO YOU NOTICE?

Focus on phrases as you zoom in on these lines from the poem "Conscientious Objector" by Edna St. Vincent Millay.

MENTOR TEXT

> I shall die, but that is all that I shall do for Death.
>
> I hear him leading his horse out of the stall; I hear the clatter on the barn-floor.

Now, ask yourself the following questions:

- What are the prepositional phrases in these lines?
- How does each prepositional phrase function in the poem: as an adjectival phrase or an adverbial phrase?

The three prepositional phrases in the poem are *for Death, out of the stall,* and *on the barn-floor.* The first two are both adverbial phrases. The phrase *for Death* modifies the verb *do,* and *out of the stall* modifies *leading. On the barn-floor* acts as an adjectival phrase that describes the noun *clatter.*

Grammar for Writers Writers are like reporters; they need to answer the questions *What? When? Where, What kind?* or *Which one?* in their writing. Prepositional phrases are keys to the answers.

Do people use prepositional phrases in conversation?

They use them "in conversation" all the time!

3.1 Phrases

When one adjective or adverb cannot convey enough information, a phrase can contribute more detail to a sentence. A **phrase** is a group of words that does not include a subject and verb and cannot stand alone as a sentence.

There are several kinds of phrases, including **prepositional phrases, appositive phrases, participial phrases, gerund phrases,** and **infinitive phrases.**

Prepositional Phrases

A **prepositional phrase** consists of a preposition and a noun or pronoun, called the object of the preposition. *Over their heads, until dark,* and *after the baseball game* are all prepositional phrases. Prepositional phrases often modify other words by functioning as adjectives or adverbs.

Sometimes, a single prepositional phrase may include two or more objects joined by a conjunction.

EXAMPLES   between the **chair** and the **table**
             preposition   object   object

             with the **snow** and **hail**
             preposition   object   object

             beside the **night table** and the **bed**
             preposition   object   object

See Practice 3.1A

Adjectival Phrases
A prepositional phrase that acts as an adjective is called an **adjectival phrase.**

> An **adjectival phrase** is a prepositional phrase that modifies a noun or pronoun by telling *what kind* or *which one*.

ADJECTIVES	ADJECTIVAL PHRASES
A beautiful picture hung in the meeting hall.	A picture of great beauty hung in the meeting hall. *(What kind of picture?)*
Anne had a heavy book.	Anne had a book that was heavy. *(What kind of book?)*

Like one-word adjectives, adjectival phrases can modify subjects, direct objects, indirect objects, or predicate nominatives.

MODIFYING
A SUBJECT

The library **across the road** has been an asset.

MODIFYING
A DIRECT OBJECT

Let's take a picture **of the Sears Tower**.

MODIFYING AN
INDIRECT OBJECT

I gave the people **on the trip** a tour.

MODIFYING
A PREDICATE
NOMINATIVE

Germany is a country **with many castles**.

A sentence may contain two or more **adjectival phrases.** In some cases, one phrase may modify the preceding phrase. In others, two phrases may modify the same word.

EXAMPLES

We bought tickets **for the trip** **to Florida**.

The statue **of the rearing horse** **in the park** was huge.

Adverbial Phrases

An **adverbial phrase** is a prepositional phrase that modifies a verb, an adjective, or an adverb by pointing out *where, why, when, in what way,* or *to what extent.*

ADVERBS	ADVERBIAL PHRASES
He walked quickly. (Walked *in what way?*)	He walked with speed .
I was worried then. (Worried *why?*)	I was worried by the weather report .
The plane flew overhead. (Flew *where?*)	The plane flew over the airport .

Adverbial phrases can modify verbs, adjectives, or adverbs.

MODIFYING
A VERB

The yarn rolled **across the floor** .

MODIFYING
AN ADJECTIVE

Amy was happy **beyond question** .

MODIFYING
AN ADVERB

She buried the feelings deep **in her mind** .

An adverbial phrase may either follow the word it modifies or be located elsewhere in the sentence. Often, two adverbs in different parts of a sentence can modify the same word.

EXAMPLES

MODIFIES

A creek disappeared **during the earthquake** .

MODIFIES

During the earthquake , a creek disappeared.

MODIFIES   MODIFIES

After the play we all met **at the restaurant** .   See Practice 3.1B

PRACTICE 3.1A > Identifying Prepositional Phrases

Read each sentence. Write the prepositional phrase or phrases in each sentence and underline the prepositions.

EXAMPLE   According to the flyer, the concert begins at dark.

ANSWER   *according to the flyer; at dark*

1. The news article announced an agreement between the two countries.

2. Cut one pound of apples into slices.

3. The people at the back of the boat got wet.

4. The wedding guests entered through a breathtaking courtyard.

5. The house down the street has a fountain.

6. We looked into the old house through a broken window.

7. Ted found the toy under the bucket.

8. Sometimes a picture from my childhood will bring back memories.

9. I like stories about other countries.

10. I wish I could return to the lake house.

PRACTICE 3.1B > Identifying Adjectival and Adverbial Phrases

Read each sentence. Write the adjectival or adverbial phrases. Then, identify each phrase as either *adjectival* or *adverbial*.

EXAMPLE   I often play at the park on Post Street.

ANSWER   *at the park* — adverbial
on Post Street — adjectival

11. Mary Cassatt was a leader among American painters.

12. Rosa chose the one with blue stripes.

13. The cavalry will reach the fort by noon.

14. We got our new puppy at an animal shelter.

15. We bought a CD by a punk rock band.

16. She drove for hours in the storm.

17. A flock of gray birds flew overhead.

18. The boat landed on an island near the coast.

19. The library is open on weekends during the day.

20. Here's a gift for you from Uncle Greg.

SPEAKING APPLICATION

Take turns with a partner. Describe the location of an object in the room. Your partner should listen for and identify three prepositions that you use.

WRITING APPLICATION

Use the prepositions in sentences 11, 14, and 18 to write three sentences of your own. Use the same prepositions, but change the other words to create new sentences.

Appositives and Appositive Phrases

The term *appositive* comes from a Latin verb that means "to put near or next to."

Appositives Using **appositives** in your writing is an easy way to give additional meaning to a noun or pronoun.

> An **appositive** is a group of words that identifies, renames, or explains a noun or pronoun.

As the examples below show, appositives usually follow immediately after the words they explain.

EXAMPLES

Mrs. Wilson, **the painter**, donated beautiful paintings.

The school committee, **the PTA**, planned the spring dance.

Notice that commas are used in the examples above because these appositives are **nonessential.** In other words, the appositives could be omitted from the sentences without altering the basic meaning of the sentences.

Some appositives, however, are not set off by any punctuation because they are **essential** to the meaning of the sentence.

EXAMPLES

The artist **da Vinci** was also a scientist.
(The appositive is essential because it identifies which specific artist.)

My sister **Kate** is a persuasive speaker.
(The appositive is essential because you might have several sisters.)

Note About Terms: Sometimes, the terms *nonrestrictive* and *restrictive* are used in place of *nonessential* and *essential.*

Appositive Phrases When an appositive is accompanied by its own modifiers, it is called an **appositive phrase.**

> An **appositive phrase** is a noun or pronoun with modifiers that adds information by identifying, renaming, or explaining a noun or pronoun.

Appositives and appositive phrases may follow nouns or pronouns used in almost any role within a sentence. The modifiers within an appositive phrase can be adjectives, adjective phrases, or other groups of words functioning as adjectives.

EXAMPLES   Mr. Jane, **my history teacher**, assigned us to watch a documentary.

Bob explained anatomy, **the study of the structure of your body**.

ROLES OF APPOSITIVE PHRASES IN SENTENCES	
Identifying a Subject	William Shakespeare, a famous author, wrote many plays.
Identifying a Direct Object	The chef prepared pitas, a Mediterranean dish.
Identifying an Indirect Object	I brought my sister, a girl of five, a T-shirt from my trip.
Identifying an Object Complement	I chose green, my favorite color, for house shutters.
Identifying a Predicate Nominative	My favorite food is romaine lettuce, an ingredient in a tasty salad.
Identifying the Object of a Preposition	Store the potatoes in the pantry, a cool, dry place.

Compound Appositives Appositives and appositive phrases can also be compound.

EXAMPLES   The class officers— **president** , **vice-president** , and **secretary** —planned the event.

Some types of shoes, **sandals** and **sneakers** , are on sale this week.

Toby used her favorite colors, **blue** , **green** , and **yellow** , to paint her room.

See Practice 3.1C

Grammar and Style Tip When **appositives** or **appositive phrases** are used to combine sentences, they help to eliminate unnecessary words. One way to streamline your writing is to combine sentences by using an appositive phrase.

TWO SENTENCES	COMBINED SENTENCE
Tel Aviv is located on the Mediterranean Sea. The city is an important Israeli seaport.	Tel Aviv, an important Israeli seaport , is located on the Mediterranean Sea.
The Lion King was performed at the Minskoff Theatre. The musical includes many original songs.	*The Lion King,* a musical performed at the Minskoff Theatre , includes many original songs.
Florida is on the East Coast. It is one of our warmest states.	Florida, one of our warmest states , is on the East Coast.

Read aloud the pairs of sentences in the chart. Notice how the combined sentences, which began as two choppy sentences, include the same information. However, they flow much more smoothly once the information in both sentences is clearly linked.

See Practice 3.1D

PRACTICE 3.1C ▷ **Identifying Appositive and Appositive Phrases**

Read each sentence. Then, write the appositive or appositive phrase in each sentence.

EXAMPLE   We look forward to the main event, tennis.

ANSWER   *tennis*

1. Doug's favorite book, <u>The Hobbit</u>, was written by J.R.R. Tolkien.

2. Rachel's hobby, skydiving, is very exciting.

3. Her bad habit, eavesdropping, is very rude.

4. The baby's new skills, walking and waving, seemed to make her very happy.

5. My dog's favorite activity, napping, takes up most of his day.

6. The strangest event, catching a greased pig, was the highlight of the day.

7. The most important task, passing the class, will take a lot of work.

8. The child's chore, cleaning her room, wore her out.

9. Kimber's career goal, teaching, seems a good fit for her.

10. Tony's friend Nico needs a ride to the airport.

PRACTICE 3.1D ▷ **Using Appositives and Appositive Phrases to Combine Sentences**

Read each pair of sentences. Then, combine the sentences using an appositive or an appositive phrase.

EXAMPLE   Bart Lukas was a detective. He arrived just in time.

ANSWER   *The detective, Bart Lukas, arrived just in time.*

11. Mars is one of the closest planets to Earth. Mars can be seen without a telescope.

12. Misty Alexander is a lawyer. She was the main speaker at the conference.

13. Rubber is an elastic substance. It quickly restores itself to its original size and shape.

14. The North Sea is an arm of the Atlantic Ocean. The North Sea is rich in fish and oil.

15. Imelda is my friend. She loves to knit.

16. Gettysburg is a town in Pennsylvania. An important battle was fought there.

17. Julius is an artist. He owns a gallery.

18. Our old house is on Larchmont Street. That house is my favorite place.

19. My cat is Clive. He loves tuna.

20. Hartford is a bustling city. It is located in Connecticut.

SPEAKING APPLICATION

Take turns saying two sentences about the same subject to a partner. Your partner should combine your sentences, using either an appositive or an appositive phrase.

WRITING APPLICATION

Write a set of sentences. Then, combine the sentences with an appositive or appositive phrase.

Verbal Phrases

When a verb is used as a noun, an adjective, or an adverb, it is called a **verbal.** Although a verbal does not function as a verb, it retains two characteristics of verbs: It can be modified in different ways, and it can have one or more complements. A verbal with modifiers or complements is called a **verbal phrase.**

Participles

Many of the adjectives you use are actually verbals known as **participles.**

RULE 3.1.5

> **A participle** is a form of a verb that can act as an adjective.

The most common kinds of participles are **present participles** and **past participles.** These two participles can be distinguished from one another by their endings. Present participles usually end in *-ing (frightening, entertaining).* Past participles usually end in *-ed (frightened, entertained),* but many have irregular endings, such as *-t* or *-en (burnt, written).*

PRESENT PARTICIPLES	PAST PARTICIPLES
The limping dancer favored her aching foot.	Confused, Joe returned to his interrupted project.

Like other adjectives, participles answer the question *What kind?* or *Which one?* about the nouns or pronouns they modify.

EXAMPLES   Jane's **tearing** eyes betrayed her sadness.
(*What kind* of eyes? Answer: *tearing* eyes)

The **shattered** tiles need to be replaced.
(*Which* tiles? Answer: *shattered* tiles)

Participles may also have a **present perfect** form.

EXAMPLES   **Having decided**, Laura made the call.

Being greeted by his friends, Mark walked off the plane.

Verb or Participle? Because **verbs** often have endings
such as *-ing* and *-ed,* you may confuse them with **participles.**
If a word ending in *-ed* or *-ing* expresses the action of the
sentence, it is a verb or part of a verb phrase. If it describes
a noun or pronoun, it is a participle.

> **A verb shows an action, a condition, or the fact that something exists. A participle acting as an adjective modifies a noun or a pronoun.**

3.1.6 RULE

See Practice 3.1E

ACTING AS VERBS	ACTING AS ADJECTIVES
The dog is growling at the intruder. (What is the dog doing?)	The growling dog attacked the intruder. (Which dog?)
The dancers delighted their audience. (What did the dancers do?)	Delighted, the audience clapped for the dancers. (What kind of audience?)

Participial Phrases
A participle can be expanded by adding modifiers and
complements to form a **participial phrase.**

> **A participial phrase is a participle modified by an adverb or adverbial phrase or accompanied by a complement. The entire participial phrase acts as an adjective.**

3.1.7 RULE

The following examples show different ways that participles may
be expanded into phrases.

WITH AN ADVERB
Traveling quickly , we made it in time for dinner.

WITH AN ADVERB PHRASE
Traveling at breakneck speed , we made it home in time for dinner.

WITH A COMPLEMENT
Avoiding bumps , we made it home for dinner.

A participial phrase that is nonessential to the basic meaning of a
sentence is set off by commas or other forms of punctuation.
A participial phrase that is essential is not set off by punctuation.

NONESSENTIAL PHRASES	ESSENTIAL PHRASES
There is Mark, waiting at the bus stop.	The boy waiting at the bus stop is Mark.
Painted in 1567, the canvas is a masterpiece.	The canvas painted in 1567 is one that needs preservation.

In the first sentence on the left side of the chart above, *waiting at the bus stop* merely adds information about Mark, so it is nonessential. In the sentence on the right, however, the same phrase is essential because many different boys might be in view.

In the second sentence on the left, *Painted in 1567* is an additional description of *canvas,* so it is nonessential. In the sentence on the right, however, the phrase is essential because it identifies the specific canvas that is being discussed.

Participial phrases can often be used to combine information from two sentences into one.

TWO SENTENCES	We were exhausted by the climb up the mountain. We rested by the side of trail.
COMBINED	**Exhausted by the climb up the mountain**, we rested by the side of the trail.
TWO SENTENCES	We drank coffee. We shared stories about our lives.
COMBINED	**Drinking coffee**, we shared stories about our lives.

Notice how part of the verb in one sentence is changed into a participle in the combined sentence.

See Practice 3.1F

PRACTICE 3.1E ▶ Identifying Participles

Read each sentence. Show that you understand verbals (participles) by writing whether the underlined word is a *verb* or a *participle*. Use the word in a new sentence.

EXAMPLE   They are <u>stopping</u> early today.

ANSWER   *verb; The police officer is stopping traffic for the parade.*

1. He gave a <u>moving</u> speech.
2. I was <u>stirring</u> the soup.
3. Barbara put away the <u>laundered</u> shirts.
4. Everyone was <u>singing</u> daily.
5. Do we have any <u>wrapping</u> paper left?
6. The <u>finished</u> artwork was auctioned off.
7. Our summer cabin has <u>running</u> water in the bathroom now.
8. She is <u>shopping</u> for a new coat today.
9. The <u>dreaming</u> student stared out the window.
10. I asked for another <u>formatted</u> disk.

PRACTICE 3.1F ▶ Recognizing Participial Phrases

Read each sentence. Write the participial phrase in each sentence. Then, write *E* for *essential* or *N* for *nonessential*.

EXAMPLE   One deputy, using a stop watch, timed the car from one marker to another.

ANSWER   *using a stop watch* — N

11. Stretching slowly, the cat jumped from the windowsill.
12. The tornado forecasted earlier today did not hit our area.
13. The dress sewn by a seamstress, that I liked was already sold.
14. Sitting in a chair, the man tells Navajo folktales.
15. Reading the assignment, she took notes carefully.
16. A bowl hollowed out of wood can be a collector's item.
17. The rabbit hopping along the fence is my pet.
18. The people waiting to see Tiger Woods whistled and clapped.
19. Cheering for the team, we celebrated the victory.
20. Living more than four hundred years ago, Leonardo da Vinci kept journals of his ideas and inventions.

SPEAKING APPLICATION

Show that you understand verbals (participles). Tell a partner about television shows that you have seen recently. Use participles as you speak. Your partner will identify each participle.

WRITING APPLICATION

Use the participial phrases in sentences 11, 13, and 16 to write three new sentences.

Gerunds

Many nouns that end in *-ing* are actually **verbals** known as **gerunds.** Gerunds are not difficult to recognize: They always end in *-ing*, and they always function as **nouns.**

> A **gerund** is a form of a verb that ends in *-ing* and acts as a **noun.**

FUNCTIONS OF GERUNDS	
Subject	Swimming is my favorite activity.
Direct Object	The English people make visiting England a pleasure.
Indirect Object	Mrs. Kay's lecture gave traveling a new perspective.
Predicate Nominative	My mom's favorite activity is cooking.
Object of a Preposition	Their puppy showed signs of extensive training.
Appositive	Anne's profession, teaching, is hard work.

Verb, Participle, or Gerund? Words ending in *-ing* may be parts of verb phrases, participles acting as adjectives, or gerunds.

> Words ending in *-ing* that act as **nouns** are called **gerunds.** Unlike verbs ending in *-ing,* gerunds do not have helping verbs. Unlike participles ending in *-ing,* they do not act as adjectives.

VERB	Kim is **sleeping** in her bed.
PARTICIPLE	The **sleeping** girl was very tired.
GERUND	**Sleeping** is very healthful.
VERB	My sister was **crying**, and that upset me.
PARTICIPLE	**Crying**, my sister upset me.
GERUND	My sister's **crying** upset me.

Gerund Phrases Like participles, gerunds may be joined by other words to make **gerund phrases.**

> A **gerund phrase** consists of a gerund and one or more modifiers or a complement. These phrases act together as a noun.

GERUND PHRASES	
With Adjectives	His constant, angry yelling made the manager difficult to tolerate.
With an Adverb	Acting quickly is not always a good idea.
With a Prepositional Phrase	Many places in the town prohibit walking dogs on the grass.
With a Direct Object	Rob was incapable of reciting the lines.
With an Indirect and a Direct Object	The English teacher tried giving her students praise.

Note About Gerunds and Possessive Pronouns: Always use the possessive form of a personal pronoun in front of a gerund.

INCORRECT   We never listen to **him** complaining.

CORRECT   We never listen to **his** complaining.

INCORRECT   **Them** refusing to wear seat belts is dangerous.

See Practice 3.1G   CORRECT   **Their** refusing to wear seat belts is dangerous.

Infinitives

The third kind of verbal is the **infinitive.** Infinitives have many different uses. They can act as nouns, adjectives, or adverbs.

> An **infinitive** is a form of a verb that generally appears with the word *to* in front of it and acts as a noun, an adjective, or an adverb.

The teacher asked the class **to work quietly** .

INFINITIVES USED AS NOUNS	
Subject	To understand history requires reading and studying.
Direct Object	The militia decided to rebel .
Predicate Nominative	The prisoner's only option was to surrender .
Object of a Preposition	The train to New York City was about to leave .
Appositive	You have only one choice, to go .

Unlike gerunds, infinitives can also act as adjectives and adverbs.

INFINITIVES USED AS MODIFIERS	
Adjective	The allies showed a willingness to cooperate .
Adverb	Some animals were unable to fight .

Prepositional Phrase or Infinitive? Although both **prepositional phrases** and **infinitives** often begin with *to,* you can tell the difference between them by analyzing the words that follow *to.*

RULE 3.1.13

A **prepositional phrase** always ends with a noun or pronoun that acts as the object of the preposition. An **infinitive** always ends with a verb.

PREPOSITIONAL PHRASE	INFINITIVE
The puppy listened to the command .	The obedience instructor's job is to command .
We took the car to the back of the shop.	Make sure to back up your work in case you lose it.

Note About Infinitives Without *to*: Sometimes infinitives do not include the word *to*. When an infinitive follows one of the eight verbs listed below, the *to* is generally omitted. However, it may be understood.

VERBS THAT PRECEDE INFINITIVES WITHOUT *TO*			
dare	help	make	see
hear	let	please	watch

EXAMPLES   He won't dare **[to] go** without asking.

Please help me **[to] leave** the package here.

Jon helped Bill **[to] complete** the project.

Infinitive Phrases Infinitives also can be joined with other words to form phrases.

> An **infinitive phrase** consists of an infinitive and its modifiers, complements, or subject, all acting together as a single part of speech.

RULE
3.1.14

INFINITIVE PHRASES	
With an Adverb	Anne's family likes to eat later .
With an Adverb Phrase	To drive in the snow is not easy.
With a Direct Object	She hated to leave Chicago .

With an Indirect and a Direct Object	They promised to show us the pictures
	  direct indirect direct
	  object object object
	 from their wedding.

With a Subject and a Complement	I want her to make her own choices . subject complement

See Practice 3.1H

PRACTICE 3.1G ▷ Identifying Gerunds and Gerund Phrases

Read each sentence. Show that you understand the function of verbals (gerunds) by writing the gerund or gerund phrase. Then, use the gerund or gerund phrase in a new sentence.

EXAMPLE   Gardening can be a good pastime.

ANSWER   *gardening; Mr. Hale enjoys gardening.*

1. On rainy days, Emma enjoys reading.

2. Losing badly is never fun to experience.

3. I helped out in the office, labeling envelopes.

4. Trimming is important to the health of most plants.

5. My mom made volunteering an important part of her life.

6. Quan has shown talent for drawing.

7. Knitting can be enjoyable and profitable.

8. The man's crime was stealing.

9. Exercising regularly can be important for good health.

10. With this machine, cleaning seems easy.

PRACTICE 3.1H ▷ Identifying Infinitives and Infinitive Phrases

Read each sentence. Show that you understand verbals (infinitives) by writing each infinitive or infinitive phrase.

EXAMPLE   Dad went to buy some meat.

ANSWER   *to buy some meat*

11. Is this the right path to take?

12. Hayden wants to walk to school.

13. You should try to listen carefully.

14. Jorge is willing to learn new things.

15. Keri asked me to hand you this book.

16. To rebuild the warehouse that burned down is important.

17. When I am in New York City, I like to shop.

18. Would you like to explain your answer?

19. Your teacher is ready to begin speaking.

20. Charlie likes to write e-mails to his friends.

SPEAKING APPLICATION

Show that you understand the function of verbals (gerunds). Use gerunds in sentences to tell a partner about your favorite activities. Ask your partner to identify the gerunds as you speak.

WRITING APPLICATION

Show that you understand the function of verbals (infinitives). Write three sentences that use infinitives and read them to a partner. Ask your partner to identify the infinitives as you speak.

3.2 Clauses

Every **clause** contains a subject and a verb. However, not every clause can stand by itself as a complete thought.

> A **clause** is a group of words that contains a subject and a verb.

3.2.1 RULE

Independent and Subordinate Clauses

The two basic kinds of clauses are **independent** or **main clauses** and **subordinate clauses.**

> An **independent** or **main clause** can stand by itself as a complete sentence.

3.2.2 RULE

Every sentence must contain an independent clause. The independent clause can either stand by itself or be connected to other independent or subordinate clauses.

STANDING ALONE
Mr. Holden teaches history .
independent clause

WITH ANOTHER INDEPENDENT CLAUSE
Mr. Holden teaches history, and
independent clause
his sister teaches math .
independent clause

WITH A SUBORDINATE CLAUSE
Mr. Holden teaches history , **while his sister**
independent clause   subordinate clause
teaches math .

When you subordinate something, you give it less importance.

> A **subordinate clause,** although it has a subject and verb, cannot stand by itself as a complete sentence.

3.2.3 RULE

Subordinate clauses can appear before or after an independent clause in a sentence or can even split an independent clause.

LOCATIONS OF SUBORDINATE CLAUSES	
In the Middle of an Independent Clause	The man to whom I introduced you teaches history.
Preceding an Independent Clause	Unless the snow stops soon , the roads will be closed.
Following an Independent Clause	Hannah asked that she be excused .

See Practice 3.2A

Like phrases, subordinate clauses can function as adjectives, adverbs, or nouns in sentences.

Adjectival Clauses

One way to add description and detail to a sentence is by adding an **adjectival clause.**

> An **adjectival clause** is a subordinate clause that modifies a noun or pronoun in another clause by telling *what kind* or *which one.*

An adjectival clause usually begins with one of the relative pronouns: *that, which, who, whom,* or *whose.* Sometimes, it begins with a relative adverb, such as *before, since, when, where,* or *why.* Each of these words connects the clause to the word it modifies.

> An **adjectival clause** often begins with a **relative pronoun** or a **relative adverb** that links the clause to a noun or pronoun in another clause.

The adjectival clauses in the examples on the next page answer the questions *What kind?* and *Which one?* Each modifies the noun in the independent clause that comes right before the adjectival clause. Notice also that the first two clauses begin with relative pronouns and the last one begins with a relative adverb.

EXAMPLES I finished watching the movie **that you lent me** .

We gave the research, **which we found fascinating** , a second look.

In Holland, we visited the village **where my father was born** .

Adjectival clauses can often be used to combine information from two sentences into one. Using adjectival clauses to combine sentences can indicate the relationship between ideas as well as add detail to a sentence.

TWO SENTENCES	COMBINED SENTENCES
The dancer is a prima ballerina. She is dressed to dance.	The dancer, who is a prima ballerina , is dressed to dance.
My sister graduated from college in less than four years. She is in medical school now.	My sister, who is in medical school now , graduated from college in less than four years.

Essential and Nonessential Adjectival Clauses Adjectival clauses, like appositives and participial phrases, are set off by punctuation only when they are not essential to the meaning of a sentence. Commas are used to indicate information that is not essential to the meaning of the sentence. When information in an adjectival clause is essential to the sentence, no commas are used.

NONESSENTIAL CLAUSES	ESSENTIAL CLAUSES
One of Shakespeare's best characters is Lady Macbeth, who is a main character in *Macbeth* .	The documentary that everyone must watch by Friday promises to be very interesting.
Anne James, who studied hard every night for a year , won the scholarship.	A student who prepares faithfully usually finds getting good grades easy.

See Practice 3.2B

PRACTICE 3.2A ▶ Identifying Independent and Subordinate Clauses

Read each sentence. Identify the underlined clause in each sentence as either *independent* or *subordinate*.

EXAMPLE   <u>Whenever we visit my aunt</u>, we always eat seafood.

ANSWER   *subordinate*

1. Marcos bought the coat, <u>although it was really too expensive</u>.

2. Italy is a country <u>that I have always wanted to visit</u>.

3. <u>When Sarah made the honor roll</u>, her father was very proud.

4. <u>I'm a big fan of the Miami Heat</u>, but I like the San Antonio Spurs even better.

5. <u>David is a terrific tennis player</u> because he practices all the time.

6. I left the present on the counter, <u>where you can find it easily</u>.

7. <u>If you want to take a walk</u>, I can go with you.

8. <u>Because of the heat</u>, the room felt uncomfortable.

9. If you want to feel a slight breeze, <u>wave a sheet of paper in front of your face</u>.

10. <u>Although the fire was blazing</u>, we were still cold.

PRACTICE 3.2B ▶ Identifying Adjectival Clauses

Read each sentence. Then, write the adjectival clause in each sentence.

EXAMPLE   Frank is the person that I met at Ronnie's party.

ANSWER   *that I met at Ronnie's party*

11. I can't see where the boat is docked.

12. Max is the one for whom I left the message.

13. Texas is a state that has a large population.

14. Edgar Allen Poe is a poet whose work was once ignored.

15. Marcus is the one who answered all the questions correctly during the game show.

16. I don't understand why raccoons wash their hands before eating food.

17. The movie, which is playing now, is scary.

18. This dish has an ingredient that I don't like.

19. Is this the year when the planets will align?

20. Sheila, whose father is a doctor, wants to be a surgeon.

SPEAKING APPLICATION

Take turns with a partner. Say sentences that have independent and subordinate clauses. Your partner should identify the clauses as either independent or subordinate.

WRITING APPLICATION

Show that you understand restrictive relative clauses (essential) and nonrestrictive relative clauses (nonessential) by writing two sentences that use either type of clause. Then, read your sentences to a partner. Ask your partner to identify the clauses as you speak.

Relative Pronouns **Relative pronouns** help link a subordinate clause to another part of a sentence. They also have a function in the subordinate clause.

> **Relative pronouns** connect adjectival clauses to the words they modify and act as subjects, direct objects, objects of prepositions, or adjectives in the subordinate clauses.

3.2.6 RULE

To tell how a relative pronoun is used within a clause, separate the clause from the rest of the sentence, and find the subject and verb in the clause.

FUNCTIONS OF RELATIVE PRONOUNS IN CLAUSES	
As a Subject	A boat that is built correctly is sure to stay afloat. subject
As a Direct Object	Jake, whom my sister met at college , is a doctor. direct object (Reworded clause: my sister met *whom* at college)
As an Object of a Preposition	This is the movie about which I heard great reviews . object of preposition (Reworded clause: I heard great reviews about *which*)
As an Adjective	The star whose actions were in question spoke to the adjective media.

Sometimes in writing and in speech, a relative pronoun is left out of an adjectival clause. However, the missing word, though simply understood, still functions in the sentence.

EXAMPLES   The novelists [**whom**] we studied were great writers.

The ideas [**that**] they suggested were implemented.

See Practice 3.2C

Relative Adverbs Like relative pronouns, **relative adverbs** help link the subordinate clause to another part of a sentence. However, they have only one use within a subordinate clause.

Relative adverbs connect adjectival clauses to the words they modify and act as adverbs in the clauses.

EXAMPLE The patient yearned for the day **when** she'd be out of the hospital.

In the example, the adjectival clause is *when she'd be out of the hospital.* Reword the clause this way to see that *when* functions as an adverb: *she'd be out of the hospital when.*

Adverbial Clauses

Subordinate clauses may also serve as adverbs in sentences. They are introduced by subordinating conjunctions. Like adverbs, **adverbial clauses** modify verbs, adjectives, or other adverbs.

Subordinate **adverbial clauses** modify verbs, adjectives, adverbs, or verbals by telling *where, when, in what way, to what extent, under what condition,* or *why.*

An adverbial clause begins with a subordinating conjunction and contains a subject and a verb, although they are not the main subject and verb in the sentence. In the chart that follows, the adverbial clauses are highlighted in orange. Arrows point to the words they modify.

ADVERBIAL CLAUSES	
Modifying a Verb	Before you visit Germany, you should read a tour book. (Read *when?*)
Modifying an Adjective	Randy seemed successful wherever he was. (Successful *where?*)
Modifying a Gerund	Diving is easy and fun if you have been well taught. (Diving *under what condition?*)

> **Adverbial clauses** begin with **subordinating conjunctions** and contain subjects and verbs.

EXAMPLE   **After** the rain fell, the flowers bloomed.
          subordinating
          conjunction

Recognizing the subordinating conjunctions will help you identify adverbial clauses. The following chart shows some of the most common subordinating conjunctions.

SUBORDINATING CONJUNCTIONS			
after	because	so that	when
although	before	than	whenever
as	even though	though	where
as if	if	unless	wherever
as long as	since	until	while

Whether an adverbial clause appears at the beginning, middle, or end of a sentence can sometimes affect the sentence meaning.

EXAMPLE   **Before she graduated**, Tia made plans to study abroad.

Tia made plans to study abroad **before she graduated**.

Like adjectival clauses, adverbial clauses can be used to combine the information from two sentences into one. The combined sentence shows a close relationship between the ideas.

TWO SENTENCES   **It snowed**. They stayed home.

See Practice 3.2D   COMBINED   **Because** it snowed, they stayed home.
                        subordinating
                        conjunction

PRACTICE 3.2C **Identifying Relative Pronouns and Adjectival Clauses**

Read each sentence. Then, write the adjectival clause in each sentence and underline the relative pronoun that introduces the clause.

EXAMPLE   Leslie is the one whose mother is the principal.

ANSWER   <u>whose</u> mother is the principal

1. That is the house in which I was born.

2. Janice, who plays the trumpet, joined the school band.

3. The moon is where the *Apollo 13* mission was headed.

4. Rob answered the question before anyone else could.

5. My father works in an office that has a friendly atmosphere.

6. A hurricane develops when a tropical storm picks up wind speed.

7. My mother, whose job is very stressful, worked all weekend.

8. The settlers couldn't understand why it was so difficult to grow crops.

9. My friend whom you liked thought you were nice also.

10. Algebra is a subject about which I know a lot.

PRACTICE 3.2D **Recognizing Adverbial Clauses**

Read each sentence. Write the adverbial clause in each sentence, and identify the subordinating conjunction.

EXAMPLE   We wanted to stop so that we could grab something to eat.

ANSWER   *so that we could grab something to eat, so that*

11. My dad will worry if we are late.

12. We posted the warning where it would reach the most people.

13. Professor Franklin tutors at the elementary school whenever he has time.

14. After the sauce has simmered, add the basil and thyme.

15. I'm sure Gloria will assist if you ask her.

16. While recovering, Rumi read several books a month.

17. Each student was better prepared than the one before.

18. The mattress was dropped off today, as the salesman had guaranteed.

19. After he gave out homework assignments, Mr. O'Malley started the lesson.

20. Wendell appears excited whenever this topic is debated.

SPEAKING APPLICATION

Take turns with a partner. Describe a book you have read. Your partner should listen for and identify the relative pronouns *that, which, who, whom, or whose* in your description.

WRITING APPLICATION

Write sentences using the following adverbial clauses: *while I waited, after the mail was delivered; since I started high school.*

Elliptical Adverbial Clauses Sometimes, words are omitted in adverbial clauses, especially in those clauses that begin with *as* or *than* and are used to express comparisons. Such clauses are said to be *elliptical.*

> An **elliptical clause** is a clause in which the verb or the subject and verb are understood but not actually stated.

3.2.10 RULE

Even though the subject or the verb (or both) may not appear in an elliptical clause, they make the clause express a complete thought.

In the following examples, the understood words appear in brackets. The sentences are alike, except for the words *he* and *him*. In the first sentence, *he* is a subject of the adverbial clause. In the second sentence, *him* functions as a direct object of the adverbial clause.

VERB UNDERSTOOD	His sister resembles their father more **than he [does]** .
SUBJECT AND VERB UNDERSTOOD	His sister resembles their father more **than [she resembles] him** .

When you read or write elliptical clauses, mentally include the omitted words to clarify the intended meaning.

See Practice 3.2E

Noun Clauses

Subordinate clauses can also act as nouns in sentences.

> A **noun clause** is a subordinate clause that acts as a noun.

3.2.11 RULE

A noun clause acts in almost the same way a one-word noun does in a sentence: It tells what or whom the sentence is about.

In a sentence, a noun clause may act as a subject, direct object, indirect object, predicate nominative, object of a preposition, or appositive.

EXAMPLES **Whatever you lost** can be found in the house.
subject

My parents remembered **what I wanted for my graduation** .
direct object

The chart on the next page contains more examples of the functions of noun clauses.

Introductory Words

Noun clauses frequently begin with the words *that, which, who, whom,* or *whose*—the same words that are used to begin adjective clauses. *Whichever, whoever,* or *whomever* may also be used as introductory words in noun clauses. Other noun clauses begin with the words *how, if, what, whatever, where, when, whether,* or *why.*

Introductory words may act as subjects, direct objects, objects of prepositions, adjectives, or adverbs in noun clauses, or they may simply introduce the clauses.

SOME USES OF INTRODUCTORY WORDS IN NOUN CLAUSES	
FUNCTIONS IN CLAUSES	EXAMPLES
Adjective	He could not decide which car was the best.
Adverb	We want to know how to get there .
Subject	I want the receipe from whoever made that pot pie !
Direct Object	Whatever my guidance counselor advised , I did.
No Function	The doctor determined that she had broken her leg .

Note that in the following chart the introductory word *that* in the last example has no function except to introduce the clause.

FUNCTIONS OF NOUN CLAUSES IN SENTENCES	
Acting as a Subject	Whoever is last must close the door.
Acting as a Direct Object	Please invite whomever you want to the wedding.
Acting as an Indirect Object	Her attitude gave whomever met her a shock.
Acting as a Predicate Nominative	Our problem is whether we should help or not.
Acting as an Object of a Preposition	Use the car for whatever purpose you choose.
Acting as an Appositive	The country rejected the plea that prisoners be cared for by personal dentists.

Some words that introduce noun clauses also introduce adjectival and adverbial clauses. It is necessary to check the function of the clause in the sentence to determine its type. To check the function, try substituting the words *it, you, fact,* or *thing* for the clause. If the sentence retains its smoothness, you probably replaced a noun clause.

NOUN CLAUSE I knew **that she wouldn't be on time**.

SUBSTITUTION I knew it.

In the following examples, all three subordinating clauses begin with *where,* but only the first is a noun clause because it functions in the sentence as a direct object.

NOUN CLAUSE Mr. Anderson told the tour group **where they would meet after the show**.
(Told the group *what?*)

ADJECTIVAL CLAUSE They took the patient to the emergency room, **where they examined him**.
(*Which* room?)

ADVERBIAL CLAUSE She lives **where the weather is rainy all year**.
(Lives *where?*)

Note About Introductory Words: The introductory word *that* is often omitted from a noun clause. In the following examples, the understood word *that* is in brackets.

EXAMPLES The security guard suggested **[that] I state my name**.

After his teacher told him he passed, Brian knew **[that] he could do anything**.

We remember **[that] you wanted Japanese food for dinner tonight**. See Practice 3.2F

PRACTICE 3.2E ▷ Identifying Elliptical Adverbial Clauses

Read each sentence. Then, write the adverbial clause in each sentence. For the adverbial clauses that are elliptical, add the understood words in parentheses.

EXAMPLE   My sculpture received more praise than his sculpture.

ANSWER   *than his sculpture (did)*

1. That building is taller than the Empire State Building.

2. My foot itches more than a bee sting itches.

3. Carrie spoke to Jason longer than to Joe.

4. Nora is as well-spoken as her mother.

5. Carl's explanation is as clear as your explanation.

6. The newly discovered star is as bright as our star.

7. Joanne is as early as you.

8. I can ski faster than Ed.

9. Jill's kite is higher than Mr. William's kite.

10. The baseball is rolling faster than the bowling ball.

PRACTICE 3.2F ▷ Recognizing Noun Clauses

Read each sentence. Then, write the noun clause in each sentence and label it *subject, direct object, indirect object, predicate nominative,* or *object of a preposition.*

EXAMPLE   We all knew that you would win.

ANSWER   *that you would win* — direct object

11. Do you know when the flight departs?

12. The king will give whoever wins a reward.

13. That she was angry was obvious to no one.

14. One concern was which field had better amenities.

15. We ask that you submit your film again.

16. What Francis documented astonished all of us.

17. Roman's main concern was whether he should study or play basketball.

18. Whoever is passionate about film will enjoy this movie.

19. The boss's predicament about how it would be possible to appease both employees demanded much thought.

20. Harold offers advice to whoever is fortunate enough to stand next to him.

SPEAKING APPLICATION

Take turns with a partner. Tell about a vivid dream. Use at least three adverbial clauses. Your partner should listen for and identify the adverbial clauses.

WRITING APPLICATION

Write a paragraph in which you review a film, using three different functions of a noun clause. Underline each noun clause in your paragraph.

3.3 The Four Structures of Sentences

Independent and subordinate clauses are the building blocks of sentences. These clauses can be combined in an endless number of ways to form the four basic sentence structures: **simple, compound, complex,** and **compound-complex.**

RULE 3.3.1

A simple sentence contains a single independent or main clause.

Although a simple sentence contains only one main or independent clause, its subject, verb, or both may be compound. A simple sentence may also have modifying phrases and complements. However, it cannot have a subordinate clause.

In the following simple sentences, the subjects are highlighted in yellow, and the verbs are highlighted in orange.

ONE SUBJECT AND VERB	The **rain fell**.
COMPOUND SUBJECT	**Dan** and **I made** the coffee.
COMPOUND VERB	The **girl jumped** and **ran**.
COMPOUND SUBJECT AND VERB	Neither the **teacher** nor the **student heard** the alarm or **saw** smoke.

RULE 3.3.2

A compound sentence contains two or more main clauses.

The main clauses in a compound sentence can be joined by a comma and a coordinating conjunction (*and, but, for, nor, or, so, yet*) or by a semicolon (;). Like a simple sentence, a compound sentence contains no subordinate clauses.

EXAMPLE   An American **bride** often **carries** flowers at her wedding, and **she throws** the flowers at the end.

See Practice 3.3A

> **A complex sentence** consists of one independent or main clause and one or more subordinate clauses.

The independent clause in a complex sentence is often called the main clause to distinguish it from the subordinate clause or clauses. The subject and verb in the independent clause are called the subject of the sentence and the main verb. The second example shows that a subordinate clause may fall between the parts of a main clause. In the examples below, the main clauses are highlighted in blue, and the subordinate clauses are highlighted in pink.

EXAMPLES   **No one answered the door** **when the bell rang**.

The bouquet of flowers **that the girl carried** **didn't have any lilies**.

Note on Complex Sentences With Noun Clauses: The subject of the main clause may sometimes be the subordinate clause itself.

EXAMPLE   **That he wanted to run** **upset them**.

> **A compound-complex sentence** consists of two or more independent clauses and one or more subordinate clauses.

In the example below, the independent clauses are highlighted in blue, and the subordinate clauses are highlighted in pink.

EXAMPLE   **The deck boards splinter** **when it snows heavily**, and **we have to repair the wood finish** **so that the splinters are covered**.

See Practice 3.3B

PRACTICE 3.3A > Distinguishing Between Simple and Compound Sentences

Read each sentence. Then, label each sentence as *simple* or *compound*.

EXAMPLE   Joe dove for the ball and missed.

ANSWER   *simple*

1. We had hoped for good news from our teacher but the scores had not been published yet.

2. Teammates and rivals alike worked side by side covering the field.

3. Sandy stood behind the podium, collected herself, and began her speech.

4. The counselors were satisfied, but the campers were not happy with the new rules.

5. Phillip completed his lessons late, so he was not free to come along with us.

6. Mr. Henderson laughed long and hard.

7. Our assignment would never be complete; nevertheless, we decided to continue.

8. We remained on the side of the road.

9. Some travelers pack well; some prepare halfheartedly; others reject the entire process.

10. Veronica had an urge to clean the kitchen.

PRACTICE 3.3B > Identifying the Four Structures of Sentences

Read each sentence. Then, label each sentence as *simple, compound, complex,* or *compound-complex*.

EXAMPLE   Chase found that he needed to spend his time wisely.

ANSWER   *complex*

11. The assembly is trying to determine how they will promote their cause.

12. The lieutenant cautioned the rookie detectives to be careful.

13. The runners approached the final lap, and the crowd cheered loudly.

14. We should be quick, or the boat will depart without us.

15. Jacqueline would be the best selection, for she debates better than I.

16. Mayor Johnson posed for photographs and greeted each visitor.

17. Although I enjoy swimming and diving, I do better outside the pool.

18. The teacher picked up the note and tossed it into the garbage can.

19. Can you find the recipe Margarita likes, or shall I have her e-mail it?

20. Laura volunteered at a food bank that offered services for needy people, and she earned praise for her caring attitude.

SPEAKING APPLICATION

Take turns with a partner. Describe your favorite activity. Your partner should listen for and identify simple and compound sentences in your description.

WRITING APPLICATION

Write a brief paragraph on any topic of your choice, using a variety of correctly structured sentences: simple, compound, complex, and compound-complex.

Cumulative Review Chapters 1–3

PRACTICE 1 ▷ **Identifying Nouns**

Read the sentences. Label each underlined noun as *concrete* or *abstract*. If the noun is concrete, label it *collective*, *compound*, or *proper*.

1. Jonathan has a <u>passion</u> for photography.

2. Next December I will be traveling to <u>Scotland</u>.

3. Preparing for his trip to <u>Lake Minnetonka</u>, Carl packed a <u>flashlight</u>.

4. It is William's <u>concern</u> for others that makes him special.

5. Gregory meets with his <u>staff</u> every Tuesday.

PRACTICE 2 ▷ **Identifying Pronouns**

Read the sentences. Then, label each underlined pronoun *reciprocal*, *demonstrative*, *relative*, *interrogative*, or *indefinite*.

1. Harold and Ben shook hands with <u>each other</u>.

2. <u>That</u> is Carla's ticket.

3. The woman <u>who</u> hired me was incredibly courteous.

4. <u>What</u> do you want to do this weekend?

5. <u>All</u> the seats were occupied at the PTA meeting.

PRACTICE 3 ▷ **Classifying Verbs and Verb Phrases**

Read the sentences. Then, write the verb or verb phrase in each sentence. Label them as *action verb* or *linking verb*, and *transitive* or *intransitive*.

1. The competitors looked intently at one another before the game.

2. The committee selected a new chairperson to head the science department.

3. Zachary always feels invigorated after taking a walk.

4. Samantha appeared excited at the news of the election.

5. Mr. Hampton greeted the Weatherman family at the door.

PRACTICE 4 ▷ **Identifying Adjectives and Adverbs**

Read the sentences. Then, label the underlined word as *adverb* or *adjective*. Write the word that is modified.

1. Hanson made a <u>powerful</u> serve to win the match.

2. The charity event attracted many <u>well-known</u> celebrities.

3. Marcus handled the situation <u>rather</u> calmly.

4. After the <u>second</u> lap, Jacqueline had a lead.

5. Gloria was <u>not</u> involved in the argument.

PRACTICE 5 ▷ **Using Conjunctions and Interjections**

Read the sentences. Then, write the conjunction or interjection. If there is a conjunction in the sentence, label it *coordinating*, *correlative*, or *subordinating*.

1. Hector searched through the couch for change as Fred ordered the pizza.

2. Kenneth's flight was canceled, so he was forced to stay another night.

3. Man! I just can't seem to finish this puzzle.

4. Not only did we catch four big fish, but we also ate them later that night.

5. Both Simon and Christine received scholarships to college.

Continued on next page ▶

Cumulative Review   Chapters 1–3

 PRACTICE 6 **Recognizing Direct and Indirect Objects and Object of a Preposition**

Identify the underlined items as a *direct object,* *indirect object,* or *object of a preposition.*

1. Meena rode the <u>train</u> to the <u>museum</u>.

2. Gary gave his <u>girlfriend</u> a <u>necklace</u>.

3. Adrian showed the <u>talent scout</u> a glimpse of his <u>portfolio</u>.

4. The principal praised <u>Rich</u> and <u>Jessica</u> for their perfect attendance.

5. Joshua asked the <u>doorman</u> for directions to the <u>arena</u>.

6. Has Flora shown <u>Luther</u> and <u>Ruth</u> her new dress?

7. Will Kent buy <u>us</u> tickets to the <u>rodeo</u>?

8. Mrs. O'Connor reads her <u>daughter</u> a <u>story</u> every night.

9. The plumber sent me a <u>bill</u> for his <u>services</u>.

10. My uncle Sean gave <u>us</u> tickets to the <u>match</u>.

PRACTICE 7 **Identifying Phrases**

Write the phrases contained in the following sentences. Identify each phrase as a *prepositional phrase, appositive phrase, participial phrase, gerund phrase,* or *infinitive phrase.*

1. Last weekend, Anya went to the circus.

2. Mark went to the post office to mail his application.

3. Mr. Newsome, my first-grade teacher, wrote me a letter.

4. Studying for the quiz is a good idea.

5. I was completely soaked by the pouring rain.

6. Working hard, the detective solved the case.

7. Coach Landry asked Thomas to join the team.

8. Playing baseball is Sean's favorite activity.

9. Constance Reynolds, our regional supervisor, gave her annual report.

10. Victor Gonzalez, a former professional athlete, took a job coaching collegiate sports.

PRACTICE 8 **Recognizing Clauses**

Label the underlined clauses in the following sentences *independent* or *subordinate.* Identify any subordinate clause as *adjectival, adverbial,* or *noun clause.* Then, label any adjectival clauses *essential* or *nonessential.*

1. <u>Although Trevor could not play ball</u>, he ran out onto the field.

2. My good friend Larry, <u>who lives in Dallas</u>, just graduated from high school.

3. After I left the gym, <u>I ran into Nathan in the parking lot</u>.

4. <u>If you want to sing well</u>, you must practice.

5. Professor Jenkins is impressive for <u>what he knows about ancient history</u>.

6. William's idea <u>that I hire you</u> was a stroke of genius.

7. You take out the garbage <u>while I clean the attic</u>.

8. Frederick, <u>who put on a hat and scarf</u>, set off into the snowstorm.

9. <u>My mom has decided to hire an interior decorator</u> because she wants to brighten the room.

10. <u>Why you forgot me</u> is hard to comprehend.

CHAPTER 4

EFFECTIVE SENTENCES

Use both shorter and longer sentences, including compound and complex sentences, to add variety to your writing.

WRITE GUY *Jeff Anderson, M.Ed.*

WHAT DO YOU NOTICE?

Investigate how ideas are combined as you zoom in on this sentence from "Rama's Initiation," an excerpt from the *Ramayana* by R. K. Narayan.

MENTOR TEXT

> When they meditated on and recited these incantations, the arid atmosphere was transformed for the rest of their passage and they felt as if they were wading through a cool stream with a southern summer breeze blowing in their faces.

Now, ask yourself the following questions:

- How did the author combine ideas in the subordinate clause that begins the sentence?
- How does the author combine the two remaining ideas in the sentence?

A compound verb connects ideas in the subordinate clause *when they meditated on and recited these incantations.* Rather than use two clauses, one about meditating and one about reciting, the author uses *and* to combine the ideas. The author then combines two main, or independent, clauses using the conjunction *and*—one about the atmosphere being transformed and the other about the subjects feeling as if they were wading through a cool stream.

Grammar for Writers Writers often combine sentences to make their writing flow smoothly. Add a graceful rhythm to your sentences by looking for different ways to combine ideas.

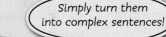

Simply turn them into complex sentences!

I have too many short sentences in this paragraph. What's a simple solution?

4.1 The Four Functions of a Sentence

Sentences can be classified according to what they do—that is, whether they state ideas, ask questions, give orders, or express strong emotions.

Declarative sentences are used to declare, or state, facts.

RULE 4.1.1 > A **declarative sentence** states an idea and ends with a period.

DECLARATIVE   Toronto is a city in Canada.

To *interrogate* means "to ask." An **interrogative sentence** is a question.

RULE 4.1.2 > An **interrogative sentence** asks a question and ends with a question mark.

INTERROGATIVE   In which countries do gorillas live?

Imperative sentences give commands or directions.

RULE 4.1.3 > An **imperative sentence** gives an order or a direction and ends with either a period or an exclamation mark.

EL9

Most imperative sentences start with a verb. In this type of imperative sentence, the subject is understood to be *you*.

IMPERATIVE   Follow the list exactly.

Exclamatory sentences are used to express emotions.

RULE 4.1.4 > An **exclamatory sentence** conveys strong emotion and ends with an exclamation mark.

EXCLAMATORY   This is ridiculous!

See Practice 4.1A
See Practice 4.1B

PRACTICE 4.1A > Identifying the Four Types of Sentences

Read each sentence. Then, label each sentence *declarative, interrogative, imperative,* or *exclamatory.*

EXAMPLE   Leave a note if no one is in the office.

ANSWER   *imperative*

1. Have you located the movie you wanted to see?
2. Sign here after you fill out the form.
3. Which of the applicants do you think deserves the job?
4. Skate parks are becoming increasingly popular.
5. Make sure the bolt is screwed on tightly.
6. What a thoughtful thing to do!
7. Walk south on Second Street and then make a right turn.
8. The heat from the oven fills the room.
9. Have you seen Luanne since yesterday?
10. What a mess!

PRACTICE 4.1B > Punctuating the Four Types of Sentences

Read each sentence. Then, label each sentence *declarative, interrogative, imperative,* or *exclamatory.* Then, in parentheses, write the correct end mark.

EXAMPLE   Porcupines use sharp quills as a defense against predators

ANSWER   *declarative (.)*

11. What a fantastic night
12. Did you return the movie
13. What a strange looking cat that is
14. Please stop staring at me
15. Tomorrow's function should be interesting
16. Who wrote that novel
17. Now that is what I call a performance
18. During the summer, I plan to read lots of books
19. Be sure to tell your mother that I returned her scarf
20. You can tour the Alamo and see artifacts that date back to the Texas Revolution

SPEAKING APPLICATION

Take turns with a partner. Say sentences that are declarative, interrogative, imperative, and exclamatory. Your partner should identify each type of sentence.

WRITING APPLICATION

Write a paragraph, using any sentence in Practice 4.1B as your topic. Use declarative, imperative, and exclamatory sentences in your paragraph.

4.2 Sentence Combining

Too many short sentences can make your writing choppy and disconnected.

One way to avoid the excessive use of short sentences and to achieve variety is to combine sentences.

RULE 4.2.1

Sentences can be combined by using a compound subject, a compound verb, or a compound object.

TWO SENTENCES	Kate enjoyed watching the movie. Mike enjoyed watching the movie.
COMPOUND SUBJECT	Kate and Mike enjoyed watching the movie.
TWO SENTENCES	Tara studied hard today. Tara passed the test.
COMPOUND VERB	Tara studied hard today and passed the test.
TWO SENTENCES	Rob saw the band. Rob saw the fans.
COMPOUND OBJECT	Rob saw the band and the fans.

See Practice 4.2A

RULE 4.2.2

Sentences can be combined by joining two main or independent clauses to create a compound sentence.

Use a compound sentence when combining ideas that are related but independent. To join main clauses, use a comma and a coordinating conjunction (*for, and, but, or, nor, yet,* or *so*) or a semicolon.

EXAMPLE	The lion was looking for prey. It seemed very hungry.
COMPOUND SENTENCE	The lion was looking for prey, and it seemed very hungry.

RULE 4.2.3

> Sentences can be combined by changing one into a subordinate clause to create a **complex sentence.**

To show the relationship between ideas in which one depends on the other, use a **complex sentence.** The subordinating conjunction will help readers understand the relationship. Some common subordinating conjunctions are *after, although, because, if, since, when,* and *while.*

EXAMPLE	We were hungry. It had been a long and active day.
COMBINED WITH A SUBORDINATE CLAUSE	We were hungry **after our long and active day** .

RULE 4.2.4

> Sentences can be combined by changing one of them into a **phrase.**

EXAMPLE	My school plays today. We play the other high school.
COMBINED WITH PREPOSITIONAL PHRASE	My school plays **against the other high school** today.
EXAMPLE	My school will play against the other high school today. They are number one.
COMBINED WITH APPOSITIVE PHRASE	My school will play against the other high school today, **the number one team** .

See Practice 4.2B
See Practice 4.2C

Combining Sentences Using Compound Subjects, Verbs, and Objects

Read each set of sentences. Then, write one sentence that combines them.

EXAMPLE   Simon doesn't like riding in elevators. Simon doesn't like flying in airplanes.

ANSWER   *Simon doesn't like riding in elevators or flying in airplanes.*

1. Skiing is often difficult for beginners. Skiing requires good balance.

2. I like to eat steak. I like to eat potatoes.

3. The book contains pictures of medieval castles. There are pictures of royal armies.

4. Brandon built the bookshelf himself. Brandon built the table himself.

5. Ray went hiking. Ray saw raccoons.

6. She is a talented vocalist. She is the best singer in the choir.

7. Randolph's daughter is a lawyer. Randolph's son is a lawyer.

8. Tony won the race. Tony won a trophy.

9. Clouds covered the sky. A huge flock of birds covered the sky.

10. The magician wanted to go backstage. His assistant wanted to go backstage.

Combining Sentences Using Phrases

Read each set of sentences. Then, combine each set by turning one sentence into a phrase that adds detail to the other.

EXAMPLE   The howling wind blew through the trees. The trees surrounded our house.

ANSWER   *The howling wind blew through the trees that surrounded our house.*

11. Hail fell persistently throughout the city. It fell for an hour.

12. William Tamery was the first captain of the soccer team. He was a major reason for the winning season.

13. Humpback whales communicate with one another. Humpback whales are endangered animals.

14. Doing calisthenics is a great way to stay in shape. Calisthenics is a form of exercise.

15. The Taggert Building was originally a fire station. The Taggert Building is now the town's museum.

SPEAKING APPLICATION

Take turns with a partner. Tell two related sentences. Your partner should combine these sentences into one sentence.

WRITING APPLICATION

Write two related sentences. Then, exchange papers with a partner. Your partner should combine the two sentences into one by turning one sentence into a phrase.

PRACTICE 4.2C ▶ **Combining Sentences by Forming Compound or Complex Sentences**

Read each pair of sentences. Then, combine the sentences, using the coordinating or subordinating conjunction indicated in parentheses.

EXAMPLE   Robert and his brother could not spend time together. They wrote letters to each other. (so)

ANSWER   *Robert and his brother could not spend time together, so they wrote letters to each other.*

1. Poetry can express emotions and ideas. Poetry stimulates and entertains the reader. (as)

2. Would you like to go to the zoo? Is reading about animals good enough for now? (or)

3. Giving your new pet plenty of attention takes time. Every moment is worth it. (but)

4. One day, Logan went to a beach. The beach offered all kinds of entertainment. (that)

5. I like horses and dogs. I get along better with cats. (although)

6. The symphony finished its performance. The audience gave it a standing ovation. (and)

7. Bethany finished her test before the rest of the class. She was allowed to go to the library. (so)

8. We had accomplished our goal. We realized there was more work to do. (yet)

9. Steve went to school early. I walked to school alone. (while)

10. Stanley finished the science project. Leonard added the bibliography. (after)

4.3 Varying Sentences

Vary your sentences to develop a rhythm, to achieve an effect, or to emphasize the connections between ideas. There are several ways you can vary your sentences.

Varying Sentence Length

To emphasize a point or surprise a reader, include a short, direct sentence to interrupt the flow of long sentences. Notice the effect of the last sentence in the following paragraph.

EXAMPLE   The Jacobites derived their name from *Jacobus,* the Latin name for King James II of England, who was dethroned in 1688 by William of Orange during the Glorious Revolution. Unpopular because of his Catholicism and autocratic ruling style, James fled to France to seek the aid of King Louis XIV. In 1690, James, along with a small body of French troops, landed in Ireland in an attempt to regain his throne. His hopes ended at the Battle of the Boyne.

Some sentences contain only one idea and can't be broken. It may be possible, however, to state the idea in a shorter sentence. Other sentences contain two or more ideas and might be shortened by breaking up the ideas.

LONGER SENTENCE   Many of James II's predecessors were able to avoid major economic problems, but James had serious economic problems.

MORE DIRECT   Unlike many of his predecessors, James II was unable to avoid major economic problems.

LONGER SENTENCE   James tried to work with Parliament to develop a plan of taxation that would be fair and reasonable, but members of Parliament rejected his efforts, and James dissolved the Parliament.

SHORTER SENTENCES   James tried to work with Parliament to develop a fair and reasonable taxation plan. However, because members of Parliament rejected his efforts, James dissolved the Parliament.

Varying Sentence Beginnings

Another way to create sentence variety is to start sentences with different parts of speech.

WAYS TO VARY SENTENCE BEGINNINGS	
Start With a Noun	Cars are difficult to rebuild.
Start With an Adverb	Naturally, cars are difficult to rebuild.
Start With an Adverbial Phrase	Because of their complexity, cars are difficult to rebuild.
Start With a Participial Phrase	Having tried to rebuild several cars, I know how hard it is.
Start With a Prepositional Phrase	For the average person, cars are very difficult to rebuild.
Start With an Infinitive Phrase	To rebuild a classic car was my goal.

See Practice 4.3A

Using Inverted Word Order

You can also vary sentence beginnings by reversing the traditional subject–verb order to create verb–subject order. You can reverse order by starting the sentence with a **participial phrase** or a **prepositional phrase.** You can also move a complement to the beginning of the sentence.

SUBJECT–VERB ORDER

The Browns waited at the traffic light.

The team marched onto the opponent's field.

The cheering of the fans filled the air.

The cheering was deafening.

VERB–SUBJECT ORDER

Waiting at the traffic light were the Browns.
participial phrase

Onto the opponent's field marched the team.
prepositional phrase

Filling the air was the cheering of the fans.
participial phrase

Deafening was the cheering.
predicate adjective

See Practice 4.3B

PRACTICE 4.3A ▷ Revising to Vary Sentence Beginnings

Read each sentence. Rewrite each sentence to begin with the part of speech or phrase indicated in parentheses. You may need to add a word or phrase.

EXAMPLE   I tossed and turned constantly and didn't sleep at all during the night. (participial phrase)

ANSWER   *Tossing and turning constantly, I didn't sleep at all during the night.*

1. Oceanographers have worked endlessly to study the sea. (adverb)

2. I lost my concentration when the phone began to ring. (adverb)

3. I asked her to visit. (infinitive phrase)

4. I roasted a turkey. (prepositional phrase)

5. I ate an apple. (participial phrase)

6. I tried to distract my mother. (adverb)

7. I proudly delivered my speech. (infinitive phrase)

8. Trees are homes to birds and other small animals. (prepositional phrase)

9. Fire can spread quickly through a dry forest. (adverbial phrase)

10. Contestants have won lots of prizes. (adverb)

PRACTICE 4.3B ▷ Inverting Sentences to Vary Subject-Verb Order

Read each sentence. Rewrite each of the following sentences by inverting the subject-verb order to verb-subject order.

EXAMPLE   Several tourists stared at the timetable in the train station.

ANSWER   *Staring at the timetable in the train station were several tourists.*

11. Burning coals and boiling lava erupted from the mouth of Mount Etna.

12. Clarissa lay on the bed with her ankle throbbing painfully.

13. The basic requirements for the merit badge are listed here.

14. The mountain loomed above us, jagged and menacing.

15. The good news spread throughout the town.

16. A family of robins settled in our maple tree.

17. Three dedicated band members practiced for hours in our garage.

18. The actor delivered the speech dramatically.

19. The first Liberty Bell cracked during testing.

20. A gentle stream flows throughout the campgrounds.

SPEAKING APPLICATION

Take turns with a partner. Say sentences aloud. Your partner should revise each sentence to have a different beginning.

WRITING APPLICATION

Write three original sentences about your plans for the future. Then, exchange papers with a partner. Your partner should invert the subject-verb order in your sentences to verb-subject order.

4.4 Avoid Fragments and Run-ons

Hasty writers sometimes omit crucial words, punctuate awkwardly, or leave their thoughts unfinished, causing two common sentence errors: **fragments** and **run-ons**.

Recognizing Fragments

Although some writers use them for stylistic effect, **fragments** are generally considered errors in standard English.

> **Do not capitalize and punctuate phrases, subordinate clauses, or words in a series as if they were complete sentences.**

Reading your work aloud to listen for natural pauses and stops should help you avoid fragments. Sometimes, you can repair a fragment by connecting it to words that come before or after it.

> **One way to correct a fragment is to connect it to the words in a nearby sentence.**

PARTICIPIAL FRAGMENT	inspired by the skill of the sensei
ADDED TO A NEARBY SENTENCE	**Inspired by the skill of the sensei**, Rick saw the karate demonstration again.
PREPOSITIONAL FRAGMENT	before his students
ADDED TO A NEARBY SENTENCE	The sensei performed his demonstration **before his students**.
PRONOUN AND PARTICIPIAL FRAGMENT	the one stuffed with vegetables
ADDED TO NEARBY SENTENCE	My favorite sandwich is **the one stuffed with vegetables**.

> Another way to correct a fragment is to add any sentence part that is needed to make the fragment a complete sentence.

Remember that every complete sentence must have both a subject and a verb and express a complete thought. Check to see that each of your sentences contains all of the parts necessary to be complete.

NOUN FRAGMENT

the group of experienced Boy Scouts

COMPLETED SENTENCES

The group of experienced Boy Scouts
subject

built their campsite here.
verb

We attentively watched
subject   verb

the group of experienced Boy Scouts .
direct object

Notice what missing sentence parts must be added to the following types of phrase fragments to make them complete.

	FRAGMENTS	COMPLETED SENTENCES
Noun Fragment With Participial Phrase	the instructions read by us	The instructions were read by us.
Verb Fragment	will be at the meeting today	I will be at the meeting today.
Prepositional Fragment	in the pantry closet	I put the pasta in the pantry closet.
Participial Fragment	found under the bed	The sneakers found under the bed are mine.
Gerund Fragment	teaching my children to cook	Teaching my children to cook is fun.
Infinitive Fragment	to eat the fresh lasagna	I expect to eat the fresh lasagna.

> You may need to attach a **subordinate clause** to a main clause to correct a fragment.

A **subordinate clause** contains a subject and a verb but does not express a complete thought and cannot stand alone as a sentence. Link it to a main clause to make the sentence complete.

ADJECTIVAL CLAUSE FRAGMENT   which was being displayed outside

COMPLETED SENTENCE   I enjoyed visiting the art exhibit, **which was being displayed outside**.

ADVERBIAL CLAUSE FRAGMENT   after he painted the new mural

COMPLETED SENTENCE   **After he painted the new mural**, he was ready for the exhibit.

NOUN CLAUSE FRAGMENT   whatever food is left in the pantry

COMPLETED SENTENCE   We will eat **whatever food is left in the pantry**.

Series Fragments A fragment is not always short. A long series of words still needs to have a subject and a verb and express a complete thought. It may be a long fragment masquerading as a sentence.

SERIES FRAGMENT	COMPLETE SENTENCE
after reading Dickens's novel, with its cynical look at poverty and greed, in the style so typical of this writer	After reading Dickens's novel, with it's cynical look at poverty and greed, in the style so typical of this writer, I was able to prepare an interesting term paper.

See Practice 4.4A

Avoiding Run-on Sentences

A **run-on** sentence is two or more sentences capitalized and punctuated as if they were a single sentence.

> **Use punctuation and conjunctions to correctly join or separate parts of a run-on sentence.**

There are two kinds of **run-ons: fused sentences**, which are two or more sentences joined with no punctuation, and **comma splices**, which have two or more sentences separated only by commas rather than by commas and conjunctions.

FUSED SENTENCE	The team practiced every day they became the best in the state.
COMMA SPLICE	The one couple arrived for dinner, the other couple never came.

As with fragments, proofreading or reading your work aloud will help you find run-ons. Once found, they can be corrected by adding punctuation and conjunctions or by rewording the sentences.

FOUR WAYS TO CORRECT RUN-ONS		
	RUN-ON	CORRECTION
With End Marks and Capitals	The party was in full swing at the house the people laughed together.	The party was in full swing. At the house, the people laughed together.
With Commas and Conjunctions	The presents needed wrapping we could not locate the tape.	The presents needed wrapping, but we could not locate the tape.
With Semicolons	New York City has many cultures living together, consequently it is called the melting pot.	New York City has many cultures living together; consequently, it is called the melting pot.
By Rewriting	The dog show began late, a judge didn't arrive on time.	The dog show began late because a judge didn't arrive on time.

See Practice 4.4B

PRACTICE 4.4A **Identifying and Correcting Fragments**

Read each sentence. If an item contains a fragment, rewrite it to make a complete sentence. If an item contains a complete sentence, write *correct*.

EXAMPLE   While she was cooking.

ANSWER   *While she was cooking, the phone rang.*

1. Loud music makes studying difficult.

2. Where cattails and reeds grew high.

3. I am sometimes funny, loud, or just silly.

4. Must have been abandoned.

5. He plans to be friendly.

6. After he took the dog to the vet.

7. A gallon of green paint should be enough for this room.

8. When the bell rang, there were students left outside.

9. Concerned about the look of the sky.

10. Because time was running short.

PRACTICE 4.4B **Revising to Eliminate Run-on Sentences**

Read each sentence. Correct each run-on by correctly joining or separating the sentence parts.

EXAMPLE   The beach is pleasant during the week, it is crowded on weekends.

ANSWER   *The beach is pleasant during the week. It is crowded on weekends.*

11. The play was good, the cast was only mediocre.

12. Michael wants to become a doctor, he is my brother.

13. You'll love that book, it is a page turner.

14. I applied for a variety of jobs, everyone said I interviewed well.

15. In general, I love to exercise running is the activity that I enjoy most.

16. Catie wrote a poem it was her homework assignment.

17. Patel took driver's education classes, he received his driver's license a few months later.

18. Days turned into years, the years quickly passed.

19. Have you heard the news Marti is moving to Miami.

20. Catherine II was a Russian empress, she was called Catherine the Great.

SPEAKING APPLICATION

Take turns with a partner. Say sentence fragments. Your partner should turn each fragment into a complete sentence.

WRITING APPLICATION

Write three run-on sentences. Then, exchange papers with a partner and correct your partner's run-on sentences.

4.5 Misplaced and Dangling Modifiers

Careful writers put modifiers as close as possible to the words they modify. When modifiers are misplaced or left dangling in a sentence, the result may be illogical or confusing.

Recognizing Misplaced Modifiers

A **misplaced modifier** is placed too far from the modified word and appears to modify the wrong word or words.

RULE 4.5.1

> A **misplaced modifier** seems to modify the wrong word in the sentence.

MISPLACED MODIFIER
The girl fell over a hurdle **running on the track**.

CORRECTION
The girl **running on the track** fell over a hurdle.

MISPLACED MODIFIER
We heard the doorbell ring **while eating dinner**.

CORRECTION
While eating dinner, we heard the doorbell ring.

Recognizing Dangling Modifiers

With **dangling modifiers,** the word that should be modified is missing from the sentence. Dangling modifiers usually come at the beginning of a sentence and are followed by a comma. The subject being modified should come right after the comma.

RULE 4.5.2

> A **dangling modifier** seems to modify the wrong word or no word at all because the word it should modify has been omitted from the sentence.

See Practice 4.5A

DANGLING PARTICIPIAL PHRASE	Measuring carefully, each ingredient was placed into the bowl.
	(Who did the measuring?)
CORRECTED SENTENCE	Measuring carefully, **the cook** placed each ingredient into the bowl.

Dangling participial phrases are corrected by adding missing words and making other needed changes.

Dangling infinitive phrases and elliptical clauses can be corrected in the same way. First, identify the subject of the sentence. Then, make sure each subject is clearly stated. You may also need to change the form of the verb.

DANGLING INFINITIVE PHRASE	To exit the highway, the toll must be paid.
	(Who is exiting and must pay?)
CORRECTED SENTENCE	To exit the highway, **drivers** must pay the toll.
DANGLING ELLIPTICAL CLAUSE	While laying on the beach, a school of dolphins was spotted.
	(Who was laying on the beach and spotted the dolphins?)
CORRECTED SENTENCE	While laying on the beach, **we** spotted a school of dolphins.

EL8

A dangling adverbial clause may also occur when the antecedent of a pronoun is not clear.

DANGLING ADVERBIAL CLAUSE	When they had been married for fifty years, Sharon and Tom planned a party for their parents.
	(Who is married for 50 years, Sharon and Tom or their parents?)
CORRECTED SENTENCE	**When their parents had been married for 50 years**, Sharon and Tom planned a party for them.

See Practice 4.5B

PRACTICE 4.5A ▷ Identifying and Correcting Misplaced Modifiers

Read each sentence. Then, rewrite each sentence, putting the misplaced modifiers closer to the words they should modify.

EXAMPLE   We were happy to find the pizza in the oven that Dad had made.

ANSWER   *We were happy to find the pizza that Dad had made in the oven.*

1. The company has a meeting for employees who want to transfer overseas at noon.

2. The dog ran to his owner panting.

3. Austin drew a picture of a squirrel using computer software.

4. Please send a letter to me about the trip.

5. Clapping and cheering, the astronauts were greeted by the audience.

6. Chandra remembered that she had forgotten the map in the middle of our hike.

7. The dress at the store is on sale.

8. Walking, we saw a bear through the woods.

9. The boys waded in the creek and waited for a fish to come along with a net.

10. Let us know if you plan to attend the party on the enclosed card.

PRACTICE 4.5B ▷ Identifying and Correcting Dangling Modifiers

Read each sentence. Then, rewrite each sentence, correcting any dangling modifiers by supplying missing words or ideas.

EXAMPLE   Having arrived late, a note from the office was needed.

ANSWER   *Having arrived late, the girl needed a note from the office.*

11. Paddling along the lake, the scenery was relaxing.

12. To locate the missing hamster, a thorough search will be necessary.

13. Practicing the piano, the kids playing baseball were distracting.

14. Before leaving, turn off the lights.

15. Having given his customer a refund, the matter seemed to be closed.

16. The landscape became lush descending into the valley.

17. While logging in California, gold was discovered.

18. Before she left, Claire kissed her mother.

19. Walking onto the patio, the swimming pool looked inviting.

20. Drinking tea, my spoon fell on the floor.

SPEAKING APPLICATION

Take turns with a partner. Tell about something interesting that you have done. Use modifiers in your sentences. Your partner should name the modifiers and tell whether they are correctly placed.

WRITING APPLICATION

Use sentences 18, 19, and 20 as models to write your own examples of dangling modifiers. Then, rewrite each sentence to correct the dangling modifier.

4.6 Faulty Parallelism

Good writers try to present a series of ideas in similar grammatical structures so the ideas will read smoothly. If one element in a series is not parallel with the others, the result may be jarring or confusing.

Recognizing the Correct Use of Parallelism

To present a series of ideas of equal importance, you should use parallel grammatical structures.

> **Parallelism** involves presenting equal ideas in words, phrases, clauses, or sentences of similar types.

4.6.1 RULE

PARALLEL WORDS	The athlete looked **strong**, **fit**, and **agile**.
PARALLEL PHRASES	The greatest feeling I know is **to run a marathon flawlessly** and **to have all my friends watch me enviously**.
PARALLEL CLAUSES	The sneakers **that you recommended** and **that my sister wants** are on sale.
PARALLEL SENTENCES	**It couldn't be**, of course. **It could never, never be**. –Dorothy Parker

Correcting Faulty Parallelism

Faulty parallelism occurs when a writer uses unequal grammatical structures to express related ideas.

> Correct a sentence containing faulty parallelism by rewriting it so that each parallel idea is expressed in the same grammatical structure.

4.6.2 RULE

Faulty parallelism can involve words, phrases, and clauses in a series or in comparisons.

Nonparallel Words, Phrases, and Clauses in a Series

Always check for parallelism when your writing contains items in a series.

Correcting Faulty Parallelism in a Series

NONPARALLEL STRUCTURES	**Scheduling**, **purchasing**, and **management**

gerund   gerund   noun

of inventory are all steps in the retail process.

CORRECTION	**Scheduling**, **purchasing**, and **managing**

gerund   gerund   gerund

inventory are all steps in the retail process.

NONPARALLEL STRUCTURES	**I could not wait to taste the new foods,**

infinitive phrase

to experience the new restaurant, and

infinitive phrase

visiting the town.

participial phrase

CORRECTION	**I could not wait to taste the new foods, to**

infinitive phrase

experience the new restaurant, and to visit

infinitive phrase

the town.

infinitive phrase

NONPARALLEL STRUCTURE	**Some experts feel that jogging is not a**

noun clause

sport, but it requires athleticism.

independent clause

CORRECTION	**Some experts feel that jogging is not a sport**

noun clause

but that it requires athleticism.

noun clause

Another potential problem involves correlative conjunctions, such as *both … and* or *not only … but also*. Though these conjunctions connect two related items, writers sometimes misplace or split the first part of the conjunction. The result is faulty parallelism.

NONPARALLEL	Bill **not only** won the tennis match **but also** the state title.
PARALLEL	Bill won **not only** the tennis match **but also** the state title.

Nonparallel Words, Phrases, and Clauses in Comparisons
As the saying goes, you cannot compare apples with oranges. In writing comparisons, you generally should compare a phrase with the same type of phrase and a clause with the same type of clause.

Correcting Faulty Parallelism in Comparisons

NONPARALLEL STRUCTURES	Most people prefer **apples** to **eating celery**. noun gerund phrase
CORRECTION	Most people prefer **apples** to **celery**. noun noun

NONPARALLEL STRUCTURES	I left work **at 12:00 P.M.** rather than prepositional phrase **staying at work until 5:00 P.M.** participial phrase
CORRECTION	I left work **at 12:00 P.M.** rather than prepositional phrase **at the usual 5:00 P.M.** prepositional phrase

NONPARALLEL STRUCTURES	**George** delights **in rainy days** as much as subject prepositional phrase sunny **days** delight other **people**. subject direct object
CORRECTION	**George** delights **in rainy days** as much as subject prepositional phrase other **people** delight **in sunny days**. subject prepositional phrase

See Practice 4.6A

4.7 Faulty Coordination

When two or more independent clauses of unequal importance are joined by *and*, the result can be faulty **coordination**.

Recognizing Faulty Coordination

To *coordinate* means to "place side by side in equal rank." Two independent clauses that are joined by the coordinating conjunction *and*, therefore, should have equal rank.

RULE

4.7.1

> Use *and* or other coordinating conjunctions only to connect ideas of equal importance.

CORRECT COORDINATION   Blake designed an airplane, **and** Jane built it.

Sometimes, however, writers carelessly use *and* to join main clauses that either should not be joined or should be joined in another way so that the real relationship between the clauses is clear. Faulty coordination puts all the ideas on the same level of importance, even though logically they should not be.

FAULTY COORDINATION   Production of ships accelerated in World War II, **and** ships became a decisive factor in the war.

I didn't do well, **and** the contest was easy.

The lion looked ferocious, **and** it was growling at me.

Occasionally, writers will also string together so many ideas with *and's* that the reader is left breathless.

STRINGY SENTENCE   The tractor that drove through the field did a few twists and turns, **and** the people on the opposite side turned their necks to watch, **and** everyone laughed.

Correcting Faulty Coordination

Faulty coordination can be corrected in several ways.

> **One way to correct faulty coordination is to put unrelated ideas into separate sentences.**

When faulty coordination occurs in a sentence in which the main clauses are not closely related, separate the clauses and omit the coordinating conjunction.

FAULTY COORDINATION	Production of ships accelerated in World War II, **and** ships became a decisive factor in the war.
CORRECTION	Production of ships increased in World War II. Ships became a decisive factor in the war.

> **You can correct faulty coordination by putting less important ideas into subordinate clauses or phrases.**

If one main clause is less important than, or subordinate to, the other, turn it into a subordinate clause. You can also reduce a less important idea to a phrase.

FAULTY COORDINATION	I didn't do well, **and** the contest was easy.
CORRECTION	I didn't do well, **even though** the contest was easy.
FAULTY COORDINATION	The lion looked angry, **and** it was growling at me.
CORRECTION	Growling at me, the lion looked angry.

Stringy sentences should be broken up and revised using any of the three methods just described. Following is one way that the stringy sentence on the previous page can be revised.

REVISION OF A STRINGY SENTENCE	The tractor that drove through the field did a few twists and turns. Turning to watch, the people on the opposite side laughed.

See Practice 4.6B

PRACTICE 4.6A > **Revising to Eliminate Faulty Parallelism**

Read each sentence. Then, rewrite the sentence to correct any nonparallel structures.

EXAMPLE We enjoy walking on the beach and to collect seashells.

ANSWER *We enjoy walking on the beach and collecting seashells.*

1. The quarterback was criticized for poor throws and that he was rushing the plays.
2. I like painting, but I do not like to draw.
3. The store wants to hire someone who will help clean up and to stock shelves.
4. Seeing the movie was fun but to write a review of it was challenging.
5. The actor played the role well but a couple of times forgetting his lines.
6. My family likes to water ski and snorkeling.
7. To make a profit, we must increase sales or by cutting costs.
8. Everyone likes to receive cards but not taking the time to send them.
9. The main duties of a pet sitter are walking, feeding, and to give baths.
10. Eating, sleeping, and fun are important to me.

PRACTICE 4.6B > **Revising to Eliminate Faulty Coordination**

Read each sentence. Then, rewrite the sentence, to correct the faulty coordination.

EXAMPLE Mom bought a new car, and it's a small sedan.

ANSWER *Mom bought a new car, a small sedan.*

11. I added illustrations and I didn't have to.
12. We arrived at the mall, and the doors were about to open.
13. The beaches are wide and white, and they attract thousands of tourists.
14. We set up our campsite, and it has tents and a cooking stove.
15. We had bought everything that we needed, and we headed for our car.
16. I was so excited that I ran out the door, and I didn't eat breakfast.
17. Tripp is buying a new bike, and he sold his old one last week.
18. We hung a bird feeder in a tree, but a squirrel ate the seeds, so we put the feeder on a pole, and now the birds are able to get to the seeds.
19. Jemal waved to me, and he left for school.
20. Your dad was late picking us up, and we got to the class on time.

SPEAKING APPLICATION

Take turns with a partner. Tell about something you plan to do with your family or friends. Your partner should point out and correct any faulty parallelism.

WRITING APPLICATION

Use sentence 14 as a model to write a sentence with faulty coordination. Exchange papers with a partner. Your partner should correct the faulty coordination in your sentence.

CHAPTER 5

VERB USAGE

Portray events as you intend by using the correct forms of verbs in your writing.

WRITE GUY *Jeff Anderson, M.Ed.*

WHAT DO YOU NOTICE?

Discover the verbs as you zoom in on this sentence from the story "How Much Land Does a Man Need?" by Leo Tolstoy and as translated by Louise and Aylmer Maude.

MENTOR TEXT

"If it were my own land," thought Pahom, "I should be independent, and there wouldn't be all this unpleasantness."

Now, ask yourself the following questions:

- Why does the author use the verb *were* instead of *was* in the subordinate clause, *If it were my own land*?
- What do the auxiliary verbs *should* and *would* tell you about the mood of the sentence?

The author uses *were* instead of *was* to create the subjunctive mood, which is used to express something contrary to what is true. The auxiliary verbs *should* and *would* indicate that the rest of the sentence is also in the subjunctive mood. The use of the subjunctive mood helps the author express Pahom's wishes about what would happen *if* he had the land.

Grammar for Writers Verbs help connect and highlight ideas as much as they help express action. Use verbs to convey a mood or state of being in your writing.

I should start my homework...

Watch out. Should can get moody.

5.1 Verb Tenses

Besides expressing actions or conditions, verbs have different **tenses** to indicate when the action or condition occurred.

RULE 5.1.1 > A **tense** is the form of a verb that shows the time of an action or a condition.

EL5

The Six Verb Tenses

There are six tenses that indicate when an action or a condition of a verb is, was, or will be in effect. Each of these six tenses has at least two forms.

RULE 5.1.2 > Each tense has a **basic** and a **progressive** form.

The chart that follows shows examples of the six tenses.

THE BASIC FORMS OF THE SIX TENSES	
Present	Meg skis for a hobby.
Past	She skied every day last year.
Future	She will ski again this year.
Present Perfect	She has skied at many different resorts all over the country.
Past Perfect	She had skied first when she was only three years old.
Future Perfect	She will have skied ten times this season by President's Day.
Present	Damon reads mysteries.
Past	He read two mysteries last week.
Future	He will read other kinds of books, too.
Present Perfect	He has read Sherlock Holmes stories.
Past Perfect	He had read Agatha Christie stories.
Future Perfect	He will have read many mystery stories by the end of the year.

See Practice 5.1A

Basic Verb Forms or Tenses

Verb tenses are identified simply by their tense names. The **progressive tenses,** however, are identified by their tense names plus the word *progressive*. Progressive tenses show that an action is or was happening for a period of time.

The chart below shows examples of the six tenses in their progressive form or tense. Note that all of these progressive tenses end in *-ing*. (See the section on verb conjugation later in this chapter for more about the progressive tense.)

THE PROGRESSIVE TENSES	
Present Progressive	Meg is ice skating now.
Past Progressive	She was ice skating yesterday morning.
Future Progressive	She will be ice skating again tomorrow.
Present Perfect Progressive	She has been ice skating since she was a young child.
Past Perfect Progressive	She had been ice skating when she broke her leg.
Future Perfect Progressive	She will have been ice skating for a decade by the end of this year.

The Emphatic Form

There is also a third form or tense, the **emphatic,** which exists only for the present and past tenses. The **present emphatic** is formed with the helping verbs *do* or *does,* depending on the subject. The **past emphatic** is formed with *did.* The purpose of the emphatic tense is to put more emphasis on, or to stress, the action of the verb.

THE EMPHATIC TENSES OF THE PRESENT AND THE PAST	
Present Emphatic	Jeff does play tennis more often than Jimmy. I do read more books than my older brother.
Past Emphatic	Michael and Jake did play guitar in a band. My mom did insist that I finish my homework before I could watch TV.

See Practice 5.1B

PRACTICE 5.1A ▷ **Identifying Verb Tenses**

Read each sentence. Then, write the verb or verbs in each sentence and label their tenses (*present, past, future, present perfect, past perfect,* or *future perfect*).

EXAMPLE   The athlete jumped over the hurdle and reached the finish line.

ANSWER   *jumped* — past; *reached* — past

1. After she had explored the island, the adventurer felt more secure.

2. The movie theater will have closed by the time we arrive.

3. The boy has always loved his dog and cat.

4. During the storm, the children slept.

5. The zoo has stayed open all winter, but the animals hibernate.

6. When the teachers heard about the panel's decision, they were very happy.

7. The actors had walked off the stage and into the audience.

8. *Dogsong* and *Hatchet* are my favorite books.

9. My grandmother answered when I called her cellphone number.

10. If the boy grows to six feet, he will be taller than his father.

PRACTICE 5.1B ▷ **Recognizing Tenses or Forms of Verbs**

Read each sentence. Then, rewrite each sentence, using the verb form shown in parentheses, and underline the verb.

EXAMPLE   My father ate lunch at 2:00 P.M. (past emphatic)

ANSWER   *My father <u>did eat</u> lunch at 2:00 P.M.*

11. By that time, the flowers will have bloomed. (past perfect progressive)

12. The teacher asked the class for their book reports. (present perfect progressive)

13. I sometimes wish that the day would never end. (present emphatic)

14. The children had been playing outside. (past)

15. Roberto washed his car for three hours! (past progressive)

16. His mother did bake a loaf of bread. (past)

17. Over time, the tree had grown taller than the fence. (future perfect progressive)

18. The guitarist played the difficult tune with ease. (present progressive)

19. The passing trains sure did make a lot of noise. (past perfect progressive)

20. Ming struggled to keep his umbrella from collapsing. (past emphatic)

SPEAKING APPLICATION

Take turns with a partner. Tell about a story that you recently read. Your partner will listen for and identify the different verb tenses that you use.

WRITING APPLICATION

Write a paragraph about a trip that you would like to take. Use at least eight different verb forms or tenses in your paragraph. Then, rewrite the sentences by changing the verb tenses. Underline the verbs you used.

The Four Principal Parts of Verbs

Every verb in the English language has four **principal parts** from which all of the tenses are formed.

> **A verb has four principal parts: the present, the present participle, the past,** and the **past participle.**

5.1.3 **RULE**

The chart below shows the principal parts of the verbs *walk, speak,* and *run.*

THE FOUR PRINCIPAL PARTS			
PRESENT	PRESENT PARTICIPLE	PAST	PAST PARTICIPLE
walk	walking	walked	(have) walked
speak	speaking	spoke	(have) spoken
run	running	ran	(have) run

The first principal part, the present, is used for the basic forms of the present and future tenses, as well as for the emphatic forms or tenses. The present tense is formed by adding an *-s* or *-es* when the subject is *he, she, it,* or a singular noun. The future tense is formed with the helping verb *will. (I will walk. Mary will speak. Carl will run.)* The present emphatic is formed with the helping verb *do* or *does. (I do walk. Mary does speak. Carl does run.)* The past emphatic is formed with the helping verb *did. (I did walk. Mary did speak. Carl did run.)*

EL6

The second principal part, the present participle, is used with helping verbs for all of the progressive forms. *(I am walking. Mary is speaking. Carl is running.)*

The third principal part, the past, is used to form the past tense. *(I walked. Mary spoke. Carl ran.)* As in the example *ran,* the past tense of a verb can change its spelling. (See the next section for more information.)

The fourth principal part, the past participle, is used with helping verbs to create the perfect tenses. *(I have walked. Mary had spoken. Carl had run.)*

See Practice 5.1C
See Practice 5.1D

PRACTICE 5.1C **Recognizing the Four Principal Parts of Verbs**

Read each sentence. Then, write the verb in each sentence that matches the principal part in parentheses.

EXAMPLE   The band was playing loudly. (present participle)

ANSWER   *playing*

1. After their victory, the team celebrated at a restaurant. (past)

2. The teacher was helping students with their homework. (present participle)

3. Since the age of twelve, Gloria has moved quite often. (past participle)

4. I have studied hard in Spanish class, and now I can speak it fluently. (past participle)

5. After reaching the summit, the climber shouted with joy. (present participle)

6. Many birds have chirped loudly since I sat down on this bench. (past participle)

7. The ice melts by spring. (present)

8. Leave the dog alone, or he will start barking. (present participle)

9. The bride walks down the aisle. (present)

10. The man made his way through the crowd. (past)

PRACTICE 5.1D **Identifying the Four Principal Parts of Verbs**

Read each set of verbs. Then, for each set, write which principal part or parts (*present, present participle, past, past participle*) are listed.

EXAMPLE   cried, have baked

ANSWER   *past, past participle*

11. boasting, calling

12. twinkled, have winked

13. crunch, munch

14. sneezed, wheezed

15. dozing, sleeping

16. blinked, have settled

17. create, escape

18. edge, wedge

19. promised, have pledged

20. placing, tracing

SPEAKING APPLICATION

Take turns with a partner. Perform a mock radio broadcast about the weather, using many verb tenses in your description. Your partner should listen for and identify the principal parts of the verbs that you use.

WRITING APPLICATION

Use at least three word pairs from Practice 5.1D to write a fictional short story. Underline and label the principal parts of all the verbs you use in your story.

Regular and Irregular Verbs

The way the past and past participle forms of a verb are formed determines whether the verb is **regular** or **irregular.**

Regular Verbs The majority of verbs are regular. Regular verbs form their past and past participles according to a predictable pattern.

> **A regular verb** is one for which the past and past participle are formed by adding *-ed* or *-d* to the present form.

5.1.4 RULE

In the chart below, notice that a final consonant is sometimes doubled to form the present participle, the past, and the past participle. A final *e* may also be dropped to form the participle.

PRINCIPAL PARTS OF REGULAR VERBS			
PRESENT	PRESENT PARTICIPLE	PAST	PAST PARTICIPLE
bat	batting	batted	(have) batted
produce	producing	produced	(have) produced
depend	depending	depended	(have) depended

See Practice 5.1E
See Practice 5.1F

Irregular Verbs Although most verbs are regular, many of the most common verbs are irregular. Irregular verbs do not use a predictable pattern to form their past and past participles.

> **An irregular verb** is one whose past and past participle are *not* formed by adding *-ed* or *-d* to the present form.

5.1.5 RULE

Usage Problems Remembering the principal parts of irregular verbs can help you avoid usage problems. One common usage problem is using a principal part that is not standard.

INCORRECT Simon **buyed** new shoes.

CORRECT Simon **bought** new shoes.

A second usage problem is confusing the past and past participle when they have different forms.

INCORRECT Ben **done** his homework.

CORRECT   Ben **did** his homework.

Some common irregular verbs are shown in the charts that follow. Use a dictionary if you are not sure how to form the principal parts of an irregular verb.

IRREGULAR VERBS WITH THE SAME PRESENT, PAST, AND PAST PARTICIPLE			
PRESENT	PRESENT PARTICIPLE	PAST	PAST PARTICIPLE
burst	bursting	burst	(have) burst
cost	costing	cost	(have) cost
cut	cutting	cut	(have) cut
hit	hitting	hit	(have) hit
hurt	hurting	hurt	(have) hurt
let	letting	let	(have) let
put	putting	put	(have) put
set	setting	set	(have) set
shut	shutting	shut	(have) shut
split	splitting	split	(have) split
spread	spreading	spread	(have) spread

Note About *Be:* *Be* is one of the most irregular of all of the verbs. The present participle of *be* is *being*. The past participle is *been*. The present and the past depend on the subject and tense of the verb.

CONJUGATION OF *BE*		
	SINGULAR	PLURAL
Present	I am. You are. He, she, or it is.	We are. You are. They are.
Past	I was. You were. He, she, or it was.	We were. You were. They were.
Future	I will be. You will be. He, she, or it will be.	We will be. You will be. They will be.

IRREGULAR VERBS WITH THE SAME PAST AND PAST PARTICIPLE			
PRESENT	PRESENT PARTICIPLE	PAST	PAST PARTICIPLE
bring	bringing	brought	(have) brought
build	building	built	(have) built
buy	buying	bought	(have) bought
catch	catching	caught	(have) caught
fight	fighting	fought	(have) fought
find	finding	found	(have) found
get	getting	got	(have) got or (have) gotten
hold	holding	held	(have) held
keep	keeping	kept	(have) kept
lay	laying	laid	(have) laid
lead	leading	led	(have) led
leave	leaving	left	(have) left
lose	losing	lost	(have) lost
pay	paying	paid	(have) paid
say	saying	said	(have) said
sell	selling	sold	(have) sold
send	sending	sent	(have) sent
shine	shining	shone or shined	(have) shone or (have) shined
sit	sitting	sat	(have) sat
sleep	sleeping	slept	(have) slept
spend	spending	spent	(have) spent
stand	standing	stood	(have) stood
stick	sticking	stuck	(have) stuck
sting	stinging	stung	(have) stung
strike	striking	struck	(have) struck
swing	swinging	swung	(have) swung
teach	teaching	taught	(have) taught
win	winning	won	(have) won
wind	winding	wound	(have) wound

IRREGULAR VERBS THAT CHANGE IN OTHER WAYS			
PRESENT	PRESENT PARTICIPLE	PAST	PAST PARTICIPLE
arise	arising	arose	(have) arisen
become	becoming	became	(have) become
begin	beginning	began	(have) begun
bite	biting	bit	(have) bitten
break	breaking	broke	(have) broken
choose	choosing	chose	(have) chosen
come	coming	came	(have) come
do	doing	did	(have) done
draw	drawing	drew	(have) drawn
drink	drinking	drank	(have) drunk
drive	driving	drove	(have) driven
eat	eating	ate	(have) eaten
fall	falling	fell	(have) fallen
fly	flying	flew	(have) flown
give	giving	gave	(have) given
go	going	went	(have) gone
grow	growing	grew	(have) grown
know	knowing	knew	(have) known
lie	lying	lay	(have) lain
ride	riding	rode	(have) ridden
ring	ringing	rang	(have) rung
rise	rising	rose	(have) risen
run	running	ran	(have) run
see	seeing	saw	(have) seen
sing	singing	sang	(have) sung
sink	sinking	sank	(have) sunk
speak	speaking	spoke	(have) spoken
swim	swimming	swam	(have) swum
take	taking	took	(have) taken
tear	tearing	tore	(have) torn
throw	throwing	threw	(have) thrown
wear	wearing	wore	(have) worn
write	writing	wrote	(have) written

See Practice 5.1G
See Practice 5.1H

Recognizing Principal Parts of Regular Verbs

Read each set of verbs. Then, for each set, write the name of the two principal parts of the verbs that are listed.

EXAMPLE   smell, (have) slumped

ANSWER   *present, past participle*

1. typing, typed
2. slap, slapped
3. asked, asking
4. assign, assigning
5. calculating, (have) calculated
6. brighten, brightened
7. repair, repairing
8. brushing, (have) brushed
9. pictured, picturing
10. plan, planning

Using the Correct Form of Regular Verbs

Read each sentence. Then, write the principal part of the verb in parentheses that best completes each sentence, and identify the principal part used.

EXAMPLE   The children are (shout) loudly outside.

ANSWER   *shouting* — *present participle*

11. During her freshman year, Calista (enjoy) college very much.
12. After eating the spicy food, the water (taste) good.
13. Rocking back and forth can (calm) a baby.
14. Once you have (press) the button, the elevator will start to ascend.
15. Stop (push) me; that is against the rules!
16. My uncle has (row) a boat from Michigan to Canada.
17. Please help me while I (try) to decipher this code.
18. I accidentally (toast) the bread too long.
19. Can you (replace) the battery in my watch?
20. The back-up singers have (hum) the national anthem.

SPEAKING APPLICATION

Take turns with a partner. Say all four principal parts of the verbs in Practice 5.1E. Then, choose one verb and use all four principal parts of that verb in four different sentences.

WRITING APPLICATION

Write a newspaper article about your hometown. Use the four principal parts of different regular verbs in your article. Underline and label the principal parts of each verb that you use.

PRACTICE 5.1G > **Recognizing Principal Parts of Irregular Verbs**

Read each verb. Then, write the four principal parts of each verb in the following order: present, present participle, past, past participle.

EXAMPLE   winning

ANSWER   *win, winning, won, (have) won*

1. chosen
2. build
3. slept
4. stood
5. losing
6. kept
7. arisen
8. bit
9. rang
10. sunk

PRACTICE 5.1H > **Supplying the Correct Form of Irregular Verbs**

Read each sentence. Then, rewrite each sentence with the correct verb form, and write the principal part of the corrected verb.

EXAMPLE   The astronomer finded a new plant species last week.

ANSWER   *The astronomer found a new plant species last week.* — past

11. The pilot has flied around the world hundreds of times.
12. My mother is speak on the phone with her sister.
13. After years of practice, the chess player has winned a major tournament.
14. Joe's sister is frustrated that she has losed her keys again.
15. My cousin rung the doorbell.
16. When the space shuttle took off, my friends standing in amazement.
17. The judge is given the defendant time to speak.
18. Sally's friend worn the same hat every day.
19. When I went to camp, I will leaved my stuffed animals at home.
20. David is throw the rope to Ann.

SPEAKING APPLICATION

Take turns with a partner. Give your partner two irregular verbs not used in Practice 5.1G. Your partner should state the four principal parts of each verb.

WRITING APPLICATION

Write a short essay about plans for a camping trip. Use at least ten irregular verbs in your description of what you will pack and what you will do. Underline each irregular verb in your essay.

Verb Conjugation

The **conjugation** of a verb displays all of its different forms.

> **A conjugation is a complete list of the singular and plural forms of a verb in a particular tense.**

5.1.6 RULE

The singular forms of a verb correspond to the singular personal pronouns (*I, you, he, she, it*), and the plural forms correspond to the plural personal pronouns (*we, you, they*).

To conjugate a verb, you need the four principal parts: the present (*see*), the present participle (*seeing*), the past (*saw*), and the past participle (*seen*). You also need various helping verbs, such as *has, have,* or *will*.

Notice that only three principal parts—the present, the past, and the past participle—are used to conjugate all six of the basic forms.

See Practice 5.1l

CONJUGATION OF THE BASIC FORMS OF *SEE*		SINGULAR	PLURAL
Present	First Person Second Person Third Person	I see. You see. He, she, or it sees.	We see. You see. They see.
Past	First Person Second Person Third Person	I saw. You saw. He, she, or it saw.	We saw. You saw. They saw.
Future	First Person Second Person Third Person	I will see. You will see. He, she, or it will see.	We will see. You will see. They will see.
Present Perfect	First Person Second Person Third Person	I have seen. You have seen. He, she, or it has seen.	We have seen. You have seen. They have seen.
Past Perfect	First Person Second Person Third Person	I had seen. You had seen. He, she, or it had seen.	We had seen. You had seen. They had seen.
Future Perfect	First Person Second Person Third Person	I will have seen. You will have seen. He, she, or it will have seen.	We will have seen. You will have seen. They will have seen.

Conjugating the Progressive Tense With *Be*

As you learned earlier, the **progressive tense** shows an ongoing action or condition. To form the progressive tense, use the present participle form of the verb (the -*ing* form) with a form of the verb *be*.

CONJUGATION OF THE PROGRESSIVE FORMS OF *SEE*			
		SINGULAR	PLURAL
Present Progressive	First Person Second Person Third Person	I am seeing. You are seeing. He, she, or it is seeing.	We are seeing. You are seeing. They are seeing.
Past Progressive	First Person Second Person Third Person	I was seeing. You were seeing. He, she, or it was seeing.	We were seeing. You were seeing. They were seeing.
Future Progressive	First Person Second Person Third Person	I will be seeing. You will be seeing. He, she, or it will be seeing.	We will be seeing. You will be seeing. They will be seeing.
Present Perfect Progressive	First Person Second Person Third Person	I have been seeing. You have been seeing. He, she, or it has been seeing.	We have been seeing. You have been seeing. They have been seeing.
Past Perfect Progressive	First Person Second Person Third Person	I had been seeing. You had been seeing. He, she, or it had been seeing.	We had been seeing. You had been seeing. They had been seeing.
Future Perfect Progressive	First Person Second Person Third Person	I will have been seeing. You will have been seeing. He, she, or it will have been seeing.	We will have been seeing. You will have been seeing. They will have been seeing.

See Practice 5.1J

PRACTICE 5.1I ▶ **Conjugating the Basic Forms of Verbs**

Read each word. Then, conjugate each verb using the subject indicated in parentheses. Write the words in the past, present, past perfect, and future perfect.

EXAMPLE   see (I)

ANSWER   *I saw, I see, I had seen, I will have seen*

1. scare (we)

2. thrive (he)

3. drift (they)

4. sniff (she)

5. buy (you)

6. imagine (I)

7. live (they)

8. sigh (you)

9. pay (we)

10. ride (I)

PRACTICE 5.1J ▶ **Conjugating the Progressive Forms of Verbs**

Read each sentence. Rewrite each sentence, using the progressive forms of the verb that are indicated in parentheses.

EXAMPLE   He strikes. (past progressive; present progressive)

ANSWER   *He was striking. He is striking.*

11. He blames. (future perfect progressive; future progressive)

12. We think. (past perfect progressive; past progressive)

13. They tease. (past progressive; future progressive)

14. She leads. (future perfect progressive; past perfect progressive)

15. You create. (present progressive; present perfect progressive)

16. They travel. (past perfect progressive; present progressive)

17. I show. (past progressive; future progressive)

18. We form. (present perfect progressive; present progressive)

19. They act. (future progressive; past progressive)

20. You breathe. (future progressive; past perfect progressive)

SPEAKING APPLICATION

Take turns with a partner. Say sentences that use one of the conjugated verb forms from Practice 5.1I. Your partner should listen for and identify each verb and its form.

WRITING APPLICATION

Use progressive verb forms to write a paragraph about your favorite band or music artist. Underline all of the progressive verb forms that you use.

5.2 The Correct Use of Tenses

The basic, progressive, and emphatic forms of the six tenses show time within one of three general categories: **present, past,** and **future.** This section will explain how each verb form has a specific use that distinguishes it from the other forms.

Present, Past, and Future Tense

Good usage depends on an understanding of how each form works within its general category of time to express meaning.

Uses of Tense in Present Time

Three different forms can be used to express present time.

> The three forms of the **present tense** show present actions or conditions as well as various continuing actions or conditions.

EXPRESSING PRESENT TENSE	
Present	I ride .
Present Progressive	I am riding .
Present Emphatic	I do ride .

The main uses of the basic form of the present tense are shown in the chart below.

EXPRESSING PRESENT TENSE	
Present Action	Jake fishes in the ocean.
Present Condition	His arm is aching .
Regularly Occurring Action	He often fishes off Cape May, New Jersey.
Regularly Occurring Condition	This boat holds six people.
Constant Action	Many kinds of fish live in the ocean.
Constant Condition	Fish have scales.

See Practice 5.2A

Historical Present The present tense may also be used to express historical events. This use of the present, called the **historical present tense,** is occasionally used in narration to make past actions or conditions sound more lively.

THE HISTORICAL PRESENT TENSE	
Past Actions Expressed in Historical Present Tense	People gather around a store window to watch the first television.
Past Condition Expressed in Historical Present Tense	People watching the television cannot believe that a picture can come through the air.

The **critical present tense** is most often used to discuss deceased authors and their literary achievements.

THE CRITICAL PRESENT TENSE	
Action Expressed in Critical Present	O. Henry writes many stories with surprise endings.
Condition Expressed in Critical Present	O. Henry is the author of several volumes of short stories.

The **present progressive tense** is used to show a continuing action or condition of a long or short duration.

USES OF THE PRESENT PROGRESSIVE TENSE	
Long Continuing Action	Mark is practicing soccer every afternoon.
Short Continuing Action	He is trying to make the team.
Continuing Condition	He wants to make the first team someday.

USES OF THE PRESENT EMPHATIC TENSE	
Emphasizing a Statement	Jane does want to go to the store.
Denying a Contrary Assertion	No, she does not want to walk downtown.
Asking a Question	Does she enjoy shopping for clothes?
Making a Sentence Negative	Jane does not want to stay at the store all day.

See Practice 5.2B

PRACTICE 5.2A Identifying the Tense in Present Time

Read each sentence. Then, write the form of the present-tense verb underlined in each sentence.

EXAMPLE   Computers <u>are</u> more popular today than they were ten years ago.

ANSWER   *present*

1. The student <u>does prepare</u> well for his presentation.
2. Maya Angelou <u>uses</u> vivid metaphors in her poetry.
3. Some people <u>are accomplishing</u> great things for future generations.
4. Susie <u>shops</u> for school supplies.
5. I <u>am going</u> to summer camp for eight weeks.
6. Surprisingly, my brother <u>does play</u> more than one instrument.
7. The birds <u>wake</u> me every morning with their chirping.
8. The doctors <u>are planning</u> to hold health seminars at their clinic.
9. Two-year-olds <u>are</u> toddlers.
10. My alarm <u>does ring</u> every morning at seven o'clock.

PRACTICE 5.2B Supplying Verbs in Present Time

Read each sentence. Then, rewrite each sentence and the underlined verb, using the tense indicated in parentheses.

EXAMPLE   The author <u>writes</u> for hours at a time. (present emphatic)

ANSWER   *The author does write for hours at a time.*

11. Sir Arthur Conan Doyle <u>wrote</u> the Sherlock Holmes mysteries. (critical present)
12. Marcia <u>gives</u> Nona a bouquet of flowers. (present progressive)
13. People in the 1700s <u>rode</u> in wagons. (historical present)
14. Fresh cherries and blueberries <u>made</u> the best snacks. (present)
15. The fan <u>waved</u> to the band onstage. (present progressive)
16. Young students on the bus <u>sing</u> songs for the bus driver. (present emphatic)
17. No matter what, I <u>will</u> attend the sporting event on Sunday. (present progressive)
18. Albert Einstein <u>revealed</u> great insights in his writings. (historical present)
19. A top <u>spins</u> on the floor. (present progressive)
20. The bread <u>baked</u> in the oven. (present)

SPEAKING APPLICATION

Take turns with a partner. Tell your point of view on which foods taste best. Use present tense verbs in your description. Your partner should listen for and identify the present tense verbs that you use.

WRITING APPLICATION

Write a few sentences about your favorite author. Use the critical present to describe his or her writing. Use the emphatic present to state your opinion about the author.

Uses of the Past Tense

There are seven verb forms that express past actions or conditions.

> The seven forms that express **past tense** show actions and conditions that began at some time in the past.

FORMS EXPRESSING PAST TENSE	
Past	I danced.
Present Perfect	I have danced.
Past Perfect	I had danced.
Past Progressive	I was dancing.
Present Perfect Progressive	I have been dancing.
Past Perfect Progressive	I had been dancing.
Past Emphatic	I did dance.

The uses of the most common form, the past, are shown below.

USES OF THE PAST TENSE	
Completed Action	Julian worked on his speech.
Completed Condition	He was an interesting speaker.

See Practice 5.2C

Notice in the chart above that the time of the action or the condition could be changed from indefinite to definite if such words as *last week* or *yesterday* were added to the sentences.

Present Perfect The **present perfect tense** always expresses indefinite time. Use it to show actions or conditions continuing from the past to the present.

USES OF THE PRESENT PERFECT TENSE	
Completed Action (Indefinite Time)	We have come to the school dance.
Completed Condition (Indefinite Time)	We have been to the school dances before.
Action Continuing to Present	Our friends are going, too.
Condition Continuing to Present	We have been excited all day.

Past Perfect The **past perfect tense** expresses an action that took place before another action.

USES OF THE PAST PERFECT TENSE	
Action Completed Before Another Action	The coaches had analyzed the other team's game before they created their own game plans.
Condition Completed Before Another Condition	They had been careful to recognize when the team became tired.

These charts show the **past progressive** and **emphatic tenses.**

USES OF THE PROGRESSIVE TENSE TO EXPRESS PAST TIME	
Past Progressive	LONG CONTINUING ACTION Wei was going to ballet class daily. SHORT CONTINUING ACTION She was talking to her teacher about her lessons. CONTINUOUS CONDITION She was being honest when she said that she practiced every day.
Present Perfect Progressive	CONTINUING ACTION Wei has been dancing since she was five years old.
Past Perfect Progressive	CONTINUING ACTION INTERRUPTED She had wanted to take jazz, but she decided that ballet was enough.

USES OF THE PAST EMPHATIC TENSE	
Emphasizing a Statement	The bicycle did work after I oiled the gears.
Denying a Contrary Assertion	Yes, I did check the chain!
Asking a Question	Why did you think I couldn't fix my old bicycle?
Making a Sentence Negative	You did not appreciate my repair skills.

See Practice 5.2D

PRACTICE 5.2C > **Identifying Tense in Past Time**

Read each item. Then, write the verbs that are in the tense indicated in parentheses.

EXAMPLE   had scooted, scooted, scouted (past)

ANSWER   *scooted, scouted*

1. had enjoyed, had halted, have praised (past perfect)

2. have tried, has worked, did attempt (present perfect)

3. had been finishing, did complete, had been missing (past perfect progressive)

4. did jump, did glide, was swooping (past emphatic)

5. has been leaving, went, disappeared (past)

6. frowned, was weeping, was sighing (past progressive)

7. had decided, had been searching, had been finding (past perfect progressive)

8. hit, kicked, was batting (past)

9. did not understand, comprehended, did care (past emphatic)

10. was skating, did skateboard, was skiing (past progressive)

PRACTICE 5.2D > **Supplying Verbs in Past Time**

Read each sentence. Then, rewrite each sentence and the underlined verb, using the verb tense indicated in parentheses.

EXAMPLE   No one <u>used</u> the computer. (past progressive)

ANSWER   *No one was using the computer.*

11. A week before, the girl <u>allowed</u> her friend to borrow her textbook. (past perfect progressive)

12. The clown <u>made</u> balloon animals for all of the children. (past progressive)

13. My brother <u>wanted</u> a bicycle for many years. (present perfect progressive)

14. The driver <u>asked</u> for directions before beginning his journey. (past emphatic)

15. Although quite enjoyable, rafting <u>was</u> less fun than hiking. (past perfect progressive)

16. I <u>was thinking</u> about his speech. (past perfect progressive)

17. The treasure hunters <u>made</u> an exciting yet dangerous discovery. (past perfect)

18. The airplane <u>backed</u> onto the runway before taking off. (past progressive)

19. The reference materials <u>show</u> step-by-step instructions. (past)

20. I <u>called</u> John. (present perfect progressive)

SPEAKING APPLICATION

Take turns with a partner. Make up rhyming sentences that use verbs (in some form of the past tense). Your partner should listen for and identify the past-tense verbs in your rhymes.

WRITING APPLICATION

Write a paragraph about something exciting that happened to you when you were a child. Use five different forms of the past tense in your paragraph.

Uses of the Future Tense

The **future tense** shows actions or conditions that will happen at a later date.

> **The future tense expresses actions or conditions that have not yet occurred.**

FORMS EXPRESSING FUTURE TENSE	
Future	I will wait .
Future Perfect	I will have waited .
Future Progressive	I will be waiting .
Future Perfect Progressive	I will have been waiting .

USES OF THE FUTURE AND THE FUTURE PERFECT TENSE	
Future	I will go home after school. I will babysit for my little brother.
Future Perfect	I will have babysat for him every day this week. Next week, I will have babysat for him for six months.

Notice in the next chart that the **future progressive** and the **future perfect progressive tenses** express only future actions.

USES OF THE PROGRESSIVE TENSE TO EXPRESS FUTURE TIME	
Future Progressive	Max will be working all weekend.
Future Perfect Progressive	He will have been working at the store for ten weeks by the end of the summer.

The basic forms of the present and the present progressive tense are often used with other words to express future time.

EXAMPLES The play **opens** next weekend.

We **are practicing** our parts.

See Practice 5.2E
See Practice 5.2F

PRACTICE 5.2E **Identifying Tense in Future Time**

Read each sentence. Then, write the future-tense verb in each sentence and the form of the tense.

EXAMPLE   The president will address Congress tonight.

ANSWER   *will address* — *future*

1. A local restaurant will be catering the event.

2. A radio station will sponsor the parade.

3. The shipment you ordered will arrive soon.

4. Surely you will be inviting Tom to the party.

5. Before the concert, we will have distributed the flyers.

6. Next semester, I will have been taking five classes.

7. The team will be playing its last game on Saturday.

8. My mother will return your call when she arrives home.

9. Kanin will have been giving his speech tonight.

10. The plane will have arrived by evening.

PRACTICE 5.2F **Supplying Verbs in Future Time**

Read each sentence. Then, rewrite each sentence, filling in the blank with the future-tense form of the verb indicated in parentheses.

EXAMPLE   Steven _____ his decision soon. (make, future progressive)

ANSWER   *Steven will be making his decision soon.*

11. We _____ different parts of Texas by next month. (tour, future perfect)

12. In another five years, scientists _____ the time capsule. (open, future progressive)

13. She _____ her report. (present, future perfect)

14. Mr. Bishop _____ our class this morning. (visit, future perfect progressive)

15. Jose _____ you his decision today. (tell, future)

16. I _____ all day. (study, future perfect)

17. She _____ school here for one year next May. (attend, future perfect progressive)

18. The caterers _____ beverages at the meeting. (provide, future)

19. The buses _____ late today because of the rain. (arrive, future progressive)

20. Tammy _____ her lines by this afternoon. (rehearse, future perfect)

SPEAKING APPLICATION

Take turns with a partner. Tell what you hope to be doing in five years. Use future-tense verbs in your sentences. Your partner should listen for and identify the future-tense verbs that you use.

WRITING APPLICATION

Rewrite your corrections for sentences 13, 18, and 19, changing the verbs to include other future-tense verbs. Make sure your sentences still make sense.

Sequence of Tenses

A sentence with more than one verb must be consistent in its
time sequence.

> **When showing a sequence of events, do not shift tenses
> unnecessarily.**

EXAMPLES Ursula **will walk** to school, and then she **will take**
the bus home.

Dan **has walked** his dogs and **fed** them.

Mom **worked** all day and **cooked** dinner at night.

Sometimes, however, it is necessary to shift tenses, especially
when a sentence is complex or compound-complex. The tense
of the main verb often determines the tense of the verb in the
subordinate clause. Moreover, the form of the participle or
infinitive often depends on the tense of the verb in the main
clause.

Verbs in Subordinate Clauses It is frequently necessary to look
at the tense of the main verb in a sentence before choosing the
tense of the verb in the subordinate clause.

> **The tense of a verb in a subordinate clause should follow
> logically from the tense of the main verb.**

INCORRECT I **will understand** that Michael **was** late.

CORRECT I **understand** that Michael **was** late.

As you study the combinations of tenses in the charts on the next
pages, notice that the choice of tenses affects the logical relationship
between the events being expressed. Some combinations indicate
that the events are **simultaneous**—meaning that they occur at
the same time. Other combinations indicate that the events are
sequential—meaning that one event occurs before or after the other.

SEQUENCE OF EVENTS

MAIN VERB	SUBORDINATE VERB	MEANING
MAIN VERB IN PRESENT TENSE		
I understand...	**PRESENT** that he explores in the woods. **PRESENT PROGRESSIVE** that he is exploring in the woods. **PRESENT EMPHATIC** that he does explore in the woods.	Simultaneous events: All events occur in present time.
I understand...	**PAST** that he explored in the woods. **PRESENT PERFECT** that he has explored in the woods. **PAST PERFECT** that he had explored in the woods. **PAST PROGRESSIVE** that he was exploring in the woods. **PRESENT PERFECT PROGRESSIVE** that he has been exploring in the woods. **PAST PERFECT PROGRESSIVE** that he had been exploring in the woods. **PAST EMPHATIC** that he did explore in the woods.	Sequential events: The exploring comes before the understanding.
I understand...	**FUTURE** that he will explore in the woods. **FUTURE PERFECT** that he will have explored in the woods. **FUTURE PROGRESSIVE** that he will be exploring in the woods. **FUTURE PERFECT PROGRESSIVE** that he will have been exploring in the woods.	Sequential events: The understanding comes before the exploring.

SEQUENCE OF EVENTS		
MAIN VERB	**SUBORDINATE VERB**	**MEANING**
MAIN VERB IN PAST TENSE		
I understood...	**PAST** that he explored in the woods. **PAST PROGRESSIVE** that he was exploring in the woods. **PAST EMPHATIC** that he did explore in the woods.	Simultaneous events: All events take place in the past.
I understood...	**PAST PERFECT** that he had explored in the woods. **PAST PERFECT PROGRESSIVE** that he had been exploring in the woods.	Sequential events: The exploring came before the understanding.
MAIN VERB IN FUTURE TENSE		
I will understand...	**PRESENT** if he explores in the woods. **PRESENT PROGRESSIVE** if he is exploring in the woods. **PRESENT EMPHATIC** if he does explore in the woods.	Simultaneous events: All events take place in future time.
I will understand...	**PAST** if he explored in the woods. **PRESENT PERFECT** if he has explored in the woods. **PRESENT PERFECT PROGRESSIVE** if he has been exploring in the woods. **PAST EMPHATIC** if he did explore in the woods.	Sequential events: The exploring comes before the understanding.

Time Sequence With Participles and Infinitives Frequently, the form of a participle or infinitive determines whether the events are simultaneous or sequential. Participles can be present (*watching*), past (*watched*), or perfect (*having won*). Infinitives can be present (*to watch*) or perfect (*to have watched*).

> **The form of a participle or an infinitive should logically relate to the verb in the same clause or sentence.**

5.2.6 RULE

To show simultaneous events, you will generally need to use the present participle or the present infinitive, whether the main verb is present, past, or future.

Simultaneous Events

IN PRESENT TIME	**Watching** the race, they **cheer**.
	present present
IN PAST TIME	**Watching** the race, they **cheered**.
	present past
IN FUTURE TIME	**Watching** the race, they **will cheer**.
	present future

To show sequential events, use the perfect form of the participle and infinitive, regardless of the tense of the main verb.

Sequential Events

IN PRESENT TIME	**Having watched** the race, they **are cheering**.
	perfect present progressive
	(The race was over *before* they cheered.)
IN PAST TIME	**Having watched** the race, they **cheered**.
	perfect past
	(The race was over *before* they cheered.)
SPANNING PAST AND FUTURE TIME	**Having watched** the race, they **will cheer**.
	perfect future
	(They will cheer *after* the race is over.)

See Practice 5.2G
See Practice 5.2H

PRACTICE 5.2G	**Identifying the Time Sequence in Sentences With More Than One Verb**

Read each sentence. Then, write the verb of the event that happens second in each sentence.

EXAMPLE   After I finished my paper, Jim arrived.

ANSWER   *arrived*

1. I will drive you to school after you eat breakfast.
2. I brushed my teeth and then went to bed.
3. My sister will study medicine, but first she needs to graduate from high school.
4. Phil started jogging after he warmed up.
5. We found the book right where we left it.
6. Maggie slept in the morning and went to work at night.
7. I landed in Portland and arrived two hours later at my hotel.
8. It has been several years since I last saw my grandfather.
9. I walked into the room and found Emily there.
10. As soon as the meeting was over, the committee announced its decision.

PRACTICE 5.2H	**Recognizing and Correcting Errors in Tense Sequence**

Read each sentence. Then, if a sentence has an error in tense sequence, rewrite it to correct the error. If a sentence is correct, write *correct*.

EXAMPLE   Sid is milking the cows now, but finished soon.

ANSWER   *Sid is milking the cows now, but will finish soon.*

11. I was finishing my homework and crawled into bed.
12. When we reached the station, the train had already left.
13. Katherine works on that poem for a week, and it's still not finished.
14. Last summer, we drive to Denver, where we toured the U.S. Mint.
15. Ling made a sandwich and puts it in her lunch box.
16. Every morning, they got up early and ran.
17. She wrote a letter and sends it to her grandmother.
18. The armadillo ran across the yard and hides behind a log.
19. The sun rose and the sky turned pink.
20. Every autumn, the leaves turn brown and fell off the trees.

SPEAKING APPLICATION

Take turns with a partner. Tell about something fun you like to do. Use two verbs in your sentences. Your partner should listen for and identify the sequence of events in your sentences.

WRITING APPLICATION ·

Use sentences 13, 14, and 15 as models to write your own sentences with incorrect tense sequence. Then, exchange papers with a partner. Your partner should rewrite the sentences, using the correct sequence in tense.

Modifiers That Help Clarify Tense

The time expressed by a verb can often be clarified by adverbs such as *often*, *sometimes*, *always*, or *frequently* and phrases such as *once in a while*, *within a week*, *last week*, or *now and then*.

> **Use modifiers when they can help clarify tense.**

RULE 5.2.7

In the examples below, the modifiers that help clarify the tense of the verb are highlighted in orange. Think about how the sentences would read without the modifiers. Modifiers help to make your writing more precise and interesting.

EXAMPLES   Richard **plays** computer games **every night** .

He **practices** **once a day** .

He **practices** **once in a while** .
(These two sentences have very different meanings.)

Occasionally , he **walks** to the library to read.

He **always** **stops** to get a drink on the way.

By next year , Richard **will have played** hundreds of different kinds of games.

Richard also **practices** basketball **every day** after school.

Basketball **is** **now** one of his favorite sports.

Sometimes , he **shoots** foul shots over and over.

He **always** **gets** many of his shots in the basket.

See Practice 5.2I
See Practice 5.2J

PRACTICE 5.2I > **Identifying Modifiers That Help Clarify Tense**

Read each sentence. Then, write the modifier in each sentence that helps clarify the verb tense.

EXAMPLE   Once again, Claire set a new school record.

ANSWER   *Once again*

1. As always, the paper was delivered on time.
2. Sometimes, wild dogs could be heard howling in the woods.
3. He never loses a tennis match.
4. We sometimes ride the bus to work.
5. Suddenly, a loud clap of thunder rumbled in the sky.
6. He always prepares for his final exams.
7. One at a time, the kittens were rescued from the tree.
8. Carefully, he opened the front door.
9. I always brush my teeth thoroughly.
10. We will learn the dance, one step at a time.

PRACTICE 5.2J > **Supplying Modifiers to Clarify Meaning**

Read each sentence. Then, fill in the blank with a modifier that will clarify the meaning of each sentence.

EXAMPLE   _____, David waited for his sister.

ANSWER   *Last Friday,*

11. My favorite watch was _____ fixed.
12. We _____ eat breakfast food for dinner.
13. The carpenter sanded each board _____.
14. _____, the deer ran into the woods.
15. Jed _____ orders fish for lunch.
16. _____, I enjoy swimming in the ocean.
17. My sister practices the piano _____.
18. Golf is _____ a very popular sport.
19. I _____ wait my turn to speak.
20. We visited a new museum _____.

SPEAKING APPLICATION

Take turns with a partner. Tell about a trip that you have taken. Use modifiers that help clarify tense in your sentences. Your partner should listen for and identify the modifiers in your sentences.

WRITING APPLICATION

Use your corrections for sentences 13, 16, and 19 as models to write your own sentences. Rewrite the sentences to include different modifiers that clarify the meaning of each sentence.

5.3 The Subjunctive Mood

There are three **moods,** or ways in which a verb can express an action or condition: **indicative, imperative,** and **subjunctive.** The **indicative** mood, which is the most common, is used to make factual statements (*Karl is helpful.*) and to ask questions (*Is Karl helpful?*). The **imperative** mood is used to give orders or directions (*Be helpful.*).

Using the Subjunctive Mood

There are two important differences between verbs in the **subjunctive** mood and those in the indicative mood. First, in the present tense, third-person singular verbs in the subjunctive mood do not have the usual *-s* or *-es* ending. Second, the subjunctive mood of *be* in the present tense is *be;* in the past tense, it is *were,* regardless of the subject.

INDICATIVE MOOD	SUBJUNCTIVE MOOD
Jaime works with me.	I suggest that he work with me.
Jaime is hardworking.	He insists that everyone be hardworking.
He was patient.	If he were not patient, he would not be so successful.

Use the subjunctive mood (1) in clauses beginning with *if* or *that* to express an idea that is contrary to fact or (2) in clauses beginning with *that* to express a request, a demand, or a proposal.

5.3.1 RULE

Expressing Ideas Contrary to Fact Ideas that are contrary to fact are commonly expressed as wishes or conditions. Using the subjunctive mood in these situations shows that the idea expressed is not true now and may never be true.

EXAMPLES

Dave wishes that the cafeteria **were** less noisy.

He wished that he **were** able to hear his friends.

He could have heard them if they **were** in the quiet corner.

Some *if* clauses do not take a subjunctive verb. If the idea expressed may be true, an indicative form is used.

EXAMPLES   I said that **if** we **won** the game, I'd buy everyone's frozen yogurt.

If I **want** to win, I'll have to practice hard.

Expressing Requests, Demands, and Proposals Verbs that request, demand, or propose are often followed by a *that* clause containing a verb in the subjunctive mood.

REQUEST   I request that the survey results **be** published.

DEMAND   It is required that the survey results **be** published.

PROPOSAL   I proposed that the survey results **be** published.   See Practice 5.3A

Auxiliary Verbs That Express the Subjunctive Mood

Because certain helping verbs suggest conditions contrary to fact, they can often be used in place of the subjunctive mood.

Could, would, or *should* can be used with a verb to express the subjunctive mood.

The sentences on the left in the chart below have the usual subjunctive form of the verb *be: were.* The sentences on the right have been reworded with *could, would,* and *should.*

THE SUBJUNCTIVE MOOD WITH AUXILIARY VERBS	
WITH FORMS OF *BE*	WITH *COULD, WOULD,* OR *SHOULD*
If I were taller, I'd play basketball.	If I could be taller, I'd play basketball.
If he were to leave the party, I'd stay.	If he would leave the party, I'd stay.
If you were to move, would you miss us?	If you should move, would you miss us?

See Practice 5.3B

PRACTICE 5.3A > **Identifying Mood (Indicative, Imperative, Subjunctive)**

Read each sentence. Then, identify whether each sentence expresses doubts, wishes, and possibilities in the *indicative*, *imperative*, or *subjunctive* mood.

EXAMPLE   If I were you, I would buy something to eat.

ANSWER   *subjunctive*

1. Do you recommend that he visit several places?

2. Harry was here yesterday.

3. The doctor may demand that the patient obtain several opinions.

4. Be here tonight at 7:00.

5. It is best that you remain calm at all times.

6. I am still sleepy.

7. It is necessary that I drive the entire trip.

8. Cook eggs for me for breakfast.

9. If were a doctor, I would like to work for the American Red Cross.

10. She will bring her books to class.

PRACTICE 5.3B > **Supplying Auxiliary Verbs to Express the Subjunctive Mood**

Read each sentence. Then, rewrite each sentence and complete it by supplying an auxiliary verb.

EXAMPLE   They _____ recommend that each car slow down at the intersection.

ANSWER   *They would recommend that each car slow down at the intersection.*

11. Dad _____ insist that they wear their jackets.

12. If you _____ be so kind as to tell me where the library is, I would appreciate it.

13. I _____ have suggested that he sit down, but I didn't.

14. It _____ be a good idea to study for the test.

15. I _____ prefer that you didn't leave dirty dishes in the sink.

16. We _____ suggest another plan for the project.

17. He _____ insist that we switch teams for today.

18. We _____ recommend that they wait six months before applying for certification.

19. I _____ insist that you call me before you leave.

20. We _____ be planning a party for your birthday.

SPEAKING APPLICATION

Take turns with a partner. Say sentences that express doubts, wishes, and possibilities. Use the subjunctive mood in your sentences. Your partner should listen for and identify the subjunctive mood that expresses wishes, doubts, and possibilities in your sentences.

WRITING APPLICATION

Write sentences that include auxiliary verbs that express the subjunctive mood. Then, exchange papers with a partner. Your partner should underline all the auxiliary verbs in your sentences.

5.4 Voice

This section discusses a characteristic of verbs called **voice.**

RULE 5.4.1

> **Voice** or tense is the form of a verb that shows whether the subject is performing the action or is being acted upon.

In English, there are two voices: **active** and **passive.** Only action verbs can indicate the active voice; linking verbs cannot.

Active and Passive Voice or Tense

If the subject of a verb performs the action, the verb is active; if the subject receives the action, the verb is passive.

Active Voice Any action verb can be used in the active voice. The action verb may be transitive (that is, it may have a direct object) or intransitive (without a direct object).

RULE 5.4.2

> **A verb is active if its subject performs the action.**

In the examples below, the subject performs the action. In the first example, the verb *telephoned* is transitive; *team* is the direct object, which receives the action. In the second example, the verb *developed* is transitive; *pictures* is the direct object. In the third example, the verb *gathered* is intransitive; it has no direct object. In the last example, the verb *worked* is intransitive and has no direct object.

ACTIVE VOICE

The captain **telephoned** the **team** .
transitive verb   direct object

Bill **developed** twenty-five **pictures** of the ocean.
transitive verb   direct object

Telephone messages **gathered** on the desk while
intransitive verb
she was away.

Bill **worked** quickly.
intransitive verb

See Practice 5.4A
See Practice 5.4B

EL6

Passive Voice Most action verbs can also be used in the passive voice.

> A verb is passive if its action is performed upon the subject.

5.4.3 RULE

In the following examples, the subjects are the receivers of the action. The first example names the performer, the captain, as the object of the preposition *by* instead of the subject. In the second example, no performer of the action is mentioned.

PASSIVE VOICE

The **team was telephoned** by the captain.
  receiver of action   verb

The **messages were gathered** into neat piles.
    receiver of action   verb

> A passive verb is always a verb phrase made from a form of *be* plus the past participle of a verb. The tense of the helping verb *be* determines the tense of the passive verb.

5.2.4 RULE

The chart below provides a conjugation in the passive voice of the verb *see* in the three moods. Notice that there are only two progressive forms and no emphatic form.

THE VERB *SEE* IN THE PASSIVE VOICE	
Present Indicative	It is seen.
Past Indicative	It was seen.
Future Indicative	It will be seen.
Present Perfect Indicative	It has been seen.
Past Perfect Indicative	It had been seen.
Future Perfect Indicative	It will have been seen.
Present Progressive Indicative	It is being seen.
Past Progressive Indicative	It was being seen.
Present Imperative	(You) be seen.
Present Subjunctive	(if) it be seen
Past Subjunctive	(if) it were seen

See Practice 5.2C

Using Active and Passive Voice

Writing that uses the active voice tends to be much more lively than writing that uses the passive voice. The active voice is usually more direct and economical. That is because active voice shows someone doing something.

RULE 5.4.5

Use the active voice whenever possible.

ACTIVE VOICE	Natasha **requested** help.
PASSIVE VOICE	Help **was requested** by Natasha.

The passive voice has two uses in English.

RULE 5.4.6

Use the passive voice when you want to emphasize the receiver of an action rather than the performer of an action.

EXAMPLE   Our team **was awarded** the championship.

RULE 5.4.7

Use the passive voice to point out the receiver of an action whenever the performer is not important or not easily identified.

EXAMPLE   The door to the garage **was opened**, and I could
see my dad's new car.

The active voice lends more excitement to writing, making it more interesting to readers. In the example below, notice how the sentence you just read has been revised to show someone doing something, rather than something just happening.

EXAMPLE   My dad **opened** the door to the garage, and I could
see his new car.
(*Who* opened the door?)

See Practice 5.4D

PRACTICE 5.4A ▷ Recognizing Active Voice (Active Tense)

Read each sentence. Write the active verb in each sentence.

EXAMPLE   The doctor warned against eating too much sugar.

ANSWER   *warned*

1. The company advertised the new product.
2. I concentrated on the program.
3. She performed publicly for the first time.
4. Several people raced through the airport.
5. I try to eat fruits and vegetables every day.
6. We began our trip this morning.
7. The football players charged the field.
8. My mother saves coupons.
9. The guest speaker explained his theory to the audience.
10. Her best friend lives in Chicago.

PRACTICE 5.4B ▷ Using Active Verbs

Read each item. Then, write different sentences, using each item as an active verb.

EXAMPLE   shared

ANSWER   *I shared my lunch with Will.*

11. bakes
12. assembled
13. reads
14. discovered
15. finished
16. attract
17. slid
18. participate
19. extract
20. blew

SPEAKING APPLICATION

Take turns with a partner. Say sentences in the active voice. Your partner should listen for and identify the active verbs in each of your sentences.

WRITING APPLICATION

Write a paragraph, describing a funny character. Underline all the active verbs in your paragraph.

PRACTICE 5.4C > **Forming the Tenses of Passive Verbs**

Read each verb. Then, using the subject indicated in parentheses, conjugate each verb in the passive voice for the present indicative, past indicative, future indicative, present perfect indicative, past perfect indicative, and future perfect indicative.

EXAMPLE   catch (I)

ANSWER   *I am caught, I was caught, I will be caught, I have been caught, I had been caught, I will have been caught*

1. find (you)

2. make (it)

3. see (he)

4. like (they)

5. drive (he)

6. give (we)

7. tell (they)

8. answer (it)

9. present (she)

10. close (it)

PRACTICE 5.4D > **Supplying Verbs in the Active Voice (Active Tense)**

Read each sentence. Then, complete each sentence by supplying a verb in the active voice.

EXAMPLE   Lauren _____ the phone.

ANSWER   *answered*

11. The chorus _____ a concert.

12. The new store _____ on Monday.

13. Dad _____ dinner tonight.

14. I _____ the contest entry application today.

15. The children _____ a kite in the wind.

16. The crowd _____ a roar.

17. The principal _____ us for our performance.

18. Did the actor _____ any kind of award?

19. My mother _____ a delicious meal.

20. I _____ at a movie theater this summer.

SPEAKING APPLICATION

Take turns with a partner. Say a sentence with an active verb. Your partner should say a sentence using the same verb but in the passive voice.

WRITING APPLICATION

Show that you understand active and passive tenses by writing four sentences, using active tenses twice and passive tenses twice. Read your sentences to a partner who will tell if the sentence is active tense or passive tense as you speak.

CHAPTER 6

PRONOUN USAGE

Knowing how to use pronouns correctly will help you clearly present ideas in your writing.

WRITE GUY *Jeff Anderson, M.Ed.*

WHAT DO YOU NOTICE?

Look for pronouns as you zoom in on this sentence from the essay "Making History With Vitamin C" by Penny Le Couteur and Jay Burreson.

MENTOR TEXT

> This small squadron of four ships was under the command of Captain James Lancaster, who carried bottled lemon juice with him on his flagship, the *Dragon*.

Now, ask yourself the following questions:

- Why do the authors use the pronoun *who* rather than *whom*?
- Why do the authors use the pronouns *him* and *his*?

The authors use *who* instead of *whom* because *who* is the subject of the clause that begins with *who carried*. *Whom* is commonly used as the object of a verb or preposition. The pronoun *him* is used because it is the object of the preposition *with*. The pronoun *his* shows that the flagship belongs to Captain James Lancaster.

Grammar for Writers Writers can use pronouns to help guide readers through complicated sentences. Use pronouns in your writing to avoid repeating the same nouns over and over.

I told him, her, and them the whole story.

Wow! You really got personal with all those pronouns.

6.1 Case

Nouns and pronouns are the only parts of speech that have **case.**

RULE 6.1.1

Case is the form of a noun or a pronoun that shows how it is used in a sentence.

The Three Cases

Nouns and pronouns have three cases, each of which has its own distinctive uses.

RULE 6.1.2

The three cases of nouns and pronouns are the **nominative,** the **objective,** and the **possessive.**

CASE	USE IN SENTENCE
Nominative	As the Subject of a Verb, Predicate Nominative, or Nominative Absolute
Objective	As the Direct Object, Indirect Object, Object of a Preposition, Object of a Verbal, or Subject of an Infinitive
Possessive	To Show Ownership

Case in Nouns
The case, or form, of a noun changes only to show possession.

NOMINATIVE The **ring** had been hidden for years.

(*Ring* is the subject of the verb *had been hidden*.)

OBJECTIVE We tried to find the **ring**.

(*Ring* is the object of the infinitive *to find*.)

POSSESSIVE The **ring's** location could not be determined.

(The form changes when *'s* is added to show possession.)

Case in Pronouns

Personal pronouns often have different forms for all three cases. The pronoun that you use depends on its function in a sentence.

NOMINATIVE	OBJECTIVE	POSSESSIVE
I	*me*	*my, mine*
you	*you*	*your, yours*
he, she, it	*him, her, it*	*his, her, hers, its*
we, they	*us, them*	*our, ours*
		their, theirs

EXAMPLES **I** read the book about gardening.

Anne sent the pictures to **me** .

See Practice 6.1A

The book about gardening is **mine** .

The Nominative Case in Pronouns

The **nominative case** is used when a personal pronoun acts in one of three ways.

> Use the **nominative case** when a pronoun is the subject of a verb, the subject of a predicate nominative, or the subject of a pronoun in a nominative absolute.

6.1.3 RULE

A **nominative absolute** consists of a noun or nominative pronoun followed by a participial phrase. It functions independently from the rest of the sentence.

EXAMPLE **We having opened our English books,** our

teacher had us turn to the sonnet on page 10.

NOMINATIVE PRONOUNS	
As the Subject of a Verb	I will consult the instructions while she fills the prescription.
As a Predicate Nominative	The finalists were she and he.
In a Nominative Absolute	We having finished the brunch, the server cleared the table.

Nominative Pronouns in Compounds

When you use a pronoun in a compound subject or predicate nominative, check the case either by mentally crossing out the other part of the compound or by inverting the sentence.

COMPOUND SUBJECT

My counselor and **I** went over college applications.

(**I** went over applications.)

He and his father played baseball.

(**He** played baseball.)

COMPOUND PREDICATE NOMINATIVE

The fastest runners were Mark and **he**.

(Mark and **he** were the fastest runners.)

The planners were Kris and **I**.

(Kris and **I** were the planners.)

Nominative Pronouns With Appositives

When an appositive follows a pronoun that is being used as a subject or predicate nominative, the pronoun should stay in the nominative case. To check that you have used the correct case, either mentally cross out the appositive or isolate the subject and verb.

SUBJECT

We mathematicians use calculators.

(**We** use calculators.)

PREDICATE NOMINATIVE

The sponsors were **we** juniors.

(**We** were the sponsors.)

APPOSITIVE AFTER NOUN

The team captains, who were **she** and **I**, ran the soccer practice.

(**She** and I ran the soccer practice.)

See Practice 6.1B

Identifying Case

Read each sentence. Then, label the underlined pronoun in each sentence *nominative, objective,* or *possessive.*

EXAMPLE   Did the waiter give <u>you</u> a menu?

ANSWER   *objective*

1. Gary has sold me <u>his</u> mountain bike.
2. Sondra is signing <u>her</u> name on the application.
3. Do all these muffins have raisins in <u>them</u>?
4. The skateboard in the driveway is <u>yours</u>.
5. The television show that <u>I</u> want to watch has been canceled.
6. The decorator is redoing <u>her</u> bathroom.
7. Basim said that you told <u>him</u> about the meeting tonight.
8. The bird flew around in <u>its</u> cage.
9. Mr. Hamm showed <u>us</u> how to use the copy machine.
10. Paco and <u>he</u> rotate in the lineup.

Supplying Pronouns in the Nominative Case

Read each sentence. Then, supply the correct pronoun from the choices in parentheses to complete each sentence.

EXAMPLE   Sally and (he, him) delivered the message.

ANSWER   *he*

11. Fabian and (I, me) assist with many office tasks.
12. The new member of the basketball squad is (he, him).
13. The least likely participants are (them, they).
14. (Her, She) received a cash reward for returning the lost kitten.
15. Frank or (he, him) can give you the directions.
16. Kayla and (us, we) are hosting the event.
17. Gordon and (me, I) went ice-skating last night.
18. (We, Us) freshmen are ordering the jackets.
19. (She, Her) and Matilda are the only ones present.
20. The winners were Laith and (I, me).

SPEAKING APPLICATION

Take turns with a partner. Describe your neighborhood. Use at least one example of a pronoun in each of the three cases. Your partner should listen for and identify your use of pronouns as nominative, objective, and possessive.

WRITING APPLICATION

Write a paragraph about something you did over the last summer vacation. Use at least three nominative pronouns in your paragraph.

The Objective Case

Objective pronouns are used for any kind of object in a sentence as well as for the subject of an infinitive.

> Use the **objective case** for the object of any verb, preposition, or verbal or for the subject of an infinitive.

OBJECTIVE PRONOUNS	
Direct Object	The soccer ball hit her on the arm.
Indirect Object	My friend Myles sent me a book from England.
Object of Preposition	The pilot sat in the cockpit in front of us on the small plane.
Object of Participle	The piranhas swimming around them were very ferocious.
Object of Gerund	Meeting them would be a great honor.
Object of Infinitive	I am obligated to help her work on Saturday.
Subject of Infinitive	The café wanted her to work the early shift.

Objective Pronouns in Compounds

As with the nominative case, errors with objective pronouns most often occur in compounds. To find the correct case, mentally cross out the other part of the compound.

EXAMPLES   The crashing thunder alerted Kris and **him**.
(Crashing thunder alerted **him**.)

Ashley wrote Kate and **me** directions to the party.
(Ashley wrote **me** directions.)

Note About *Between:* Be sure to use the objective case after the preposition *between*.

INCORRECT   This secret is between you and **I**.

CORRECT   This secret is between you and **me**.

Objective Pronouns With Appositives

Use the objective case when a pronoun that is used as an object or as the subject of an infinitive is followed by an appositive.

EXAMPLES   The art project overwhelmed **us** students.

My mother brought **us** boys sweaters.

See Practice 6.1C   The guide warned **us** hikers to be careful.

The Possessive Case

One use for the **possessive case** is before gerunds. A **gerund** is a verbal form ending in *-ing* that is used as a noun.

> Use the **possessive case** before gerunds.

6.1.5 RULE

EXAMPLES   **Your** outlining of the notes was sloppy.

We objected to **her** insinuating that we cheated.

Kate insists on **our** attending the conference.

Common Errors in the Possessive Case

Be sure not to use an apostrophe with a possessive pronoun because possessives already show ownership. Spellings such as *her's, our's, their's,* and *your's* are incorrect.

In addition, be sure not to confuse possessive pronouns and contractions that sound alike. *It's* (with an apostrophe) is the contraction for *it is* or *it has. Its* (without the apostrophe) is a possessive pronoun that means "belonging to it." *You're* is a contraction of *you are*; the possessive form of *you* is *your.*

POSSESSIVE PRONOUNS   The graph had served **its** purpose.

Don't forget **your** essay.

CONTRACTIONS   **It's** not likely to snow today.

See Practice 6.1D   **You're** the only ones who were late for dinner today.

PRACTICE 6.1C Supplying Pronouns in the Objective Case

Read each sentence. Then, supply an objective pronoun to complete each sentence.

EXAMPLE   Quinn taught _____ singers a new song.

ANSWER   *us*

1. Lacy borrowed this pen from _____.
2. The discovery was made by Charlie and _____.
3. Give _____ students an opportunity.
4. This discussion is between you and _____.
5. Are these magazines for Keith or _____?
6. I didn't tell _____ the bad news.
7. Will you show this to _____?
8. Give _____ some assistance.
9. Did you hear _____?
10. The waiter asked _____ for our orders.

PRACTICE 6.1D Recognizing Pronouns in the Possessive Case

Read each sentence. Then, write the correct pronoun from the choices in parentheses to complete each sentence.

EXAMPLE   (Our, Us) squad lost the competition.

ANSWER   *Our*

11. I could be wrong, but isn't this locker (mine, my)?
12. After graduation, the seniors usually store away (they're, their) cap and gown.
13. (You, Your) squeaking brakes need to be repaired.
14. I would like to know which of those houses is (hers, she).
15. Richard asked Joe for (him, his) recipe.
16. The soldiers were given medals for (their, they're) bravery.
17. Nellie claimed that the calculator was (my, mine).
18. Ping was proud to hear them singing (he, his) song.
19. The handlers were elated when (our, ours) dog won the competition.
20. The hurricane left destruction in (it's, its) wake.

SPEAKING APPLICATION

Take turns with a partner. Describe an interesting scene from a book that you have read. Include at least three objective pronouns in your description.

WRITING APPLICATION

Write a paragraph about something fun you plan to do in the next year. Make sure to include three possessive pronouns in your paragraph.

6.2 Special Problems With Pronouns

Choosing the correct case is not always a matter of choosing the form that "sounds correct," because writing is usually more formal than speech. For example, it would be incorrect to say, "John is smarter than *me*." because the verb is understood in the sentence: "John is smarter than *I [am]*."

Using *Who* and *Whom* Correctly

In order to decide when to use *who* or *whom* and the related forms *whoever* and *whomever*, you need to know how the pronoun is used in a sentence and what case is appropriate.

> **Who** is used for the nominative case. **Whom** is used for the objective case.

6.2.1 RULE

CASE	PRONOUNS	USE IN SENTENCES
Nominative	*who* *whoever*	As the Subject of a Verb or Predicate Nominative
Objective	*whom* *whomever*	As the Direct Object, Object of a Verbal, Object of a Preposition, or Subject of an Infinitive
Possessive	*whose* *whosever*	To Show Ownership

EXAMPLES

I know **who** made that stew.

Kodie snuggled with **whoever** was on the couch.

Bob did not know **whom** the coach chose.

Whose coat is in the kitchen?

The nominative and objective cases are the source of certain problems. Pronoun problems can appear in two kinds of sentences: direct questions and complex sentences.

In Direct Questions

Who is the correct form when the pronoun is the subject of a simple question. *Whom* is the correct form when the pronoun is the direct object, object of a verbal, or object of a preposition.

Questions in subject–verb word order always begin with *who*. However, questions in inverted order never correctly begin with *who*. To see if you should use *who* or *whom*, reword the question as a statement in subject–verb word order.

EXAMPLES	**Who** wants a ticket to the new museum?
	Whom did you invite tonight?
	(You did invite **whom** tonight.)

In Complex Sentences

Follow these steps to see if the case of a pronoun in a subordinate clause is correct. First, find the subordinate clause. If the complex sentence is a question, rearrange it in subject–verb order. Second, if the subordinate clause is inverted, rearrange the words in subject–verb word order. Finally, determine how the pronoun is used in the subordinate clause.

EXAMPLE	**Who**, may I ask, has read the book?
REARRANGED	I may ask **who** has read the book.
USE OF PRONOUN	(subject of the verb *has read*)

EXAMPLE	Is the president the one **whom** they chose?
REARRANGED	They chose **whom** could be president.
USE OF PRONOUN	(object of the verb *chose*)

Note About *Whose*: The word *whose* is a possessive pronoun; the contraction *who's* means "who is" or "who has."

| POSSESSIVE PRONOUN | **Whose** pen is this? |
| CONTRACTION | **Who's** [who has] taken my pen? |

See Practice 6.2A

Pronouns in Elliptical Clauses

An **elliptical clause** is one in which some words are omitted but still understood. Errors in pronoun usage can easily be made when an elliptical clause that begins with *than* or *as* is used to make a comparison.

> In **elliptical clauses** beginning with *than* or *as*, use the form of the pronoun that you would use if the clause were fully stated.

6.2.2 RULE

The case of the pronoun is determined by whether the omitted words fall before or after the pronoun. The omitted words in the examples below are shown in brackets.

WORDS OMITTED BEFORE PRONOUN

You told Anna more than **me**.

(You told Anna more than [you told] **me**.)

WORDS OMITTED AFTER PRONOUN

Ben is as persistent as **he**.

(Ben is as persistent as **he** [is].)

Mentally add the missing words. If they come *before* the pronoun, choose the objective case. If they come *after* the pronoun, choose the nominative case.

CHOOSING A PRONOUN IN ELLIPTICAL CLAUSES
1. Consider the choices of pronouns: nominative or objective.
2. Mentally complete the elliptical clause.
3. Base your choice on what you find.

The case of the pronoun can sometimes change the entire meaning of the sentence.

NOMINATIVE PRONOUN

She likes reading more than **I**.

She liked reading more than **I** [did].

OBJECTIVE PRONOUN

She liked reading more than **me**.

She liked reading more than [she liked] **me**.

See Practice 6.2B

PRACTICE 6.2A > **Choosing *Who* or *Whom* Correctly**

Read each sentence. Then, write *who* or *whom* to complete each sentence.

EXAMPLE   Jasmine is the one _____ I came to visit.

ANSWER   *whom*

1. _____ did the coach select as team captain?

2. Those are the volunteers _____ the mayor will honor.

3. The trip is open to anyone _____ can read a map.

4. To _____ did you give the key?

5. A good educator must be someone _____ enjoys teaching.

6. _____ have you asked to the dance?

7. The prize was given to the person _____ answered the most questions correctly.

8. Jeannette is the person _____ I supported during the campaign.

9. He is the same man _____ I met at the conference.

10. Terry Heath is a student _____ gets lots of praise.

PRACTICE 6.2B > **Identifying the Correct Pronoun in Elliptical Clauses**

Read each sentence. Then, complete each elliptical clause with an appropriate pronoun.

EXAMPLE   Burke is as loud as _____.

ANSWER   *she*

11. Damon plays the drums better than _____ plays.

12. The panel chose Kendra rather than _____.

13. The test results delighted Brian as much as _____ delighted his parents.

14. I do not understand German as well as _____ understands French.

15. That comment impressed Fred as much as _____ impressed Alicia.

16. Leonard decided to ask Zalaima to be his running mate rather than _____.

17. Nathan is as committed to the cause as _____.

18. The Falcons scored as many points as _____ had scored during the playoffs.

19. Corey runs the hurdles faster than _____.

20. Rosa likes her puppy more than _____ brother likes the puppy.

SPEAKING APPLICATION

Take turns with a partner. Ask questions using both *who* and *whom*. Your partner should respond by also using *who* and *whom* correctly in his her response.

WRITING APPLICATION

Write a true or fictional paragraph describing any type of competition. Use at least two elliptical clauses in your paragraph.

CHAPTER 7

AGREEMENT

Understanding how nouns relate to verbs and pronouns will help you achieve agreement in your sentences.

WRITE GUY *Jeff Anderson, M.Ed.*

WHAT DO YOU NOTICE?

Look for examples of agreement as you zoom in on this sentence from the play *Antigone* by Socrates, as translated by Dudley Fitts and Robert Fitzgerald.

MENTOR TEXT

> **HAIMON.** The ideal condition would be, I admit, that men should be right by instinct; but since we are all too likely to go astray, the reasonable thing is to learn from those who can teach.

Now, ask yourself the following questions:

- Which noun does the pronoun *we* refer to? How do they agree?
- How do the verbs *are* and *is* agree with their subjects?

The pronoun *we* refers to the noun *men*. Because *men* and *we* are both plural, they agree in number. The verb *are* is plural and agrees with the plural pronoun *we* that precedes it. The verb *is* is singular, so it agrees with the singular noun *thing*.

Grammar for Writers Writers are more articulate when they make subjects and verbs and nouns and pronouns agree. Make your writing easier for readers to follow by focusing on agreement.

Your sentences are so agreeable

That's because I use friendly subjects and verbs.

7.1 Subject–Verb Agreement

For a subject and a verb to agree, both must be singular, or both must be plural. In this section, you will learn how to make sure singular and plural subjects and verbs agree.

Number in Nouns, Pronouns, and Verbs

In grammar, **number** indicates whether a word is singular or plural. Only three parts of speech have different forms that indicate number: nouns, pronouns, and verbs.

RULE

7.1.1

> **Number** shows whether a noun, pronoun, or verb is singular or plural.

Recognizing the number of most nouns is seldom a problem because most form their plurals by adding *-s* or *-es*. Some, such as *mouse* or *ox*, form their plurals irregularly: *mice, oxen.*

Pronouns, however, have different forms to indicate their number. The chart below shows the different forms of personal pronouns in the nominative case, the case that is used for subjects.

PERSONAL PRONOUNS		
SINGULAR	PLURAL	SINGULAR OR PLURAL
I	*we*	*you*
he, she, it	*they*	

The grammatical number of verbs is sometimes difficult to determine. That is because the form of many verbs can be either singular or plural, and they may form plurals in different ways.

SINGULAR   He **runs**.

He **has run**.

PLURAL   We **run**.

We **have run**.

Some verb forms can be only singular. The personal pronouns *he*, *she*, and *it* and all singular nouns call for singular verbs in the present and the present perfect tense.

ALWAYS
SINGULAR

He **jumps**.

He **has jumped**.

Ben **yells**.

Chris **has yelled**.

She **runs**.

She **has run**.

The verb *be* in the present tense has special forms to agree with singular subjects. The pronoun *I* has its own singular form of *be*; so do *he, she, it*, and singular nouns.

ALWAYS
SINGULAR

I **am** starving.

She **is** short.

Ben **is** late.

She **is** waiting.

All singular subjects except *you* share the same past tense verb form of *be*.

ALWAYS
SINGULAR

I **was** going to work.

He **was** class president.

Keith **was** late for work.

See Practice 7.1A

He **was** getting on the train.

A verb form will always be singular if it has had an *-s* or *-es* added to it or if it includes the words *has, am, is*, or *was*. The number of any other verb depends on its subject.

The chart on the next page shows verb forms that are always singular and those that can be singular or plural.

VERBS THAT ARE ALWAYS SINGULAR	VERBS THAT CAN BE SINGULAR OR PLURAL
(he, she, Jane) sees (he, she, Jane) has seen (I) am (he, she, Jane) is (I, he, she, Jane) was	(I, you, we, they) see (I, you, we, they) have seen (you, we, they) are (you, we, they) were

Singular and Plural Subjects

When making a verb agree with its subject, be sure to identify the subject and determine its number.

RULE 7.1.2

A singular subject must have a singular verb. A plural subject must have a plural verb.

SINGULAR SUBJECT AND VERB	PLURAL SUBJECT AND VERB
The doctor works in South Africa.	These doctors work in South Africa.
She was being secretive about the date of the party.	They were being secretive about the date of the party.
Benji looks through a magazine for ideas about gardening.	Benji and Brice look through a magazine for ideas about gardening.
France is a large country in Europe.	France and Italy are large countries in Europe.
Kira takes biology and anatomy.	Kira and Kim take biology and anatomy.
Bethany is planning a vacation to Australia.	Our cousins are planning a vacation to Australia.
Tiff plays defense on the soccer team.	Tiff and Terry play on the soccer team.
She looks through the plane window.	They look through the plane window.
Benjamin has been studying human anatomy.	We have been studying human anatomy.

See Practice 7.1B

PRACTICE 7.1A > **Identifying Number in Nouns, Pronouns, and Verbs**

Read each word or group of words. Write whether the word or words are *singular*, *plural*, or *both*.

EXAMPLE   was sleeping

ANSWER   *singular*

1. shuts
2. women
3. adore
4. you
5. they
6. have
7. desk
8. flies above
9. discuss
10. moose

PRACTICE 7.1B > **Identifying Singular and Plural Subjects and Verbs**

Read each sentence. Then, write the subject and verb in each sentence and label them *plural* or *singular*.

EXAMPLE   The papers have been ruined in the flood.

ANSWER   *subject:* **papers**; *verb:* **have been ruined** — *plural*

11. The dance starts at seven o'clock tonight.
12. Rick has begun his final art project.
13. New houses have many modern features.
14. This summer, our rosebushes have started to bloom.
15. The old bookshelves from the basement were being sold at our yard sale.
16. My sister often plays with her friends after school.
17. Before the planting season, I clean all the flower pots.
18. Gentle waves slap against the dock.
19. The floor mats in my car are getting worn.
20. The egg has fallen from the carton.

SPEAKING APPLICATION

Take turns with a partner. Tell about what you did this morning before coming to school. Your partner should listen for and name the plural and singular nouns and verbs that you use.

WRITING APPLICATION

For each sentence in Practice 7.1B, change the subject from singular to plural or plural to singular. Make sure that the verb in each sentence agrees with your new subject.

Intervening Phrases and Clauses

When you check for agreement, mentally cross out any words that separate the subject and verb.

7.1.3

> **A phrase or clause that interrupts a subject and its verb does not affect subject–verb agreement.**

In the first example below, the singular subject *discovery* agrees with the singular verb *interests* despite the intervening prepositional phrase *of ancient scrolls,* which contains a plural noun.

EXAMPLES   The **discovery** of ancient scrolls **interests** many people.

The **researchers** , whose research is nearly complete, **require** more funding.

Intervening parenthetical expressions—such as those beginning with *as well as, in addition to, in spite of,* or *including*—also have no effect on the agreement of the subject and verb.

EXAMPLES   Your **research** , in addition to the data gathered by those working in the lab, **is helping** to cure many diseases.

Christina's **trip** , including visits to Florida and California, **is lasting** six months.

See Practice 7.1C

Relative Pronouns as Subjects

When *who, which,* or *that* acts as a subject of a subordinate clause, its verb will be singular or plural depending on the number of the antecedent.

7.1.4

> **The antecedent of a relative pronoun determines its agreement with a verb.**

EXAMPLES   She is the only **one** of the professors **who has** experience teaching American literature.

(The antecedent of *who* is *one*.)

She is the only one of several **professors who have** experience teaching American literature.

(The antecedent of *who* is *professor*.)

Compound Subjects

A **compound subject** has two or more simple subjects, which are usually joined by *or* or *and*. Use the following rules when making compound subjects agree with verbs.

Subjects Joined by *And*

Only one rule applies to compound subjects connected by *and:* The verb is usually plural, whether the parts of the compound subject are all singular, all plural, or mixed.

A compound subject joined by *and* is generally plural and must have a plural verb.

7.1.5
RULE

TWO SINGULAR SUBJECTS   A **snowstorm** and an **ice storm hit** the mountain.

TWO PLURAL SUBJECTS   **Tulips** and **daisies are** growing in my garden.

A SINGULAR SUBJECT AND A PLURAL SUBJECT   A purple **tulip** and many yellow **daisies make** a beautiful arrangement.

There are two exceptions to this rule. The verb is singular if the parts of a compound subject are thought of as one item or if the word *every* or *each* precedes the compound subject.

Peanut butter and jelly was all the child

would eat.

Every weather center and emergency

network in the United states issues warnings for

severe weather.

Singular Subjects Joined by *Or* or *Nor*

When both parts of a compound subject connected by *or* or *nor* are singular, a singular verb is required.

> **RULE 7.1.6**
>
> **Two or more singular subjects joined by *or* or *nor* must have a singular verb.**

EXAMPLE   A **sandwich** or **salad makes** a great lunch.

Plural Subjects Joined by *Or* or *Nor*

When both parts of a compound subject connected by *or* or *nor* are plural, a plural verb is required.

> **RULE 7.1.7**
>
> **Two or more plural subjects joined by *or* or *nor* must have a plural verb.**

EXAMPLE   Neither **blizzards** nor **snowstorms cause** as

many power outages as ice storms.

Subjects of Mixed Number Joined by *Or* or *Nor*

If one part of a compound subject is singular and the other is plural, the verb agrees with the subject that is closer to it.

> **RULE 7.1.8**
>
> **If one or more singular subjects are joined to one or more plural subjects by *or* or *nor*, the subject closest to the verb determines agreement.**

EXAMPLES   Neither **Anastasia** nor my **parents are excited**.

Neither my **parents** nor **Anastasia is excited**.   See Practice 7.1D

PRACTICE 7.1C > **Identifying Intervening Phrases and Clauses**

Read each sentence. Underline the intervening phrase or clause between the subject and the verb in each sentence.

EXAMPLE   The book by Dr. Seuss is well-known by all.

ANSWER   *The book by Dr. Seuss is well-known by all.*

1. A bouquet of red roses was given to Jan.

2. Olivia, the only one of four children, has inherited her mother's eye color.

3. The salespeople, who are working in the shoe department, are at a meeting.

4. The pages of the book, as well as the back and front covers, are in great condition.

5. The lake where trout can be found is being overfished.

6. A house built near the ocean is likely to have beautiful views of the water.

7. The giant trees that tower over the forest floor offer shade to the animals.

8. Three kids from my class were sent acceptance letters from prestigious universities.

9. The storyboards that the student created were helpful in her presentation.

10. The birds, including the fledglings, had to fly south for the winter.

PRACTICE 7.1D > **Making Verbs Agree With Singular and Compound Subjects**

Read each sentence. Then, fill in the blank with the form of a verb that agrees with the singular or compound subject.

EXAMPLE   Neither Helen nor I _____ to the meeting.

ANSWER   *went*

11. My mother and father _____ late for the movie.

12. Both fish and ducks _____ in that pond.

13. Broccoli and spinach _____ green vegetables.

14. Either worms or insects _____ the plant crops.

15. Both oil and vinegar _____ used in this salad dressing.

16. Shorts, T-shirts, and sunglasses _____ needed for your vacation.

17. He _____ the hard drive.

18. Neither rain nor snow _____ us from taking this field trip.

19. Blueberries or any other berry _____ good on oatmeal.

20. Writers and illustrators often _____ together to create a book.

SPEAKING APPLICATION

Take turns with a partner. Use sentences with intervening clauses to tell about your best holiday experience. Your partner should identify the intervening clauses in your sentences.

WRITING APPLICATION

Use sentences 14, 16, and 19 as models to write similar sentences. Exchange papers with a partner. Your partner should complete the sentences with the correct form of a verb that agrees with the subject.

Confusing Subjects

Some kinds of subjects have special agreement problems.

Hard-to-Find Subjects and Inverted Sentences
Subjects that appear after verbs are said to be **inverted.**
Subject–verb order is usually inverted in questions. To find out
whether to use a singular or plural verb, mentally rearrange the
sentence into subject–verb order.

RULE 7.1.9

> A verb must still agree in number with a subject that comes
> after it.

EXAMPLE	On the counter **are** two coffee **mugs** .
REARRANGED IN SUBJECT–VERB ORDER	Two coffee **mugs are** on the counter.

The words *there* and *here* often signal an inverted sentence.
These words never function as the subject of a sentence.

EXAMPLES	There **are** the family **photos** .
	Here **is** the updated **information** .

Note About *There's* and *Here's*: Both of these contractions
contain the singular verb *is: there is* and *here is.* They should be
used only with singular subjects.

CORRECT	**There's** only one **meeting** scheduled.
	Here's a black **suit** to try on.

See Practice 7.1E

Subjects With Linking Verbs
Subjects with linking verbs may also cause agreement problems.

RULE 7.1.10

> A linking verb must agree with its subject, regardless of the
> number of its predicate nominative.

EXAMPLES   **Apples are** my favorite fruit.

One **reason** we expect a snowstorm **is** that
the air is freezing.

In the first example, the plural verb *are* agrees with the plural
subject *apples*. In the next example, the singular subject *reason*
takes the singular verb *is*.

Collective Nouns

Collective nouns name groups of people or things. Examples
include *audience*, *class*, *club*, and *committee*.

> A collective noun takes a singular verb when the group it
> names acts as a single unit. A collective noun takes a plural
> verb when the group acts as individuals.

7.1.11 RULE

SINGULAR   The special **forces embarked** at night.

(The members act as a unit.)

PLURAL   The special **forces were going** on separate
missions.

(The members act individually.)

Nouns That Look Like Plurals

Some nouns that end in *-s* are actually singular. For example,
nouns that name branches of knowledge, such as *civics*, and
those that name single units, such as *mumps*, take singular verbs.

> Use singular verbs to agree with nouns that are plural in form
> but singular in meaning.

7.1.12 RULE

SINGULAR   **Social studies is** my favorite subject.

When words such as *ethics* and *politics* do not name branches of
knowledge but indicate characteristics, their meanings are plural.
Similarly, such words as *eyeglasses*, *pants*, and *scissors* generally
take plural verbs.

PLURAL   Ronnie's **ethics change** all the time.

Indefinite Pronouns
Some indefinite pronouns are always singular, some are always plural, and some may be either singular or plural. Prepositional phrases do not affect subject–verb agreement.

> **Singular indefinite pronouns take singular verbs. Plural indefinite pronouns take plural verbs.**

SINGULAR   *anybody, anyone, anything, each, either, everybody, everyone, everything, neither, nobody, no one, nothing, somebody, someone, something*

PLURAL   *both, few, many, others, several*

SINGULAR   **Everyone** in the concert arena **has left**.

PLURAL   **Many** of the flowers **were planted**.

> **The pronouns *all, any, more, most, none*, and *some* usually take a singular verb if the antecedent is singular, and a plural verb if it is plural.**

SINGULAR   **Some** of the house **was finished** by nightfall.

PLURAL   **Some** of the damaged houses **are** being repaired.

Titles of Creative Works and Names of Organizations
Plural words in the title of a creative work or in the name of an organization do not affect subject–verb agreement.

> **A title of a creative work or name of an organization is singular and must have a singular verb.**

EXAMPLES   **The March of Dimes is** a wonderful charity.
(organization)

Starry Night by Vincent Van Gogh **is** a famous painting.
(creative work)

Amounts and Measurements

Although they appear to be plural, most amounts and measurements actually express single units or ideas.

> **A noun expressing an amount or measurement is usually singular and requires a singular verb.**

7.1.16   RULE

EXAMPLES   **Four hundred million dollars is** the cost to build a new bridge.

(Four hundred million dollars is one sum of money.)

Four miles was our distance from the nearest shopping mall.

(Four miles is a single distance.)

Three quarters of the house **was rebuilt** by the end of the week.

(Three quarters is one part of a house.)

Half of the weeds **were uprooted**.

(Half refers to a number of individual weeds, and not part of an individual garden, so it is plural.)

See Practice 7.1F

PRACTICE 7.1E > **Identifying Subjects and Verbs in Inverted Sentences**

Read each sentence. Then, identify the subject and verb in each sentence.

EXAMPLE   Here is your assignment.

ANSWER   subject: *assignment*; verb: *is*

1. Onto the playground rushed the excited children.

2. How will we ever get back to the road?

3. There are no mistakes in your report.

4. In the cupboard are the fancy dishes.

5. Where did you leave your sneakers?

6. There was the exit from the building.

7. Here are some ideas for your class project.

8. Was the coffee on the counter?

9. May I have another sheet of paper, please?

10. Somewhere between those trees lives the fox.

PRACTICE 7.1F > **Making Verbs Agree With Confusing Subjects**

Read each sentence. Then, write the correct subject or verb from the choices in parentheses to complete each sentence.

EXAMPLE   The committee (is, are) disagreeing among themselves about the plans.

ANSWER   *are*

11. Everyone in the room (is ,are) registered to vote.

12. Half of the chairs (has, have) cushions on them.

13. The (jury, juries) sit in separate courtrooms.

14. *War and Peace* (is, are) a classic literary novel.

15. Three miles (is, are) the distance we will walk during the hike.

16. (Storms, A storm) at sea cause high waves that crash against the shore.

17. A group of Vikings (is, are) setting sail for the New World.

18. Few of the tourists (go, goes) to the museum.

19. Social studies (has, have) always been my best subject.

20. In the trees, at the top of the hill, (lives, live) the family of deer.

SPEAKING APPLICATION

Take turns with a partner. Say five inverted sentences. Your partner should identify the subject and verb in each of your sentences.

WRITING APPLICATION

Write three sentences that include confusing subjects. Underline the subject in each sentence, and make sure that the verb agrees with the subject.

7.2 Pronoun–Antecedent Agreement

Like a subject and its verb, a pronoun and its antecedent must agree. An **antecedent** is the word or group of words for which the pronoun stands.

Agreement Between Personal Pronouns and Antecedents

While a subject and verb must agree only in number, a personal pronoun and its antecedent must agree in three ways.

> **A personal pronoun must agree with its antecedent in number, person, and gender.**

7.2.1 RULE

The **number** of a pronoun indicates whether it is singular or plural. **Person** refers to a pronoun's ability to indicate either the person speaking (first person), the person spoken to (second person), or the person, place, or thing spoken about (third person). **Gender** is the characteristic of nouns and pronouns that indicates whether the word is *masculine* (referring to males), *feminine* (referring to females), or *neuter* (referring to neither males nor females).

The only pronouns that indicate gender are third-person singular personal pronouns.

GENDER OF THIRD-PERSON SINGULAR PRONOUNS	
Masculine	*he, him, his*
Feminine	*she, her, hers*
Neuter	*it, its*

In the example below, the pronoun *her* agrees with the antecedent *Lori Smith* in number (both are singular), in person (both are third person), and in gender (both are feminine).

EXAMPLE   Lori Smith has opened **her** office to the employees.

Agreement in Number

There are three rules to keep in mind to determine the number of compound antecedents.

Use a singular personal pronoun when two or more singular antecedents are joined by *or* or *nor.*

EXAMPLES Either Amber **or** Tina will bring **her** copy of the *Mona Lisa* to class.

Neither Sophie **nor** Allie will sleep in **her** new bed.

Use a plural personal pronoun when two or more antecedents are joined by *and.*

EXAMPLE Brittany **and** I are studying for **our** driver's test.

An exception occurs when a distinction must be made between individual and joint ownership. If individual ownership is intended, use a singular pronoun to refer to a compound antecedent. If joint ownership is intended, use a plural pronoun.

SINGULAR **Adam and Cathy** played **her** piano.

PLURAL **Adam and Cathy** paid for **their** piano.

SINGULAR Neither **Terry nor Todd** let me drive **his** car.

PLURAL Neither **Terry nor Todd** let me drive **their** car.

The third rule applies to compound antecedents whose parts are mixed in number.

Use a plural personal pronoun if any part of a compound antecedent joined by *or* or *nor* is plural.

EXAMPLE   If either the **vendor** or the **presenters** arrive, take **them** to the meeting.

See Practice 7.2A

Agreement in Person and Gender Avoid shifts in person or gender of pronouns.

> As part of pronoun–antecedent agreement, take care not to shift either person or gender.

RULE 7.2.5

SHIFT IN PERSON   **Kevin** is planning to visit California because **you** can see how the Navy Seals train.

CORRECT   **Kevin** is planning to visit California because **he** wants to see how the Navy Seals train.

SHIFT IN GENDER   The **dog** wagged **its** tail back and forth and barked **his** head off.

CORRECT   The **dog** wagged **its** tail back and forth and barked **its** head off.

Generic Masculine Pronouns Traditionally, a masculine pronoun has been used to refer to a singular antecedent whose gender is unknown. Such use is called *generic* because it applies to both masculine and feminine genders. Many writers now prefer to use *his or her, he or she, him or her,* or to rephrase a sentence to eliminate the situation.

> When gender is not specified, either use *his or her* or rewrite the sentence.

RULE 7.2.6

EXAMPLES   Each **student** found a useful periodical on which to research **his or her report** on WWII.

Students found useful periodicals on which to research **their reports** on WWII.

See Practice 7.2B

PRACTICE 7.2A > **Making Personal Pronouns
Agree With Their Antecedents**

Read each sentence. Then, for each sentence,
choose the personal pronoun in parentheses that
agrees with the antecedent.

EXAMPLE   Peter and I enjoyed (our, his) trip to
New York City.

ANSWER   *our*

1. The butterfly is tasting the sap with (her, its)
feet.

2. Neither Dee nor Barbara uses (their, her)
calculator very often.

3. The manager gets to choose (his, their) office.

4. Joe and Melissa work after school to prove
that (he or she, they) can get good grades and
earn money.

5. A skunk's odor is (its, their) defense.

6. Maura has washed (her, their) son's hair.

7. Neither Jose nor Laura remembered to bring
(their, his or her) swimsuit.

8. Police officers should wear (his or her, their)
badges.

9. Neither Mike nor Kyung rode (his, their) bike
to practice.

10. Each boy designed (his, their) own robot.

PRACTICE 7.2B > **Revising for Agreement in
Person and Gender**

Read each sentence. Then, revise each sentence
so that the personal pronoun agrees with the
antecedent.

EXAMPLE   If you need more information, I will
be glad to send them.

ANSWER   *If you need more information, I will
be glad to send it.*

11. Neither Jenny nor Ashley brought their books
to school.

12. I like the kind of movie that leaves you
guessing.

13. If Laura doesn't understand the directions, she
should ask the teacher to explain it to them.

14. The dog behaved as if she had an injured paw.

15. Manuel writes his assignments in a notebook,
a habit that helps you remember them.

16. Each of the salesmen reported their sales
figures.

17. One of my neighbors runs to improve the
muscle tone in their legs.

18. If a person wants to succeed, you have to be
willing to work hard.

19. I am happy for Frank because they won the
tournament.

20. The coach expects a lot from us, but you
started to appreciate him after a while.

SPEAKING APPLICATION

**Take turns with a partner. Tell about members
of your families. Use several different personal
pronouns in your sentences. Your partner
should name the personal pronouns you
use and tell whether they agree with their
antecedents.**

WRITING APPLICATION

**Use sentences 14, 15, and 16 as models to
write similar sentences. Then, exchange
papers with a partner. Your partner should
revise each sentence to make the personal
pronoun agree with the antecedent.**

Agreement With Indefinite Pronouns

When an indefinite pronoun, such as *each*, *all*, or *most*, is used with a personal pronoun, the pronouns must agree.

> **Use a plural personal pronoun when the antecedent is a plural indefinite pronoun.**

EXAMPLES **Many** of the students were excited about **their** art lessons.

All the girls forgot to bring **their** uniforms.

When both pronouns are singular, a similar rule applies.

> **Use a singular personal pronoun when the antecedent is a singular indefinite pronoun.**

In the first example, the personal pronoun *her* agrees in number with the singular indefinite pronoun *one*. The gender (feminine) is determined by the word *actresses*.

EXAMPLES Only **one** of the actresses practiced **her** lines.

One of the actresses remembered to bring **her** script.

If other words in the sentence do not indicate a gender, you may use *him or her*, *he or she*, *his or her* or rephrase the sentence.

EXAMPLES **Each** of the athletes wore **his or her** new track uniform.

The **athletes** wore **their** new track uniforms.

For indefinite pronouns that can be either singular or plural, such as *all*, *any*, *more*, *most*, *none*, and *some*, agreement depends on the antecedent of the indefinite pronoun.

EXAMPLES **Most** of the fruit had lost **its** appeal.
(The antecedent of *most* is *fruit,* which is singular.)

Most of the shoppers wanted **their** money back.
(The antecedent of *most* is *shoppers,* which is plural.)

Some of the lasagna **was** too hot.
(The antecedent of *some* is *lasagna,* which is singular.)

All of the passports **were** in the suitcase.
(The antecedent of *all* is *passports,* which is plural.)

In some situations, strict grammatical agreement may be illogical. In these situations, either let the meaning of the sentence determine the number of the personal pronoun, or reword the sentence.

ILLOGICAL When **each of the doorbells** rang, I answered **it** as quickly as possible.

MORE LOGICAL When **each of the doorbells** rang, I answered **them** as quickly as possible.

MORE LOGICAL When **all of the doorbells** rang, I answered **them** as quickly as possible.

See Practice 7.2C

Agreement With Reflexive Pronouns

Reflexive pronouns, which end in *-self* or *-selves,* should only refer to a word earlier in the same sentence.

RULE 7.2.9

A reflexive pronoun must agree with an antecedent that is clearly stated.

EXAMPLES **Patricia** made dinner for **herself**.

You should consider **yourself** blessed.

Star **athletes** enjoy making a spectacle of **themselves**.

See Practice 7.2D

PRACTICE 7.2C > **Supplying Indefinite Pronouns**

Read each sentence. Then, rewrite each sentence, filling in the blank with an appropriate indefinite pronoun that agrees with the antecedent.

EXAMPLE   Has _____ called for me today?

ANSWER   *Has anyone called for me today?*

1. _____ of my friends plan to enter their essays in the writing contest.

2. _____ of my sisters wants her own room.

3. Only _____ of the horses has its mane brushed.

4. _____ of the books on the shelves need their covers dusted.

5. _____ of the baseball players had his uniform cleaned.

6. _____ of the fish still had a hook in its mouth.

7. _____ of the plants have black spots on their leaves.

8. _____ of the rugs were handmade.

9. _____ of the rooms had curtains covering the windows.

10. _____ of the ducks was black.

PRACTICE 7.2D > **Supplying Reflexive Pronouns**

Read each sentence. Then, write the correct reflexive pronoun that agrees with the antecedent in each sentence.

EXAMPLE   Ladies and gentlemen, please help _____ to some apple cider.

ANSWER   *yourselves*

11. We told _____ that we were improving things.

12. The panel members decided among _____ that they wanted to end the meeting.

13. Jeremy did finish the job by _____.

14. We found _____ wondering what to do after the game.

15. I made _____ a sandwich for lunch.

16. She left the room so that the reporters could talk among _____.

17. The children amused _____ by playing a game.

18. Lance made _____ a race car for the science fair.

19. I told my mom to prepare _____ for good news.

20. The tourists suddenly found _____ in a historic part of town.

SPEAKING APPLICATION

Take turns with a partner. Choose three indefinite pronouns. Your partner should say sentences, using a personal pronoun that agrees with each indefinite pronoun.

WRITING APPLICATION

Use sentences 11, 12, and 15 as models to write similar sentences. Then, exchange papers with a partner. Your partner should rewrite each sentence, using the correct reflexive pronoun that agrees with the antecedent.

7.3 Special Problems With Pronoun Agreement

This section will show you how to avoid some common errors that can obscure the meaning of your sentences.

Vague Pronoun References

One basic rule governs all of the rules for pronoun reference.

> **7.3.1** **To avoid confusion, a pronoun requires an antecedent that is either stated or clearly understood.**

The pronouns *which, this, that,* and *these* should not be used to refer to a vague or overly general idea.

In the following example, it is impossible to determine exactly what the pronoun *these* stands for because it may refer to three different groups of words.

VAGUE
REFERENCE
Emma was hungry, the baby was restless, and the air conditioner was broken. **These** made our trip to the beach unpleasant.

This vague reference can be corrected in two ways. One way is to change the pronoun to an adjective that modifies a specific noun. The second way is to revise the sentence so that the pronoun *these* is eliminated.

CORRECT
Emma was hungry, the baby was restless, and the air conditioner was broken. **These conditions** made our trip to the beach unpleasant.

CORRECT
Emma's hunger, the baby's restlessness, and the air conditioner's breakdown made our trip to the beach unpleasant.

The personal pronouns *it*, *they*, and *you* should always have a clear antecedent.

In the next example, the pronoun *it* has no clearly stated antecedent.

VAGUE REFERENCE | Harold is visiting art museums next month. **It** should be very enlightening.

Again, there are two methods of correction. The first method is to replace the personal pronoun with a specific noun. The second method is to revise the sentence entirely in order to make the whole idea clear.

CORRECT | Harold is visiting art museums next month. **The experience** should be very enlightening

CORRECT | **Harold's visit** to art museums next month should be very enlightening

In the next example, the pronoun *they* is used without an accurate antecedent.

VAGUE REFERENCE | I loved tasting the Italian dish, but **they** never explained what ingredients were used.

CORRECT | I loved tasting the Italian dish, but **the chef** never explained what ingredients were used.

VAGUE REFERENCE | When we arrived at the mall, **they** told us which store was having a sale today.

CORRECT | When we arrived at the mall, **the sales associate** told us which store was having a sale today.

Use *you* only when the reference is truly to the reader or listener.

VAGUE REFERENCE   **You** couldn't understand a word Steve sang.

CORRECT   **We** couldn't understand a word Steve sang.

VAGUE REFERENCE   On the team my brother played for, **you** were expected to win all the time.

CORRECT   On the team my brother played for, **athletes** were expected to win all the time.

Note About *It*: In many idiomatic expressions, the personal pronoun *it* has no specific antecedent. In statements such as "It is late," *it* is an idiom that is accepted as standard English.

See Practice 7.3A

Ambiguous Pronoun References

A pronoun is **ambiguous** if it can refer to more than one antecedent.

A pronoun should never refer to more than one antecedent.

In the following sentence, *he* is confusing because it can refer to either *Jim* or *Wayne*. Revise such a sentence by changing the pronoun to a noun or rephrasing the sentence entirely.

AMBIGUOUS REFERENCE   Jim told Wayne about the game **he** attended.

CORRECT   Jim told Wayne about the game Jim attended.

(Jim knew about the game.)

Do not repeat a personal pronoun in a sentence if it can refer to a different antecedent each time.

AMBIGUOUS REPETITION	When Kate asked her mother if **she** could borrow the cellphone, **she** said that **she** needed it.
CLEAR	When Kate asked her mother if **she** could borrow the cellphone, **Kate** said that **she** needed it.
CLEAR	When Kate asked her mother if **she** could borrow the cellphone, her **mother** said that **she** needed it **herself**.

Notice that in the first sentence above, it is unclear whether *she* is referring to Kate or to her mother. To eliminate the confusion, Kate's name was used in the second sentence. In the third sentence, the reflexive pronoun *herself* helps to clarify the meaning.

Avoiding Distant Pronoun References

A pronoun should be placed close to its antecedent.

> **A personal pronoun should always be close enough to its antecedent to prevent confusion.**

7.3.6 RULE

A distant pronoun reference can be corrected by moving the pronoun closer to its antecedent or by changing the pronoun to a noun. In the example below, *it* is too far from the antecedent *leg*.

DISTANT REFERENCE	Blake shifted his weight from his injured leg. Four days ago, he had tripped, scraping himself on the pavement. Now **it** was wrapped with bandages.
CORRECT	Blake shifted his weight from his injured leg. Four days ago, he had fallen, scraping himself on the pavement. Now his **leg** was wrapped with bandages.

See Practice 7.3B

(*Leg* replaces the pronoun *it*.)

PRACTICE 7.3A ▷ **Correcting Vague Pronouns**

Read each sentence. Then, rewrite each sentence
to avoid the use of vague pronouns.

EXAMPLE   After the test, they tell you your
           score.

ANSWER   *After the test, the examiners tell
           you your score.*

1. They predict that spring will come early this
   year.

2. Omaya worked in the library and enjoyed
   it very much.

3. The movie was funny, but they could have
   made it shorter.

4. To train for a marathon, you must run
   very often.

5. On the news it mentioned that unemployment
   has declined.

6. You must speak Spanish to qualify for
   that job.

7. At the meeting, they spoke about fire safety.

8. In this book, it suggests that the funding was
   part of a recovery plan.

9. During colonial times, you had to grow your
   own crops in order to survive.

10. Before each meal, you should wash your
    hands.

PRACTICE 7.3B ▷ **Recognizing Ambiguous
Pronouns**

Read each sentence. Then, rewrite each sentence
to avoid the use of ambiguous pronouns.

EXAMPLE   Remove the sandwich from the bag
           and throw it away.

ANSWER   *Remove the sandwich from the bag
           and throw the bag away.*

11. Remove the stamps from the envelopes and
    give them to me.

12. Her mother told Hailey the news as soon as
    she got home.

13. Uncle Tim read to Zachary until he fell asleep.

14. Please take the towel from the drying rack and
    fold it.

15. Michelle told Patty that she had to leave by
    noon.

16. Plant the bush by the new tree and water it.

17. Mother gave Emma a dress that she had made
    for the dance.

18. After Mrs. Gonzalez talks to Ms. Brewer, ask
    her to come to my office.

19. Mary talked to Suzanne until she was ready
    for school.

20. Take the last egg out of the container and
    recycle it.

SPEAKING APPLICATION

Take turns with a partner. Use sentences
from Practice 7.3A as models to say similar
sentences that contain vague pronoun
references. Your partner should reword each
sentence to make it clearer.

WRITING APPLICATION

Use sentences 11, 12, and 15 as models to write
similar sentences. Then, exchange papers with
a partner. Your partner should rewrite each
sentence, correcting the ambiguous pronoun
references.

USING MODIFIERS

Knowing how to use adjectives and adverbs correctly will help you make clear comparisons.

CHAPTER 8

WRITE GUY *Jeff Anderson, M.Ed.*

WHAT DO YOU NOTICE?

Look for modifiers as you zoom in on this sentence from the essay "An American Idea" by Theodore H. White.

MENTOR TEXT

> By the time Jefferson drafted his call, men were in the field fighting for those new-learned freedoms, killing and being killed by English soldiers, the best-trained troops in the world, supplied by the world's greatest navy.

Now, ask yourself the following questions:

- To what are the English soldiers and the navy being compared?
- What are the comparative forms of the modifiers *best* and *greatest*?

The author compares the English soldiers and the navy to all other soldiers and navies using the adjectives *best* and *greatest*. *Best* and *greatest* are the superlative forms of *good* and *great*; the superlative form compares three or more things. The comparative forms are *better* and *greater*; the comparative form compares two things.

Grammar for Writers Writers use comparisons to add to their descriptions and to state opinions. Be sure to check how many items you are comparing so that you use the correct form of a modifier.

Good or best? Which of these adjectives should I use?

Whichever you think is better!

8.1 Degrees of Comparison

In the English language, there are three degrees, or forms, of most adjectives and adverbs that are used in comparisons.

Recognizing Degrees of Comparison

In order to write effective comparisons, you first need to know the three degrees.

> **RULE 8.1.1** The three degrees of comparison are the **positive**, the **comparative**, and the **superlative**.

The following chart shows adjectives and adverbs in each of the three degrees. Notice the three different ways that modifiers are changed to show degree: (1) by adding *-er* or *-est*, (2) by adding *more* or *most*, and (3) by using entirely different words.

DEGREES OF ADJECTIVES		
POSITIVE	COMPARATIVE	SUPERLATIVE
high	higher	highest
eager	more eager	most eager
good	better	best
DEGREES OF ADVERBS		
early	earlier	earliest
eagerly	more eagerly	most eagerly
well	better	best

See Practice 8.1A

Regular Forms

Adjectives and adverbs can be either **regular** or **irregular,** depending on how their comparative and superlative degrees are formed. The degrees of most adjectives and adverbs are formed regularly. The number of syllables in regular modifiers determines how their degrees are formed.

> **RULE 8.1.2** Use *-er* or *more* to form the comparative degree and *-est* or *most* to form the superlative degree of most one- and two-syllable modifiers.

EXAMPLES

green	greener	greenest
healthful	more healthful	most healthful

> **All adverbs that end in -ly form their comparative and superlative degrees with *more* and *most*.**

EXAMPLES

happily	more happily	most happily
painfully	more painfully	most painfully

> **Use *more* and *most* to form the comparative and superlative degrees of all modifiers with three or more syllables.**

EXAMPLES

tolerant	more tolerant	most tolerant
protective	more protective	most protective

Note About Comparisons With *Less* and *Least*: *Less* and *least* can be used to form another version of the comparative and superlative degrees of most modifiers.

See Practice 8.1B

EXAMPLES

tolerant	less tolerant	least tolerant
protective	less protective	least protective

Irregular Forms

The comparative and superlative degrees of a few commonly used adjectives and adverbs are formed in unpredictable ways.

> **The irregular comparative and superlative forms of certain adjectives and adverbs must be memorized.**

In the chart on the following page, the form of some irregular modifiers differs only in the positive degree. The modifiers *bad*, *badly*, and *ill*, for example, all have the same comparative and superlative degrees *(worse, worst)*.

IRREGULAR MODIFIERS		
POSITIVE	COMPARATIVE	SUPERLATIVE
bad, badly, ill	worse	worst
far (distance)	farther	farthest
far (extent)	further	furthest
good, well	better	best
late	later	last or latest
little (amount)	less	least
many, much	more	most

RULE 8.1.6

Bad is an adjective. Do not use it to modify an action verb. **Badly** is an adverb. Use it after an action verb but not after a linking verb.

INCORRECT Sam plays soccer **bad**.

CORRECT Sam plays soccer **badly**.

INCORRECT Maya felt **badly** about moving.

CORRECT Maya felt **bad** about moving

Note About *Good* and *Well*: *Good* is always an adjective and cannot be used as an adverb after an action verb. It can, however, be used as a predicate adjective after a linking verb.

INCORRECT Matt plays the guitar **good**.

CORRECT That guitar sounds **good**.

Well is generally an adverb. However, when *well* means "healthy," it is an adjective and can be used after a linking verb.

CORRECT Keisha did **well** on her math test.

CORRECT Keisha should be **well** soon.

See Practice 8.1C
See Practice 8.1D

PRACTICE 8.1A > **Recognizing Positive, Comparative, and Superlative Degrees of Comparison**

Read each sentence. Then, identify the degree of comparison of the underlined word or words as *positive, comparative,* or *superlative.*

EXAMPLE   The patient's fever is <u>lower</u> this morning.

ANSWER   *comparative*

1. Amy is <u>shorter</u> than her older sister.
2. The weather has been perfectly <u>beautiful</u> all weekend.
3. This has been the <u>wettest</u> summer on record.
4. The Turner's house is the <u>oldest</u> one on our street.
5. The waters of Cedar Lake are <u>more calm</u> than the other nearby lakes.
6. The Snipes have the <u>most carefully</u> trimmed shrubs on the block.
7. The teacher greeted each student <u>warmly</u>.
8. Billy just blew the <u>biggest</u> balloon I have ever seen.
9. Lana felt <u>better</u> after she had talked things over with her mother.
10. The fans gave an <u>enthusiastic</u> roar of approval.

PRACTICE 8.1B > **Forming Regular Comparative and Superlative Degrees of Comparison**

Read each sentence. Then, rewrite each sentence with the correct comparative or superlative degree of the modifier indicated in parentheses.

EXAMPLE   She is the _____ person on the team. (tall)

ANSWER   *She is the tallest person on the team.*

11. My father works _____ than I do. (hard)
12. The novel by Charles Dickens is one of the _____ I've ever read. (impressive)
13. The fussy baby will be _____ after a long nap. (agreeable)
14. The banker is the _____ person in town. (funny)
15. This is the _____ article I've read. (interesting)
16. Is Mark _____ than Rob? (fast)
17. Lori is the _____ person I know. (happy)
18. My dog is _____ than my cat. (lazy)
19. She signed her name _____ than the other members. (carefully)
20. In your opinion, which of the paintings is _____? (attractive)

SPEAKING APPLICATION

Take turns with a partner. Compare the size of objects in your classroom. Use comparative, superlative, and positive degrees of comparisons. Your partner should listen for and identify which degree of comparison you are using in each of your descriptions.

WRITING APPLICATION

Rewrite sentences 11, 15, and 16, changing the modifiers in parentheses. Then, exchange papers with a partner. Your partner should write the correct degree of the modifiers you provided.

PRACTICE 8.1C > **Supplying Irregular Comparative and Superlative Forms**

Read each modifier. Then, write its irregular comparative and superlative forms.

EXAMPLE   good

ANSWER   *better, best*

1. bad
2. far (distance)
3. many
4. well
5. far (extent)
6. little (amount)
7. much
8. late
9. ill
10. badly

PRACTICE 8.1D > **Supplying Irregular Modifiers**

Read each sentence. Then, fill in the blank with the form of the modifier indicated in parentheses that best completes each sentence.

EXAMPLE   I took medicine, and now I feel _____ today than yesterday. (well)

ANSWER   *better*

11. We won't know who received _____ votes until after the recount is made. (many)
12. I ran _____ today than I have ever run before. (far)
13. Even though there had been some rainfall, the crop yield was the _____ that farmers had seen. (bad)
14. The _____ way to keep herbs fresh is to wrap them in paper towels. (good)
15. _____ people came to the festival in the evening than during the afternoon. (many)
16. The _____ amount of dust can make me sneeze. (little)
17. The city council plans to study the problem _____ before taking a vote. (far)
18. Because Dennis had a late start, he crossed the finish line _____. (late)
19. If the weather gets _____, I plan to leave early. (bad)
20. The experiment will probably work better if you apply _____ heat. (little)

SPEAKING APPLICATION

Take turns with a partner. Say sentences with irregular comparative and superlative forms. Your partner should indicate if incorrect comparisons have been used and suggest corrections.

WRITING APPLICATION

Write pairs of sentences using each of the following modifiers correctly: *farthest* and *furthest*, *more* and *most*, *worse* and *worst*, *bad* and *badly*.

8.2 Making Clear Comparisons

The comparative and superlative degrees help you make comparisons that are clear and logical.

Using Comparative and Superlative Degrees

One basic rule that has two parts covers the correct use of comparative and superlative forms.

> Use the **comparative degree** to compare two persons, places, or things. Use the **superlative degree** to compare three or more persons, places, or things.

8.2.1 **RULE**

The context of a sentence should indicate whether two items or more than two items are being compared.

COMPARATIVE   My sailboat is **faster** than Jerry's.

Mom's cooking is **more delicious** than Dad's.

This comedian is **less funny** than the first one.

SUPERLATIVE   My sailboat is the **fastest** on the bay.

Mom's dinners are her **most delicious** meals.

The **least funny** comedian performed first.

In informal writing, the superlative degree is sometimes used just for emphasis, without any specific comparison.

EXAMPLE   Champ has the **silkiest** coat.

Note About Double Comparisons: A double comparison is caused by using both -er and *more* or both -est and *most* to form a regular modifier or by adding an extra comparison form to an irregular modifier.

INCORRECT   It's **more harder** to swim than to dive.

CORRECT   It's **harder** to swim than to dive.

See Practice 8.2A
See Practice 8.2B

PRACTICE 8.2A > **Supplying the Comparative and Superlative Degrees of Modifiers**

Read each sentence. Then, fill in the blank with the correct form of the underlined modifier.

EXAMPLE   Biographies are <u>good</u>, but autobiographies are _____.

ANSWER   *better*

1. Cole is <u>shy</u>, but Tara is the _____ in the group.

2. All of Mrs. Erezuma's kids are <u>successful</u>, but Edward is the _____.

3. There are <u>many</u> flowers in the garden and even _____ in the greenhouse.

4. Iris is <u>friendly</u>, but of all students, Maddie is the _____.

5. I have <u>little</u> interest in opera and even _____ in jazz.

6. Jerry came <u>later</u> than Vanessa and was the _____ to arrive at the party.

7. We had hiked quite <u>far</u>, but we hadn't much _____ to hike.

8. The new restaurant is <u>fancy</u>, but the old one was _____.

9. Geo is <u>faster</u> than Ivan, but Aaron is the _____ of all.

10. Craig is <u>better</u> at chess than Roberto, but Nancy is the _____.

PRACTICE 8.2B > **Revising Sentences to Correct Errors in Modifier Usage**

Read each sentence. Then, rewrite each sentence, correcting any errors in the usage of modifiers to make comparisons. If a sentence contains no errors, write *correct*.

EXAMPLE   The dish he prepares best than any other is roast chicken.

ANSWER   *The dish he prepares better than any other is roast chicken.*

11. Perry swam farthest than Sam.

12. The blizzard was even worst the second day.

13. The less noise in the house keeps Brigitte awake.

14. We caught the more late train before the station closed.

15. I need to develop the hypothesis more further.

16. This statue is the best thing I have ever made in class.

17. Barbie sang more better when her parents were in the audience.

18. Some people need most sleep than others.

19. This car is safer than that one.

20. The movie I saw yesterday was the more uplifting one of all.

SPEAKING APPLICATION

Take turns with a partner. Compare two television shows that you have seen recently. Your partner should listen for and identify the comparisons in your sentences.

WRITING APPLICATION

Write three sentences with errors in modifier usage. Then, exchange papers with a partner. Your partner should correct your sentences.

Using Logical Comparisons

Two common usage problems are the comparison of unrelated items and the comparison of something with itself.

Balanced Comparisons
Be certain that things being compared in a sentence are similar.

> Your sentences should only compare items of a similar kind.

8.2.2
RULE

The following unbalanced sentences illogically compare dissimilar things.

UNBALANCED   **Shelly's voice** is stronger than **Ted**.

CORRECT   **Shelly's voice** is stronger than **Ted's**.

UNBALANCED   The **height of the chair** is greater than the **table**.

CORRECT   The **height of the chair** is greater than the **height of the table**.

Note About *Other* **and** *Else* **in Comparisons**
Another illogical comparison results when something is inadvertently compared with itself.

> When comparing one of a group with the rest of the group, make sure that your sentence contains the word *other* or the word *else*.

8.2.3
RULE

Adding *other* or *else* when comparing one person or thing with a group will make the comparison clear and logical.

ILLOGICAL   Peanuts are more profitable than any crop.
         (Peanuts cannot be more profitable than themselves.)

See Practice 8.2C
See Practice 8.2D

LOGICAL   Peanuts are more profitable than any **other** crop.

PRACTICE 8.2C > **Revising to Make
Comparisons Balanced
and Logical**

Read each sentence. Then, rewrite each
sentence, correcting the unbalanced or illogical
comparison.

EXAMPLE   Was his essay as good as a
professional writer?

ANSWER   *Was his essay as good as a
professional writer's?*

1. The blue boat has more horsepower than
the red.

2. Jeb's cat is bigger than Monica.

3. Allison's opinion of this book is even less
favorable than Dan.

4. The song of a bluebird is more familiar to me
than a robin.

5. Randy's car is in better condition than Arthur.

6. The pitch of a piccolo is higher than a flute.

7. Tom and Vicki's mural is much more colorful
than any mural in the gallery.

8. This month's electricity bill is lower than last
month.

9. Jerry's essay had better organization than
William.

10. Aunt Diane's spaghetti sauce is spicier
than any spaghetti sauce.

PRACTICE 8.2D > **Writing Clear Comparisons**

Read each sentence. Then, rewrite each sentence,
filling in the blanks to make a comparison that is
clear and logical.

EXAMPLE   Your report was better than _____
report in the class.

ANSWER   *Your report was better than any
other report in the class.*

11. The committee's new plan needs more
funding than _____ town program.

12. They spent more time talking about their
vacations than _____ topic.

13. Cindy's story was longer than _____.

14. Is she a better speaker than _____ on the
debate team?

15. The length of Jermaine's arm is longer than
_____.

16. Mee Kim's project is more scientific than
_____ in the school.

17. The pizza at that restaurant is more delicious
than _____ pizza in town.

18. Niall spends more time on the tennis court
than _____ in his family.

19. Taller than _____, my brother can be spotted
in any crowd.

20. Cara's hamster is smaller than _____.

SPEAKING APPLICATION

**Take turns with a partner. Say sentences that
have unbalanced or illogical comparisons. Your
partner should restate your sentences, using
balanced and logical comparisons.**

WRITING APPLICATION

**Use sentences 11, 13, and 15 as models to write
similar sentences. Then, exchange papers with
a partner. Your partner should fill in the blanks
to make the comparison in each sentence clear
and logical.**

Avoiding Comparisons With Absolute Modifiers

Some modifiers cannot be used logically to make comparisons because their meanings are *absolute*—that is, their meanings are entirely contained in the positive degree. For example, if a line is *vertical*, another line cannot be *more* vertical. Some other common absolute modifiers are *dead, entirely, fatal, final, identical, infinite, opposite, perfect, right, straight,* and *unique.*

> **Avoid using absolute modifiers illogically in comparisons.**

RULE 8.2.4

INCORRECT	That house is **more opposite** ours than any other house on the street.
CORRECT	That house is **opposite** ours on the street.

Often, it is not only the word *more* or *most* that makes an absolute modifier illogical; sometimes it is best to replace the absolute modifier with one that expresses the intended meaning more precisely.

ILLOGICAL	Your facts are **more correct** than my brother's.
CORRECT	Your facts are **more reliable** than my brother's.

Sometimes an absolute modifier may overstate the meaning that you want.

ILLOGICAL	The amount of time I spent playing baseball caused **most fatal** damage to my grades.
CORRECT	The amount of time I spent playing baseball caused the **most severe** damage to my grades.

See Practice 8.2E
See Practice 8.2F

In the preceding example, *most fatal* is illogical because something is either fatal or it is not. However, even *fatal* is an overstatement. *Most severe* better conveys the intended meaning.

PRACTICE 8.2E **Revising Sentences to Correct Comparisons Using Absolute Modifiers**

Read each sentence. Then, correct each illogical comparison by replacing the absolute modifier with more precise words.

EXAMPLE   The new outfit she chose was most beautiful.

ANSWER   *The new outfit she chose was beautiful.*

1. The explanation she gave was most entirely not true.

2. The influenza epidemic of 1918 was more fatal.

3. The test results were most final.

4. The two fingerprints are more identical.

5. The sky seems to be most clear.

6. The houses across from each other are the most opposite in layout.

7. The birthday gift is more perfect.

8. The measurement of the more right angle is 90 degrees.

9. That line is more straight.

10. My neighbor's flower garden is more dead.

PRACTICE 8.2F **Revising Overstated Absolute Modifiers**

Read each sentence. Then, rewrite each sentence, revising the overstated absolute modifier.

EXAMPLE   The judge's decision is more final.

ANSWER   *The judge's decision is absolute.*

11. The plan to build a new bridge is completely dead.

12. The extra use of electricity more overwhelmed the system.

13. If the ending were different, this movie would be more perfect.

14. Regardless of gender, all people should be treated more equally.

15. A dictator's rule is more absolute.

16. In science, gravity is a very universal principle.

17. Didn't Romeo claim that his love for Juliet was extremely eternal?

18. In Greek mythology, humans are more mortal than gods.

19. Buffy's decorating ideas are more opposite from Jane's.

20. Although it was out of water for a few minutes, the fish is somewhat living.

SPEAKING APPLICATION

Take turns with a partner. Say sentences that incorrectly use absolute modifiers. Your partner should restate your sentences correctly.

WRITING APPLICATION

Write three sentences with overstated absolute modifiers. Then, exchange papers with a partner. Your partner should revise the overstated absolute modifiers in your sentences.

CHAPTER 9

MISCELLANEOUS PROBLEMS *in* USAGE

Apply grammar usage rules to add clarity to your writing.

WRITE GUY *Jeff Anderson, M.Ed.*

WHAT DO YOU NOTICE?

Spot the negatives as you zoom in on a sentence from "Sundiata: An Epic of Old Mali: Childhood, The Lion's Awakening" by D. T. Niane, translated by G.D. Pickett.

MENTOR TEXT

It was no use Doua's defending the king's will which reserved the throne for Mari Djata, for the council took no account of Naré Maghan's wish.

Now, ask yourself the following questions:

- Is it correct for two negatives to appear in the same sentence?
- Why would the clause *for the council did not take no account of Naré Maghan's wish* be incorrect?

A sentence can contain two negatives if each negative appears in a separate clause. In this sentence the author uses *no* in two different clauses. The clause *for the council did not take no account of Naré Maghan's wish* would be incorrect because it contains a double negative. Only one negative word is needed to express a negative idea.

Grammar for Writers Writers can use negatives to create emphasis and express strong ideas. Check your negatives carefully to ensure you use them correctly.

I'm trying to stay positive.

Then definitely don't double your negatives!

9.1 Negative Sentences

In English, only one *no* is needed in a sentence to deny or refuse something. You can express a negative idea with words such as *not* or *never* or with contractions such as *can't, couldn't,* and *wasn't.* (The ending *-n't* in a contraction is an abbreviation of *not.*)

Recognizing Double Negatives

Using two negative words in a sentence when one is sufficient is called a **double negative.** While double negatives may sometimes be used in informal speech, they should be avoided in formal English speech and writing.

Do not use double negatives in formal writing.

The following chart provides examples of double negatives and two ways each can be corrected.

DOUBLE NEGATIVE	CORRECTIONS
Phil don't like no amusement parks.	Phil doesn't like amusement parks. Phil likes no amusement parks.
He won't even go to no new ones.	He won't even go to any new ones. He will go to no new ones.
He says he won't never like them.	He says he won't ever like them. He says he will never like them.

Sentences that contain more than one clause can correctly contain more than one negative word. Each clause, however, should contain only one negative word.

EXAMPLES   Donna **didn't** go to the fair because she **didn't** have any money.

She **wouldn't** tell Ellen her real reason, so she said she **didn't** want to go.

Forming Negative Sentences Correctly

There are three common ways to form negative sentences.

Using One Negative Word The most common ways to make a statement negative are to use one **negative word,** such as *never*, *no*, or *none*, or to add the contraction *-n't* to a helping verb.

> Use only one **negative word** in each clause.

9.1.2 RULE

DOUBLE NEGATIVE	The storm **didn't** damage **nothing** .
PREFERRED	The storm **didn't** damage **anything** .
	The storm damaged **nothing** .

Using *But* in a Negative Sense When *but* means "only," it usually acts as a negative. Do not use it with another negative word.

DOUBLE NEGATIVE	There **wasn't but** one sock left in my drawer.
PREFERRED	There was **but** one sock left in my drawer.
	There was **only** one sock left in my drawer.

Using *Barely, Hardly,* and *Scarcely* Each of these words is negative. If you use one of these words with another negative word, you create a double negative.

> Do not use *barely, hardly,* or *scarcely* with another negative word.

9.1.3 RULE

DOUBLE NEGATIVE	She **hadn't barely** mastered the new language.
PREFERRED	She **had barely** mastered the new language.
DOUBLE NEGATIVE	He **couldn't hardly** see beyond the hill
PREFERRED	He **could hardly** see beyond the hill.
DOUBLE NEGATIVE	We **couldn't scarcely** believe our eyes.
PREFERRED	We **could scarcely** believe our eyes.

See Practice 9.1A

Using Negatives to Create Understatement

Sometimes a writer wants to express an idea indirectly, either to minimize the importance of the idea or to draw attention to it. One such technique is called **understatement.**

> Understatement can be achieved by using a negative word and a word with a negative prefix, such as *un-*, *in-*, *im-*, *dis-*, and *under-*.

EXAMPLES   Bill did **not underestimate** Norm's speed.

My mom is **hardly inexperienced** at volleyball.

It's **not impossible** that we'll have a good time at the party.

These examples show that the writer is praising the people or things he or she is discussing. In the first example, the writer states that Bill expected Norm's speed. In the second example, the writer states that mom is experienced at volleyball. In the third example, the writer states that the people involved may have a good time at the party.

If you choose to use understatement, be sure to use it carefully so that you do not sound critical when you wish to praise.

EXAMPLES   Mary does **not dislike** her new uniform.

Even though it was not the color or style she preferred, she decided it was **not too bad** .

In both examples above, the writer is actually making a negative statement. In the first example, although the writer "does not dislike" her uniform, he or she clearly doesn't like it very much, either. In the second example, the writer seems to think that, although it is not the color or style she prefers, it is all right.

See Practice 9.1B

Revising Sentences to Avoid Double Negatives

Read each sentence. Then, rewrite each sentence to correct the double negative.

EXAMPLE   You shouldn't have told nobody where I was going.

ANSWER   *You shouldn't have told anybody where I was going.*

1. We couldn't hardly make our way through the brush.

2. Are you sure you don't have but one day free this week?

3. There wasn't no cloud in the sky.

4. Vanessa didn't have no trouble choosing a topic.

5. The article didn't include no biographical information.

6. I don't have room for but one elective in my schedule.

7. Casey can't never walk away from a stray animal.

8. There wasn't scarcely enough breeze to ruffle a leaf.

9. Ravi didn't go nowhere last night.

10. Stavros hasn't eaten none of his food.

Using Negatives to Create Understatement

Read each item. Then, use each item to create understatement.

EXAMPLE   Unpopular

ANSWER   *The captain of the football team is not an unpopular student.*

11. displace

12. undisciplined

13. undernourished

14. impoverished

15. incapable

16. disinterested

17. undissolved

18. unruly

19. inadmissible

20. underweight

SPEAKING APPLICATION

Take turns with a partner. Say sentences that contain double negatives. Your partner should listen to and correct your sentences.

WRITING APPLICATION

Use items 13, 16, and 18 to write other sentences that contain double negatives. Then, exchange papers with a partner. Your partner should correct your sentences.

(1) a, an The use of the article *a* or *an* is determined by the sound of the word that follows it. *A* is used before consonant sounds, while *an* is used before vowel sounds. Words beginning with *hon-, o-,* or *u-* may have either a consonant or a vowel sound.

EXAMPLES
a hairstyle (*h* sound)

a one-minute exercise (*w* sound)

an honorable person (no *h* sound)

an open door (*o* sound)

an understanding person (*u* sound)

(2) accept, except *Accept,* a verb, means "to receive." *Except,* a preposition, means "to leave out" or "other than."

VERB She **accepted** the gift generously.
PREPOSITION She gave everyone a gift **except** me.

(3) adapt, adopt *Adapt* means "to change." *Adopt* means "to take as one's own."

EXAMPLES The dog **adapted** to its new home.

People often **adopt** animals from shelters.

(4) affect, effect *Affect* is almost always a verb meaning "to influence." *Effect,* usually a noun, means "a result." Sometimes, *effect* is a verb meaning "to bring about" or "to cause."

VERB The storm **affected** the parade.

NOUN It had the **effect** of reducing the size of the crowd.

VERB The leader **effected** a change in the program.

(5) aggravate *Aggravate* means "to make worse." Avoid using this word to mean "annoy."

INCORRECT The grade I received on the test **aggravated** me.
PREFERRED That grade is **aggravating** my risk of failing.

(6) ain't *Ain't,* which was originally a contraction for *am not,* is no longer considered acceptable in standard English. Always use *am not,* and never use *ain't.* The exception is in certain instances of dialogue.

(7) all ready, already *All ready,* which consists of two separate words used as an adjective, means "ready." *Already,* which is an adverb, means "by or before this time" or "even now."

ADJECTIVE I am **all ready** to go scuba diving.

ADVERB I have **already** checked my gear.

(8) all right, alright *Alright* is a nonstandard spelling. Make sure you use the two-word form.

INCORRECT Even though I wasn't well yesterday, I'm feeling **alright** today.

PREFERRED Even though I wasn't well yesterday, I'm feeling **all right** today.

(9) all together, altogether *All together* means "together as a single group." *Altogether* means "completely" or "in all."

EXAMPLES Fish in schools travel **all together**.

They swam in **altogether** fascinating patterns.

(10) among, between Both of these words are prepositions. *Among* shows a connection between three or more items. *Between* generally shows a connection between two items.

EXAMPLES The debating club argued **among** themselves about which team would face the competition.

The competition **between** Central and East Side promised to be fierce.

See Practice 9.2A

(11) anxious This adjective implies uneasiness, worry, or fear. Do not use it as a substitute for *eager.*

INCORRECT The band was **anxious** for the concert to begin.

PREFERRED The musicians were **anxious** about their performance.

(12) anyone, any one, everyone, every one   *Anyone* and *everyone* mean "any person" or "every person." *Any one* means "any single person (or thing)"; *every one* means "every single person (or thing)."

EXAMPLES   **Anyone** at the school is able to join a club.

Any one of the clubs might be interesting and rewarding to join.

Everyone who is interested in sports can be on a team.

Every one of the players has to practice every day.

(13) anyway, anywhere, everywhere, nowhere, somewhere   These adverbs should never end in *-s*.

INCORRECT   I know my homework is hiding **somewheres** in my locker.

PREFERRED   I know my homework is hiding **somewhere** in my locker.

(14) as   Do not use the conjunction *as* to mean "because" or "since."

INCORRECT   Sue didn't make the team **as** she couldn't run fast enough.

PREFERRED   Sue didn't make the team **because** she couldn't run fast enough.

(15) as to   *As to* is awkward. Replace it with *about*.

INCORRECT   The miners had no worries **as to** the amount of iron ore in the mountain.

PREFERRED   The miners had no worries **about** the amount of iron ore in the mountain.

(16) at   Do not use *at* after *where*. Simply eliminate *at*.

INCORRECT   Do you know **where** we are **at**?

PREFERRED   Do you know **where** we are?

(17) at, about   Avoid using *at* with *about*. Simply eliminate *at* or *about*.

INCORRECT	Phil is going to try to go to bed **at about** 10:00.
PREFERRED	Phil is going to try to go to bed **at** 10:00.

(18) awful, awfully   *Awful* is used informally to mean that something is "extremely bad." *Awfully* is used informally to mean "very." Both words are overused and should be replaced with more descriptive words. In standard English speech and writing, *awful* should only be used to mean "inspiring fear or awe in someone."

OVERUSED	That movie was really **awful**.
PREFERRED	That movie was really **terrible**.
OVERUSED	The fighters seemed **awfully** fierce.
PREFERRED	The fighters seemed **very** fierce.
OVERUSED	The howling winds were **awful**.
PREFERRED	The howling winds were **scary**.

(19) awhile, a while   *Awhile* is an adverb that means "for a short time." *A while,* which is a noun, means "a period of time." It is usually used after the preposition *for* or *after*.

ADVERB	Lie down **awhile** and rest.
	Angie waited **awhile** to watch the votes being counted.
NOUN	If you can lie still for **a while**, your headache will go away.
	Angie stayed for **a while** to see who would win.

(20) beat, win   When you *win*, you "achieve a victory in something." When you *beat* someone or something, you "overcome an opponent."

INCORRECT	Our team **won** all the others in the meet.
PREFERRED	Our team **beat** all the others in the meet.
	Our team wants to **win** the tournament.

See Practice 9.2B

PRACTICE 9.2A **Recognizing Usage Problems 1–10**

Read each sentence. Then, choose the correct item to complete each sentence.

EXAMPLE   Shannon said that she (ain't, isn't) going to watch the game.

ANSWER   *Isn't*

1. The new tax bill could (affect, effect) all employed workers.

2. The animals (adopted, adapted) to their new surroundings.

3. The press has given (all together, altogether) too much attention to the candidate's family.

4. The coach's pregame speech had a great (effect, affect) on the team's performance.

5. After an hour of instruction, we decided that we were (all ready, already) to take the test.

6. Kevin wouldn't (except, accept) the reward money for finding the lost wallet.

7. I packed both an orange and (a, an) apple.

8. Arturo and I shared the sandwiches (among, between) us.

9. Is it (alright, all right) if I take my dog to the park?

10. The smoke in the building (aggravated, annoyed) my sinus condition.

PRACTICE 9.2B **Recognizing Usage Problems 11–20**

Read each sentence. Then, choose the correct item to complete each sentence.

EXAMPLE   Maggie didn't recognize (anyone, any one) of the teachers.

ANSWER   *any one*

11. Once in (awhile, a while) a great thinker comes along to challenge traditional ideas.

12. Mary's ideas (about, as to) a theme for the party sounded exciting.

13. Naomi baked (everyone, every one) of these casseroles.

14. Megan did chores all day long and felt (awfully, extremely) satisfied with her accomplishments.

15. Desmond earned the trophy after (winning, beating) every opponent handily.

16. We will meet you (at about, at) noon.

17. Lucinda was so (eager, anxious) to take her first driving lesson that she felt queasy.

18. My brother couldn't go on the ride (as, because) he was not tall enough.

19. (Everyone, Every one) piled into the car.

20. I need to hurry because I have (somewheres, somewhere) important to go.

SPEAKING APPLICATION

Take turns with a partner. Choose the pair of words from either sentence 1 or sentence 8, and tell your partner your choices. Your partner should say two sentences, using both words correctly.

WRITING APPLICATION

Write two sentences that include usage problems. Exchange papers with a partner. Your partner should correct your sentences.

(21) because Do not use *because* after the phrase *the reason*. Say "The reason is that" or reword the sentence.

INCORRECT   The **reason** I am sad **is because** our trip to the islands was canceled.

PREFERRED   I am sad **because** our trip to the islands was canceled.

(22) being as, being that   Avoid using either of these expressions. Use *because* instead.

INCORRECT   **Being as** the sky was cloudy, we did not go to the beach.

PREFERRED   **Because** the sky was cloudy, we did not go to the beach.

(23) beside, besides   *Beside* means "at the side of" or "close to." *Besides* means "in addition to."

EXAMPLES   We picnicked **beside** the mountain stream.

             No one **besides** ourselves knew we were there.

(24) bring, take   *Bring* means "to carry from a distant place to a nearer one." *Take* means "to carry from a near place to a far one."

EXAMPLES   Please **bring** me that pile of books.
             I'll **take** them back after I've used them.

(25) can, may   Use *can* to mean "have the ability to." Use *may* to mean "have permission to" or "to be likely to."

ABILITY   Some rain-forest animals **can** climb trees.
PERMISSION   Everyone **may** work to save the rain forest.
POSSIBILITY   There **may** be a chance to save this wildlife habitat.

(26) clipped words   Avoid using clipped or shortened words, such as *gym* and *photo* in formal writing.

INFORMAL   Where are the **photos** of my family?

FORMAL   Where are the **photographs** of my family?

(27) different from, different than   *Different from* is preferred in standard English.

INCORRECT   Geometry was **different than** what I expected.

PREFERRED   Geometry was **different from** what I expected.

(28) doesn't, don't   Do not use *don't* with third-person singular subjects. Instead, use *doesn't*.

INCORRECT   This machine **don't** work well.

PREFERRED   This machine **doesn't** work well.

(29) done   *Done* is the past participle of the verb *do*. It should always take a helping verb.

INCORRECT   Billy **done** his assignment.

PREFERRED   Billy **had done** his assignment.

(30) due to   *Due to* means "caused by" and should be used only when the words *caused by* can be logically substituted.

INCORRECT   **Due to** the lack of rainfall, my garden didn't grow.

PREFERRED   My garden didn't grow **due to** the lack of rainfall.

See Practice 9.2C

(31) each other, one another   These expressions usually are interchangeable. At times, however, *each other* is more logically used in reference to only two and *one another* in reference to more than two.

EXAMPLES   The animals and plants in an ecosystem often benefit **one another**.
Bees and flowers benefit **each other** when bees pollinate flowers.

(32) farther, further   *Farther* refers to distance. *Further* means "additional" or "to a greater degree or extent."

EXAMPLES   Margaret walked much **farther** than Henry.
Once he yelled at her to stop, she listened no **further**.

(33) fewer, less   Use *fewer* with things that can be counted. Use *less* with qualities and quantities that cannot be counted.

EXAMPLES   **fewer** assignments, **less** homework

(34) get, got, gotten   These forms of the verb *get* are acceptable in standard English, but a more specific word is preferable.

INCORRECT   **get** thirsty, **got** water, **have gotten** cooler

PREFERRED   **become** thirsty, **drank** water, **have become** cooler

(35) gone, went   *Gone* is the past participle of the verb *go* and is used only with a helping verb. *Went* is the past tense of *go* and is never used with a helping verb.

INCORRECT   My brothers **gone** to the store today.

They really should **have went** yesterday.

PREFERRED   My brothers **went** to the store today.

They really should **have gone** yesterday.

(36) good, lovely, nice   Replace these overused words with a more specific adjective.

WEAK   **good** garden, **lovely** flowers, **nice** color

BETTER   **beautiful** garden, **tall** flowers, **brilliant red** color

(37) in, into   *In* refers to position. *Into* suggests motion.

EXAMPLES   My notebook is **in** my backpack.

I'll put my books **into** my locker.

(38) irregardless   Avoid this word in formal speech and writing. Instead, use *regardless*.

(39) just   When you use *just* as an adverb to mean "no more than," place it immediately before the word it modifies.

INCORRECT   Bill **just** received one prize at the meet.

PREFERRED   Bill received **just** one prize at the meet.

(40) kind of, sort of   Do not use these phrases in formal speech. Instead, use *rather* or *somewhat*.

See Practice 9.2D

PRACTICE 9.2C > **Recognizing Usage Problems 21–30**

Read each sentence. Then, choose the correct item to complete each sentence.

EXAMPLE (May, Can) I bring something to the party?

ANSWER *May*

1. The real painting looks quite different (from, than) the reproductions.

2. I (can, may) sleep through any type of noise.

3. I (brought, took) some sandwiches to eat at the game.

4. (Because, Being that) we overslept, Mom drove us to school.

5. Was there anyone (beside, besides) Jerry who saw the lunar eclipse?

6. One reason to eat fruit (is that, is because) fruit is nutritious.

7. Carmelo (doesn't, don't) plan to enter the contest.

8. My camera's special lens helps me take great (photos, photographs).

9. Ms. Lopez said that everyone (done, had done) a great job preparing for the debate.

10. The coach sat (besides, beside) my brother on the bench.

PRACTICE 9.2D > **Revising Sentences to Correct Usage Problems 31–40**

Read each sentence. Then, rewrite each sentence, correcting the errors in usage.

EXAMPLE Sara's costume is sort of different from Evelyn's.

ANSWER *Sara's costume is somewhat different from Evelyn's.*

11. We cannot hold the class if less than six students sign up.

12. We had went at least six miles out of our way.

13. Will you travel further tonight?

14. Each of my brothers got a new bike for his birthday.

15. I will buy a new coat irregardless of the cost.

16. The firefighter rushed in the burning building and saved the family pet.

17. The freshly baked bread gave off a good aroma.

18. I just have one thing to say to you: Hello!

19. There was fewer participation in the fishing derby this year.

20. The three friends wrote letters to each other.

SPEAKING APPLICATION

Take turns with a partner. Say sentences with usage problems. Your partner should correct each of your sentences.

WRITING APPLICATION

Take turns with a partner. Use two sentences from Practice 9.2D as models to write similar sentences with usage problems. Exchange papers with a partner. Your partner should correct your sentences.

(41) lay, lie   The verb *lay* means "to put or set (something) down." Its principal parts—*lay, laying, laid, laid*—are followed by a direct object. The verb *lie* means "to recline." Its principal parts—*lie, lying, lay, lain*—are not followed by a direct object.

LAY   Please **lay** the luggage in the station wagon.

              The driver **is laying** the bags next to each other.

              The passengers **laid** their carry-on bags next to them.

              The luggage will stay where the driver **has laid** it.

LIE   After their trip, the passengers just wanted to **lie** down.

              They **are lying** on the beach and listening to music.

              The child **lay** down across her father's lap.

              She hadn't **lain** down all night.

(42) learn, teach   *Learn* means "to receive knowledge." *Teach* means "to give knowledge."

EXAMPLES   A person has to **learn** many skills to live in the Arctic.

              It's best to be **taught** by experienced explorers.

(43) leave, let   *Leave* means "to allow to remain." *Let* means "to permit."

INCORRECT   **Leave** my little brother alone!

PREFERRED   **Let** my little brother alone!

(44) like, as   *Like* is a preposition meaning "similar to" or "such as." It should not be used in place of the conjunction *as*.

INCORRECT   We painted **like** we were skilled artists.

PREFERRED   We painted **as if** we were skilled artists.

              We painted **like** skilled artists.

(45) loose, lose   *Loose* is usually an adjective or part of such idioms as *cut loose, turn loose,* or *break loose. Lose* is always a verb and usually means "to miss from one's possession."

EXAMPLES   Please don't let your dog **loose** in the neighborhood.

              If you don't walk her on a leash, you might **lose** her.

(46) maybe, may be   *Maybe* is an adverb meaning "perhaps."
May be is a helping verb connected to a main verb.

ADVERB   **Maybe** I'll be able to get a good grade on this test.

VERB   I **may be** asking my teacher for some extra help.

(47) of   Do not use *of* after a helping verb such as *should, would,
could,* or *must.* Use *have* instead. Do not use *of* after *outside,
inside, off,* and *atop.* Simply eliminate *of.*

INCORRECT   A good sheepdog **would of** protected the sheep.

PREFERRED   A good sheepdog **would have** protected the sheep.

(48) OK, O.K., okay   In informal writing, *OK, O.K.,* and *okay* are
acceptably used to mean "all right." Do not use them in standard
English speech or writing, however.

INFORMAL   Sam said today's lunch choice was **okay**.

PREFERRED   Sam said today's lunch choice was **tasty**.

(49) only   *Only* should be placed immediately before the word it
modifies. Placing it elsewhere can lead to confusion.

EXAMPLES   **Only** Rich wanted to go to the gym.
              (No one else wanted to go.)

              Rich **only** wanted to go to the gym.
              (He didn't want to go anywhere else.)

(50) ought   Do not use *ought* with *have* or *had.*

INCORRECT   We **hadn't ought** to have cut down the trees.

PREFERRED   We **ought not** to have cut down the trees.

See Practice 9.2E

(51) outside of   Do not use this expression to mean "besides"
or "except."

INCORRECT   Many birds are found nowhere **outside of** tropical rain
              forests.

PREFERRED   Many birds are found nowhere **except** in tropical
              rain forests.

(52) plurals that do not end in -*s* The English plurals of
certain nouns from Greek and Latin are formed as they were
in their original language. Words such as *criteria, media,* and
phenomena are plural. Their singular forms are *criterion, medium,*
and *phenomenon*.

INCORRECT	Today, the news **media** includes newspapers, television, radio, and the Internet.
PREFERRED	Today, the news **media** include newspapers, television, radio, and the Internet.
	Today, newspapers, television, radio, and the Internet are all part of the news **media** .

(53) precede, proceed *Precede* means "to go before." *Proceed*
means "to move or go forward."

EXAMPLES	Jamie **preceded** Mary Beth into the library.
	The two girls then **proceeded** to begin work on their history project.

(54) principal, principle As an adjective, *principal* means "most
important" or "chief." As a noun, it means "a person who has
controlling authority," as in a school. *Principle* is always a noun
that means "a fundamental law."

ADJECTIVE	Evergreens are the **principal** trees on the mountain.
NOUN	Ms. Rodriguez is the **principal** in our school.
NOUN	The student council drew up the **principles** for improved sportsmanship at games.

(55) real *Real* means "authentic." In formal writing, avoid using
real to mean "very" or "really."

INCORRECT	My dad was **real** disappointed with the new recipe.
PREFERRED	My dad was **deeply** disappointed with the new recipe.

(56) says *Says* should not be used as a substitute for *said*.

INCORRECT	"Why," Ben **says** , "do we have to go home now?"
PREFERRED	"Why," Ben **said** , "do we have to go home now?"

(57) seen   *Seen* is a past participle and must be used with a helping verb.

INCORRECT   The judge **seen** a number of contestants.

PREFERRED   The judge **had seen** a number of contestants.

(58) set, sit   *Set* means "to put (something) in a certain place." Its principal parts—*set, setting, set, set*—are usually followed by a direct object. *Sit* means "to be seated." Its principal parts—*sit, sitting, sat, sat*—are never followed by a direct object.

SET   Please **set** the flowers on the table.

Mimi **is setting** the table for dinner.

I'd like you to **set** the candles on the table.

I **have set** the timer to ring at 6:30.

SIT   My mom **will sit** at the head of the table.

We **will be sitting** at the big table tonight.

Tony **sat** quietly and waited for dinner.

We **have sat** in the same places at the table for years.

(59) so   When *so* is used as a coordinating conjunction, it means *and* or *but*. Avoid using *so* when you mean "so that."

INCORRECT   I use sunglasses **so** I can see in the sunlight.

PREFERRED   I use sunglasses **so that** I can see in the sunlight.

(60) than, then   Use *than* in comparisons. Use *then* as an adverb to refer to time.

EXAMPLES   I'm taller **than** my older sister.

She measured us once; **then** , she measured us again.

(61) that, which, who   Use these relative pronouns in the following ways: *that* and *which* refer to things; *who* refers only to people.

EXAMPLES   I saw the humpback whales **that** you described.

Their mouths, **which** are huge, take in tons of water.

The marine biologist, **who** studies whales, told us about the whales' feeding behavior.

(62) their, there, they're *Their,* a possessive pronoun, always modifies a noun. *There* can be used either as an expletive at the beginning of a sentence or as an adverb showing place or direction. *They're* is a contraction of *they are.*

PRONOUN	The actors spent a lot of time memorizing **their** parts in the new play.
EXPLETIVE	**There** are so many actors in the play that the rehearsals last a long time.
ADVERB	The table and chairs will be placed over **there** on the stage.
CONTRACTION	**They're** going to be used in several scenes in the play.

(63) them Do not use *them* as a substitute for *those.*

INCORRECT	**Them** sandwiches are delicious.
PREFERRED	**Those** sandwiches are delicious.

(64) to, too, two *To,* a preposition, begins a phrase or an infinitive. *Too,* an adverb, modifies adjectives and other adverbs and means "very" or "also." *Two* is a number.

PREPOSITION	**to** the moon, back **to** Earth
INFINITIVE	**to** see the stars, **to** find the constellations
ADVERB	**too** far away, **too** hard to see
NUMBER	**two** space probes, **two** astronauts

(65) when, where Do not use *when* or *where* immediately after a linking verb. Do not use *where* in place of *that.*

INCORRECT	Block parties are **when** you can meet your neighbors. In the street is **where** everyone meets.
PREFERRED	Block parties are **occasions** to meet your neighbors. In the street is **the place** everyone meets.

See Practice 9.2F

PRACTICE 9.2E > **Recognizing Usage Problems 41–50**

Read each sentence. Then, choose the correct item to complete each sentence.

EXAMPLE   Yesterday, I saw a jellyfish (laying, lying) on the beach.

ANSWER   *lying*

1. If you don't sew up your pocket, you may (lose, loose) all of your money.

2. Because I had (laid, lay, lain) my drink in the sun, all the ice cubes melted.

3. Who (learned, taught) you that magic trick?

4. He acted (like, as if) he was sleepy.

5. Because bad weather is predicted, there (maybe, may be) very few people at the game.

6. Of all the people in the audience, (Tatum only, only Tatum) knew the answer.

7. Mom said, "(Let, Leave) the dog outside."

8. The Supreme Court ruled that it is (okay, legal) to delay paying your taxes.

9. Hassan knew that he should (of, have) studied harder for the test.

10. We (ought to have, should have) paid for our own tickets.

PRACTICE 9.2F > **Revising Sentences to Correct Usage Problems 51–65**

Read each sentence. Then, rewrite each sentence correcting the usage errors.

EXAMPLE   Yesterday, it was to hot to do any work.

ANSWER   *Yesterday, it was too hot to do any work.*

11. My parents said that their on there way home.

12. Only three people, outside of my uncle, know where the treasure is buried.

13. The man that wrote the book must be a genius.

14. Please put them candles on the table.

15. Four o'clock is when the club meets.

16. Reliant Stadium is where the Houston Texans play football.

17. I can see them houses across the water.

18. Many people had proceeded us, leaving their footprints in the sand.

19. Luke was real hungry after completing the race.

20. Mary seen the play twice already.

SPEAKING APPLICATION

Reread the sentences in Practice 9.2E and your completed sentences. Discuss with a partner which sentences were hard to complete. Explain why those sentences were challenging.

WRITING APPLICATION

Use sentences 13, 17, 18, and 19 as models to write similar sentences with usage problems. Exchange papers with a partner. Your partner should correct your sentences.

Cumulative Review Chapters 4–9

PRACTICE 1 ▷ Combining and Varying Sentences

Read the sentences. Then, rewrite each sentence according to the instructions in parentheses.

1. He studied anatomy and physiology. He learned how to categorize and label the parts of the human body. (Create a compound sentence; use a conjunction.)

2. The class visited Philadelphia. They saw the Liberty Bell. They attended a Philadelphia Phillies baseball game. (Create a complex sentence; include a compound direct object.)

3. The explorers approached the Mississippi River. They discovered a river too high to ford. (Create a complex sentence.)

4. Dinosaur bones are on display at the museum. Other ancient species of animals are also on display. (Create a compound sentence.)

5. The football team practiced on the field. (Invert the subject-verb order.)

6. Brian is my little brother. He is eight years younger than I am. (Create a complex sentence; use an appositive.)

7. Elizabeth volunteers at an animal shelter. She also works at a dog grooming shop to help animals. (Create a compound verb; start the sentence with an infinitive.)

8. Elise was worried about making a good impression. The woman interviewing her for the job thought she was great. (Create a compound sentence.)

9. Sandra is captain of the swim team and has swum for years. She won the state title in 2009. (Create a complex sentence; use an appositive.)

10. Across the sky flew a flock of geese. (Invert the subject-verb order.)

PRACTICE 2 ▷ Revising Pronoun and Verb Usage

Read the sentences. Then, revise each sentence to correct pronoun and verb usage. You may need to reorder, add, or eliminate words.

1. Only someone who likes magic will enjoy their visit to a magic show.

2. Whom, do you think, is the best debater on the debate team?

3. Ben and Adam always asks permission before inviting friends over.

4. Somebody has left their purse on the seat of the city bus.

5. The Math Club, as well as the Chess Club, meet after school on Tuesdays.

6. Not only the students but also their parents has been pleased with the new schedule.

7. Mom left the decision up to him and I.

8. To who did you give the extra ticket?

9. Chris made a shot in the final seconds, and the crowd cheered their approval.

10. He didn't seem to worry much about we kids.

PRACTICE 3 ▷ Revising for Correct Use of Active and Passive Voice

Read the sentences. Then, revise each sentence to be in the active voice. You may need to reorder, add, or delete words.

1. Lisa's hair was cut by a well-known stylist.

2. The national anthem is being sung by Jason at the game tomorrow.

3. The track was being swept by the coach before the track meet.

4. The accident was witnessed by Mrs. Thompson's neighbor.

5. The squirrels were being chased by dogs.

Continued on next page ▶

Cumulative Review   Chapters 4—9

PRACTICE 4 > **Correcting Errors in Pronoun and Verb Usage**

Read the sentences. Then, revise them, correcting all errors in agreement, verb usage, and pronoun usage. If a sentence is already correct, write *correct*.

1. Samantha and her cousins had went to the zoo to see the giant pandas the week before.

2. Neither Lucy nor Cara has choosed their classes for next semester.

3. Miguel learned his brother how to skate.

4. It was her who was asked to gives the speech at the graduation ceremony.

5. After not seeing they for a few days, we realized that her and Maria had moved away.

6. That piece of cake was for me, not him.

7. You didn't tell we that them were here first.

8. I wonder what he could have said to she.

9. "You have to ask you," Dad said, "what would yourself do in his situation?"

10. If any one of your friend needs a ride to dance rehearsal, they can call me.

PRACTICE 5 > **Using Comparative and Superlative Forms Correctly**

Read the sentences. Then, write the appropriate comparative or superlative degree of the modifier in parentheses.

1. Between the two, Juan is the (good) musician.

2. Rome is (far) from Dublin than from London.

3. I think New York is the (exciting) city in the world.

4. She is probably the (cheerful) person I know.

5. Mt. Everest is (high) than Mt. Fuji.

PRACTICE 6 > **Avoiding Double Negatives**

Read the sentences. Then, choose the word in parentheses that makes each sentence negative without forming a double negative.

1. Sadly, I didn't have (any, none) money left to contribute.

2. Michelle won't talk to (nobody, anybody) about the surprise.

3. She hadn't studied, so she (could, couldn't) hardly finish her test in the time allotted.

4. They aren't going (nowhere, anywhere) special for summer vacation this year.

5. Students are permitted to use neither their books (nor, or) their notes during the exam.

PRACTICE 7 > **Avoiding Usage Problems**

Read the sentences. Then, choose the correct expression to complete each sentence.

1. Rachel's birthday (preceded, proceeded) John's by one day.

2. Laura's grandmother wears a hearing aid (so, so that) she can understand the conversation

3. Steve is more athletic (than, then) his brother.

4. (Lay, Lie) down on the beach blanket.

5. Most first graders can (learn, teach) to read.

6. If you (let, leave) the dog alone, he will bark.

7. He is likely to (loose, lose) his way.

8. The storm will (affect, effect) their plans.

9. The (principal, principle) was newly hired.

10. Sam was (all ready, already) late to lunch.

CAPITALIZATION

Use capitalization to present ideas clearly to your readers.

WHAT DO YOU NOTICE?

Focus on capitalization as you zoom in on these sentences from the story "The Monkey's Paw" by W. W. Jacobs.

MENTOR TEXT

> "Sounds like the *Arabian Nights*," said Mrs. White, as she rose and began to set the supper. "Don't you think you might wish for four pairs of hands for me?"

Now, ask yourself the following questions:

- What do these sentences demonstrate about using capitalization with quotations?
- Why are the words *Arabian Nights* and *Mrs. White* capitalized?

These sentences show that the first word in a quotation is always capitalized. When a sentence in a quotation is interrupted and then continued, the first word in the continued portion is not capitalized. However, the second sentence in this quotation is a complete sentence, so the first word needs to be capitalized. *Arabian Nights* is capitalized because it is a proper noun that names the title of a book. *Mrs. White* is capitalized because it is a proper noun that includes a woman's title and her last name.

Grammar for Writers Writers can use capitalization to alert their readers to specific people, places, things, and events in the text as well as to words people say. When you edit your writing, carefully check your capitalization.

Would you listen to me read my lines in the play?

Okay, but be sure to start each sentence with a capital letter!

10.1 Capitalization in Sentences

Just as road signs help to guide people through a town, capital letters help to guide readers through sentences and paragraphs. Capitalization signals the start of a new sentence or points out certain words within a sentence to give readers visual clues that aid in their understanding.

Using Capitals for First Words

Always capitalize the first word in a sentence.

RULE 10.1.1

Capitalize the first word in **declarative, interrogative, imperative,** and **exclamatory** sentences.

DECLARATIVE **B**ob went to the game yesterday.

INTERROGATIVE **H**ow will you ever tell her about it?

IMPERATIVE **B**e careful when crossing.

EXCLAMATORY **H**ow could we ever have guessed!

RULE 10.1.2

Capitalize the first word in **interjections** and **incomplete questions.**

INTERJECTIONS **J**ust great!

INCOMPLETE QUESTIONS **W**ho? **W**hen?

The word *I* is always capitalized, whether it is the first word in a sentence or not.

RULE 10.1.3

Always capitalize the pronoun *I.*

EXAMPLE Alice and **I** went to the dance.

RULE 10.1.4

Capitalize the first word after a colon only if the word begins a complete sentence. Do not capitalize the word if it begins a list of words or phrases.

SENTENCE FOLLOWING A COLON
She mumbled some words: **S** he was unable to continue speaking.

LIST FOLLOWING A COLON
I put all the supplies in the box: **c** ereal, coffee, and bread.

RULE 10.1.5

Capitalize the first word in each line of traditional poetry, even if the line does not start a new sentence.

EXAMPLE
I think that I shall never see

See Practice 10.1A

A poem lovely as a tree. – Joyce Kilmer

Using Capitals With Quotations

There are special rules for using capitalization with **quotations.**

RULE 10.1.6

Capitalize the first word of a **quotation.** However, do not capitalize the first word of a continuing sentence when a quotation is interrupted by identifying words or when the first word of a quotation is the continuation of a speaker's sentence.

EXAMPLES
Jeff said, " **G** olf is my favorite sport."

" **W** hen the train came in," Bob said, " **t** he people on the platform charged forward."

Fred commented that she was " **t** he prettiest girl he ever saw."

See Practice 10.1B

PRACTICE 10.1A **Capitalizing Words**

Read each sentence. Then, write the word or words that should be capitalized in each sentence.

EXAMPLE   i hoped that i would be the first one picked to play on the team.

ANSWER   *I, I*

1. keep your head up while you are dancing.

2. her mother packed Lucy's suitcase for summer camp: shirts, shorts, bathing suit, and sneakers.

3. shall i compare thee to a summer's day? thou art more lovely and more temperate.

4. deb didn't like swimming class because she doesn't like getting her hair wet.

5. are you going to the fair this weekend?

6. she repeated her question loudly: who needs help completing the registration form?

7. excellent! now you can join our group!

8. who? who said that?

9. make eye contact with the person you are talking to.

10. we enjoyed the concert very much; it was given by our favorite musician.

PRACTICE 10.1B **Using Capitals With Quotations**

Read each sentence. Then, write the word or words in each sentence that should be capitalized.

EXAMPLE   tammy wondered, "is this the proper way to crochet?"

ANSWER   *Tammy, Is*

11. abraham Lincoln once said, "a house divided against itself cannot stand."

12. "she has already had her chance," he replied. "it is time for someone else to take a turn."

13. he told me, "you're a fantastic cook!"

14. josie replied, "i will not be attending the conference this week."

15. "just as the weatherman predicted," Cole said, "the hurricane has become a tropical storm."

16. "yvonne always asks questions," said Candace. "she is very inquisitive."

17. simon tells me that he is "always on time."

18. "meanwhile," Shannon said, "we waited patiently for the movie to start."

19. "she left early this morning," Brian said. "i think she was headed for a track meet."

20. the bus driver said, "have a nice day!"

SPEAKING APPLICATION

Take turns with a partner. Recite a short poem. Your partner should indicate when he or she thinks a word in the poem should be capitalized.

WRITING APPLICATION

Write a dialogue between two family members in which they discuss their family's history. Be sure to use conventions of capitalization correctly.

10.2 Proper Nouns

Capitalization make important words stand out in your writing, such as the names of people, places, countries, book titles, and other proper names. Sometimes proper names are used as nouns and sometimes as adjectives modifying nouns or pronouns.

Using Capitals for Proper Nouns

Nouns, as you may remember, are either **common** or **proper.**

Common nouns, such as *sailor, brother, city,* and *ocean,* identify classes of people, places, or things and are not capitalized.

Proper nouns name specific examples of people, places, or things and should be capitalized.

> Capitalize all **proper** nouns.

RULE 10.2.1

EXAMPLES   **J**effrey   **D**octor **C**allow   **G**overnor **T**ate

First **S**treet   **A**rlington **H**ouse   **R**eno

*A **T**ale of **T**wo **C**ities*   **U**.**S**.**S**. **C**onstitution

Names

Each part of a person's name—the given name, the middle name or initial standing for that name, and the surname—should be capitalized. If a surname begins with *Mc* or *O',* the letter following it is capitalized (McAdams, O'Reilly).

> Capitalize each part of a person's name even when the full name is not used.

RULE 10.2.2

EXAMPLES   **J**ohn **B**rown   **E**. **B**. **F**rome   **E**mil **C**. **T**aft

Capitalize the proper names that are given to animals.

EXAMPLES   **S**pot   **F**luffy   **L**assie

Geographical and Place Names

If a place can be found on a map, it should generally be capitalized.

> **Capitalize geographical and place names.**

Examples of different kinds of geographical and place names are listed in the following chart.

GEOGRAPHICAL AND PLACE NAMES	
Streets	Madison Avenue, First Street, Green Valley Road
Towns and Cities	Dallas, Oakdale, New York City
Counties, States, and Provinces	Champlain County, Texas, Quebec
Nations and Continents	Austria, Kenya, the United States of America, Asia, Mexico, Europe
Mountains	the Adirondack Mountains, Mount Washington
Valleys and Deserts	the San Fernando Valley, the Mojave Desert, the Gobi
Islands and Peninsulas	Aruba, the Faroe Islands, Cape York Peninsula
Sections of a Country	the Northeast, Siberia, the Great Plains
Scenic Spots	Gateway National Park, Carlsbad Caverns
Rivers and Falls	the Missouri River, Victoria Falls
Lakes and Bays	Lake Cayuga, Gulf of Mexico, the Bay of Biscayne
Seas and Oceans	the Sargasso Sea, the Indian Ocean
Celestial Bodies and Constellations	Mars, the Big Dipper, moon, Venus
Monuments and Memorials	the Tomb of the Unknown Soldier, Kennedy Memorial Library, the Washington Monument
Buildings	Madison Square Garden, Fort Hood, the Astrodome, the White House
School and Meeting Rooms	Room 6, Laboratory 3B, the Red Room, Conference Room C

Capitalizing Directions

Words indicating direction are capitalized only when they refer to a section of a country.

EXAMPLES   Trevor rode through the **S**outh.

              The airport is four miles **e**ast of the city.

Capitalizing Names of Celestial Bodies

Capitalize the names of celestial bodies except *moon* and *sun*.

EXAMPLE   The **s**un is ten times larger than **J**upiter.

Capitalizing Buildings and Places

Do not capitalize words such as *theater, hotel, university,* and *park,* unless the word is part of a proper name.

EXAMPLES   My son went to Rutgers **U**niversity.

              I will drop you off at the **u**niversity.

Events and Times

Capitalize references to historic events, periods, and documents as well as dates and holidays. Use a dictionary to check capitalization.

> Capitalize the names of specific events and periods in history.

10.2.4   RULE

SPECIAL EVENTS AND TIMES	
Historic Events	the Battle of Waterloo, World War I
Historical Periods	the Manchu Dynasty, Reconstruction
Documents	the Bill of Rights, the Magna Carta
Days and Months	Monday, June 22, the third week in May
Holidays	Labor Day, Memorial Day, Veterans Day
Religious Holidays	Rosh Hashanah, Christmas, Easter
Special Events	the World Series, the Holiday Antiques Show

Capitalizing Seasons

Do not capitalize seasons unless the name of the season is being used as a proper noun or adjective.

EXAMPLES I love to ski in the Winter.

I hope to compete in the Winter Olympics.

Capitalize the names of organizations, government bodies, political parties, races, nationalities, languages, and religions.

VARIOUS GROUPS	
Clubs and Organizations	Rotary, Knights of Columbus, the Red Cross, National Organization for Women
Institutions	the Museum of Fine Arts, the Mayo Clinic
Schools	Kennedy High School, University of Texas
Businesses	General Motors, Prentice Hall
Government Bodies	Department of State, Federal Trade Commission, House of Representatives
Political Parties	Republicans, the Democratic party
Nationalities	American, Mexican, Chinese, Israeli, Canadian
Languages	English, Italian, Polish, Swahili
Religions and Religious References	Christianity: God, the Holy Spirit, the Bible
	Judaism: the Lord, the Prophets, the Torah
	Islam: Allah, the Prophets, the Qur'an, Mohammed
	Hinduism: Brahma, the Bhagavad Gita, the Vedas
	Buddhism: the Buddha, Mahayana, Hinayana

References to Mythological Gods When referring to mythology, do not capitalize the word *god* (the *gods* of Olympus).

Capitalize the names of awards; the names of specific types of air, sea, and spacecraft; and brand names.

EXAMPLES   the Nobel Prize   the Purple Heart

Chewy Treats   Mercury V

See Practice 10.2A
See Practice 10.2B

236   Capitalization

PRACTICE 10.2A **Identifying Proper Nouns**

Read each sentence. Then, write the proper noun or nouns in each sentence.

EXAMPLE   The actress Katherine Hepburn has won many acting awards.

ANSWER   *Katherine Hepburn*

1. Spending the summer in the Northwest, we stayed in Seattle, Washington.

2. I have never visited the Statue of Liberty, but I have always wanted to.

3. Nadira's mother is from India and her father is from Spain.

4. The Dust Bowl of the 1930's was a severe drought that damaged farmland.

5. My dentist is a member of the American Dental Association.

6. Alpha Centauri is a binary star system in the constellation Centaurus.

7. Joan of Arc fought for France during the Hundred Years' War.

8. The Department of Homeland Security was created in 2002.

9. His favorite brand of pen, SmoothLine, never smudges.

10. The RMS *Titanic* hit an iceberg on April 14, 1912.

PRACTICE 10.2B **Capitalizing Proper Nouns**

Read each sentence. Then, write the word or words in each sentence that should be capitalized.

EXAMPLE   Last memorial day, we visited my grandparents in florida.

ANSWER   *Memorial Day, Florida*

11. We always eat at my favorite restaurant, amelia's, on friday nights.

12. Have you ever seen the great wall of china?

13. samuel o'reilly saw a production of *miss saigon* in new york city many years ago.

14. mary and george have lived in the south for as long as i can remember.

15. james k. polk was born in north carolina.

16. i hope the houston astros go to the world series this year.

17. When you go to rome, be sure to see the trevi fountain and the pantheon.

18. Last summer, we went camping and saw the big dipper and orion's belt as we gazed up at the stars.

19. My grandmother's ancestors came from wales and ireland.

20. The kimbell art museum in fort worth, texas, has a collection of paintings by el greco.

SPEAKING APPLICATION

Take turns with a partner. Tell about a foreign country that you would like to visit. Describe what you would see and do there. Your partner should identify the proper nouns that you use.

WRITING APPLICATION

Use sentence 17 as a model to write three similar sentences. Replace the proper nouns in sentence 17 with other proper nouns.

Using Capitals for Proper Adjectives

A **proper adjective** is either an adjective formed from a proper
noun or a proper noun used as an adjective.

10.2.7

Capitalize most **proper adjectives.**

PROPER ADJECTIVES FORMED FROM PROPER NOUNS	**A**ustralian boomerang **S**hakespeare theater
	German **B**asset hound **A**sian settlers
	French ambassador **M**exican food
PROPER NOUNS USED AS ADJECTIVES	the **S**enate floor the **C**linton speeches
	Miller festival a **B**ible class
	the **W**angs' house **N**ew **Y**ork bagels

Some proper adjectives have become so commonly used that they
are no longer capitalized.

EXAMPLES	**h**erculean **e**ffort **f**rench **f**ries
	pasteurized **m**ilk **q**uixotic **h**ope
	venetian **b**linds **t**eddy **b**ear

Brand names are often used as proper adjectives.

10.2.8

Capitalize a **brand name** when it is used as an adjective, but
do not capitalize the common noun it modifies.

EXAMPLES	**T**imo **w**allets **S**witzles **f**ruit bars
	Super **C**ool **j**eans **L**onglasting **r**efrigerator

Multiple Proper Adjectives

When you have two or more proper adjectives used together, do not capitalize the associated common nouns.

> **Do not capitalize a common noun used with two proper adjectives.**

10.2.9 RULE

ONE PROPER ADJECTIVE	TWO PROPER ADJECTIVES
Missouri River	Arkansas and Missouri rivers
First Street	First, Second, and Third streets
Erie Canal	Erie and Augusta canals
Conservation Act	Conservation and Clean Air acts
Indian Ocean	Indian and Pacific oceans
Passaic County	Passaic and Warren counties
Hawaiian Islands	Hawaiian and Canary islands

Prefixes and Hyphenated Adjectives

Prefixes and hyphenated adjectives cause special problems. Prefixes used with proper adjectives should be capitalized only if they refer to a nationality.

> **Do not capitalize prefixes attached to proper adjectives unless the prefix refers to a nationality. In a hyphenated adjective, capitalize only the proper adjective.**

10.2.10 RULE

EXAMPLES

all-American   Anglo-American

Mexican-speaking   pro-French

American Polish-language newspaper

pre-Romanesque   Sino-Tibetan

pre-Islamic architecture   Indo-Aryan

See Practice 10.2C

See Practice 10.2D

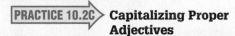

PRACTICE 10.2C **Capitalizing Proper Adjectives**

Read the sentence. Then, write the word or words in each sentence that should be capitalized.

EXAMPLE   I have toured a mayan pyramid in mexico.

ANSWER   *Mayan, Mexico*

1. The jefferson memorial is forty minutes from my house.

2. The heroine in the movie lives in a georgian manor.

3. The falkland islands are located in the atlantic ocean near argentina.

4. She had a great time in spanish class last year.

5. The american eagle is still a threatened species.

6. President Franklin Delano Roosevelt's dog was a scottish terrier.

7. The cabinet is made of french oak.

8. The malaysian ambassador was last in the receiving line.

9. irish immigrants, who came to america in the nineteenth century, are an important part of the culture.

10. My neighbor's son is a shakespearean actor.

PRACTICE 10.2D **Revising Sentences to Correct Capitalization Errors**

Read each sentence. Then, rewrite each sentence using the conventions of capitalization.

EXAMPLE   harry read an article in the spanish newspaper.

ANSWER   *Harry read an article in the Spanish newspaper.*

11. kevin ran all the way to walker avenue.

12. cynthia just finished reading a book by f. scott fitzgerald.

13. bill wanted to install french doors on the porch.

14. father says we will celebrate the fourth of july with aunt melba.

15. montpelier is the capital of vermont.

16. while on vacation, leo bought a swiss watch.

17. bavarian-made cuckoo clocks are designed differently than black forest cuckoo clocks.

18. antoni gaudí was the genius who designed many buildings in barcelona, spain.

19. thompson's gazelle and the african elephant are native to africa.

20. during the civil war, the first shots fired were at fort sumter in south carolina.

SPEAKING APPLICATION

Discuss with a partner the reason why the words *Internet* and the *Web* are capitalized.

WRITING APPLICATION

Write five sentences. In each sentence, include a proper adjective.

10.3 Other Uses of Capitals

Even though the purpose of using capital letters is to make writing clearer, some rules for capitalization can be confusing. For example, it may be difficult to remember which words in a letter you write need to start with a capital, which words in a book title should be capitalized, or when a person's title—such as Senator or Reverend—needs to start with a capital. The rules and examples that follow should clear up the confusion.

Using Capitals in Letters

Capitalization is required in parts of personal letters and business letters.

> **Capitalize the first word and all nouns in letter salutations and the first word in letter closings.**

10.3.1 RULE

SALUTATIONS
Dear **W**illiam,

Dear **M**adame:

Dear **M**rs. **L**awrence:

My **D**ear **U**ncle,

CLOSINGS
With **g**reat **r**espect,

Yours **v**ery **t**ruly,

Forever **y**ours,

All **m**y **b**est,

Using Capitals for Titles

Capitals are used for titles of people and titles of literary and artistic works. The charts and rules on the following pages will guide you in capitalizing titles correctly.

> Capitalize a person's title only when it is used with the person's name or when it is used as a proper name by itself.

WITH A PROPER
NAME
Yesterday, **G**overnor **B**arth signed the bill.

AS A PROPER
NAME
I'm glad you can join us, **G**randpa.

IN A GENERAL
REFERENCE
The **k**ing rewarded his loyal subjects.

The following chart illustrates the correct form for a variety of titles. Study the chart, paying particular attention to compound titles and titles with prefixes or suffixes.

SOCIAL, BUSINESS, RELIGIOUS, MILITARY, AND GOVERNMENT TITLES	
Commonly Used Titles	Sir, Madam, Miss, Professor, Doctor, Reverend, Bishop, Sister, Father, Rabbi, Corporal, Major, Admiral, Mayor, Governor, Ambassador
Abbreviated Titles	*Before names*: Mr., Mrs., Ms., Dr., Hon. *After names*: Jr., Sr., Ph.D., M.D., D.D.S., Esq.
Compound Titles	Vice President, Secretary of State, Lieutenant Governor, Commander in Chief
Titles With Prefixes or Suffixes	ex-Congressman Randolph, Governor-elect Loughman

Some honorary titles are capitalized. These include First Lady of the United States, Speaker of the House of Representatives, Queen Mother of England, and the Prince of Wales.

> **Capitalize certain honorary titles even when the titles are not followed by a proper name.**

10.3.3 RULE

EXAMPLE   The **p**resident and **F**irst **L**ady visited with the **q**ueen of England.

Occasionally, the titles of other government officials may be capitalized as a sign of respect when referring to a specific person whose name is not given. However, you usually do not capitalize titles when they stand alone.

EXAMPLES   We thank you, **G**overnor, for speaking to us this morning.

Only two **s**enators voted against the bill.

> **Relatives are often referred to by titles. These references should be capitalized when used with or as the person's name.**

10.3.4 RULE

WITH THE PERSON'S NAME   In that summer, **U**ncle **B**ob visited us almost every day.

AS A NAME   She said that **G**randmother loved to cook.

> **Do not capitalize titles showing family relationships when they are preceded by a possessive noun or pronoun.**

10.3.5 RULE

EXAMPLES   his **a**unt   her **m**other   Sam's **u**ncle

Capitalize the first word and all other key words in the titles of books, periodicals, poems, stories, plays, paintings, and other works of art.

The following chart lists examples to guide you in capitalizing titles and subtitles of various works. Note that the articles (*a, an,* and *the*) are not capitalized unless they are used as the first word of a title or subtitle. Conjunctions and prepositions are also left uncapitalized unless they are the first or last word in a title or subtitle or contain four letters or more. Note also that verbs, no matter how short, are always capitalized.

TITLES OF WORKS	
Books	*The Red Badge of Courage,* *Profiles in Courage,* *All Through the Night,* *John Ford: The Man and His Films* *Heart of Darkness*
Periodicals	*International Wildlife, Allure,* *Better Homes and Gardens*
Poems	"The Raven" "The Rime of the Ancient Mariner" "Flower in the Crannied Wall"
Stories and Articles	"Editha" "The Fall of the House of Usher" "Here Is New York"
Plays and Musicals	*The Tragedy of Macbeth* *Our Town* *West Side Story*
Paintings	*Starry Night* *Mona Lisa* *The Artist's Daughter With a Cat*
Music	*The Unfinished Symphony* "Heartbreak Hotel" "This Land Is Your Land"

> Capitalize titles of educational courses when they are language courses or when they are followed by a number or preceded by a proper noun or adjective. Do not capitalize school subjects discussed in a general manner.

10.3.7 RULE

WITH CAPITALS	**G**erman	**H**onors **C**hemistry
	Biology 205	**M**ath 3
	Economics 100	**R**ussian

WITHOUT CAPITALS	**h**ealth	**p**sychology
	woodworking	**h**istory
	biology	**m**ath

EXAMPLES   This year, I will be taking **m**ath, **F**rench, **H**onors **B**iology, and **w**orld **h**istory.

Margaret's favorite classes are **a**rt **h**istory, **I**talian, and **b**iology.

She does not like **p**hysical **e**ducation and **s**cience as much.

After **F**rench class, I have to rush across the building to **h**istory.

See Practice 10.3A
See Practice 10.3B

PRACTICE 10.3A **Capitalizing Titles**

Read each sentence. Then, write the word or words in each sentence that should be capitalized.

EXAMPLE   Here comes doctor Preston.

ANSWER   *Doctor*

1. I'm looking for captain Pierce.

2. My aunt linda makes the best lasagna.

3. Karen Aiken, president of winger's department store, presided over the meeting.

4. The article was called "beyond the seas"; it was well written.

5. "Excuse me, mr. secretary, would you answer one question?" asked the reporter.

6. I have a research report due in my honors biology class.

7. My Spanish teacher, senora gonzalez, organized a fiesta for the entire school.

8. The honorable judge Robinson will be presiding.

9. Edgar Allen Poe's poem annabel lee may have been written about his wife.

10. It was general Eisenhower who led the allies to victory at Normandy.

PRACTICE 10.3B **Using All of the Rules of Capitalization**

Read each sentence. Then, rewrite each sentence, using conventions of capitalization.

EXAMPLE   i've never seen mr. gutierrez in a suit.

ANSWER   *I've never seen Mr. Gutierrez in a suit.*

11. mr. kent asked us to read *the iliad* by homer.

12. I remember dr. laramy was a professor of african history at the university of Texas.

13. The speech was given by ex-mayor rawlins.

14. "oh no!" said gia. "my pen is out of ink!"

15. The sunshine skyway bridge is located in tampa, florida.

16. After a brief halt, major stevens led the troops back to camp.

17. the san diego zoo is home to two giant pandas from china.

18. Nancy attended the ball with mr. edmond sills.

19. The 2004 republican national convention was held in madison square garden.

20. The triassic period ended about 199 million years ago.

SPEAKING APPLICATION

Discuss with a partner the situations when words, such as *general* or *aunt*, are capitalized and when they are not capitalized. What different meaning does the capital indicate?

WRITING APPLICATION

Write a short fictional story about any topic of your choice. Be sure to include dialogue, titles, and proper nouns.

CHAPTER 11

PUNCTUATION

Use punctuation to create sentences that readers can navigate easily.

WRITE GUY *Jeff Anderson, M.Ed.*

WHAT DO YOU NOTICE?

Focus on punctuation as you zoom in on these sentences from *A Connecticut Yankee in King Arthur's Court* by Mark Twain.

MENTOR TEXT

> Presently this thought occurred to me: how heedless I have been! When the boy gets calm, he will wonder why a great magician like me should have begged a boy like him to help me get out of this place; he will put this and that together, and will see that I am a humbug.

Now, ask yourself the following questions:

- What purposes do the colon and the exclamation mark serve in the first sentence?
- How are commas and a semicolon used in the second sentence?

The colon introduces the narrator's thought; the exclamation mark demonstrates strong emotion. In the second sentence, the first comma sets off the subordinate clause *When the boy gets calm,* whereas the second comma is used to place emphasis on the phrase *will see that I am a humbug.* The author uses a semicolon to separate two related ideas.

Grammar for Writers Writers have several punctuation marks available to help them craft a variety of complex sentences. Be sure to use punctuation marks that guide readers through your writing.

What did the comma say to the semicolon?

"When did you start wearing that cap on your head?"

11.1 End Marks

End marks tell readers when to pause and for how long. They signal the end or conclusion of a sentence, word, or phrase. There are three end marks: the **period (.)**, the **question mark (?)**, and the **exclamation mark (!)**.

Using Periods

A **period** indicates the end of a declarative or imperative sentence, an indirect question, or an abbreviation. The period is the most common end mark.

RULE 11.1.1

> **Use a period** to end a declarative sentence, a mild imperative sentence, and an indirect question.

A **declarative sentence** is a statement of fact or opinion.

DECLARATIVE SENTENCE	This is a wonderful day.

An **imperative sentence** gives a direction or command. Often, the first word of an imperative sentence is a verb.

MILD IMPERATIVE SENTENCE	Finish sanding the table.

An **indirect question** restates a question in a declarative sentence. It does not give the speaker's exact words.

INDIRECT QUESTION	John asked me whether I could come.

Other Uses of Periods

In addition to signaling the end of a statement, periods can also signal that words have been shortened, or abbreviated.

RULE 11.1.2

> **Use a period after most abbreviations and after initials.**

PERIODS IN ABBREVIATIONS	
Titles	Dr., Sr., Mrs., Mr., Gov., Maj., Rev., Prof.
Place Names	Ave., Bldg., Blvd., Mt., Dr., St., Ter., Rd.
Times and Dates	Sun., Dec., sec., min., hr., yr., A.M.
Initials	E. B. White, Robin F. Brancato, R. Brett

Some abbreviations do not end with periods. Metric measurements, state abbreviations used with ZIP Codes, and most standard measurements do not need periods. The abbreviation for inch, *in.,* is the exception.

EXAMPLES   mm, cm, kg, L, C, CA, TX, ft, gal

The following chart lists some abbreviations with and without periods.

ABBREVIATIONS WITH AND WITHOUT END MARKS	
approx. = approximately	misc. = miscellaneous
COD = cash on delivery	mph = miles per hour
dept. = department	No. = number
doz. = dozen(s)	p. or pg. = page; pp. = pages
EST = Eastern Standard Time	POW = prisoner of war
FM = frequency modulation	pub. = published, publisher
gov. or govt. = government	pvt. = private
ht. = height	rpm = revolutions per minute
incl. = including	R.S.V.P. = please reply
ital = italics	sp. = spelling
kt. = karat or carat	SRO = standing room only
meas. = measure	vol. = volume
mfg. = manufacturing	wt. = weight

Sentences Ending With Abbreviations When a sentence ends with an abbreviation that uses a period, do not put a second period at the end. If an end mark other than a period is required, add the end mark.

EXAMPLES	Make sure to write Mike Brinks Jr **.**
	Is that Andy Jens Sr **. ?**

See Practice 11.1A

Do not use periods with acronyms, words formed with the first or first few letters of a series of words.

ACRONYMS	USA (United States of America)
	CCC (Civilian Conservation Corps)

Use a period after numbers and letters in outlines.

EXAMPLE	I **.** Maintaining your pet's health
	A **.** Diet
	1 **.** For a puppy
	2 **.** For a mature dog
	B **.** Exercise

Using Question Marks

A **question mark** follows a word, phrase, or sentence that asks a question. A question is often in inverted word order.

Use a question mark to end an interrogative sentence, an incomplete question, or a statement intended as a question.

INTERROGATIVE SENTENCE	Was the project completed yet **?**
	What time are we having company **?**
INCOMPLETE QUESTION	Small dogs stay with their moms longer. Why **?**
	I'll make you a sandwich. What kind **?**

Use care, however, in ending statements with question marks. It is better to rephrase the statement as a direct question.

STATEMENT WITH A QUESTION MARK	The night hasn't ended yet**?**
	We are having steak for dinner**?**
REVISED INTO A DIRECT QUESTION	Hasn't the night ended yet**?**
	Are we having steak for dinner**?**

Use a period instead of a question mark with an **indirect question**—a question that is restated as a declarative sentence.

EXAMPLE	Bella wanted to know when the plane would arrive**.**
	She wondered if it would be on time**.**

Using Exclamation Marks

An **exclamation mark** signals an exclamatory sentence, an imperative sentence, or an interjection. It indicates strong emotion and should be used sparingly.

> Use an **exclamation mark** to end an exclamatory sentence, a forceful imperative sentence, or an interjection expressing strong emotion.

RULE 11.1.6

EXCLAMATORY SENTENCE	Look at the huge mountain**!**
FORCEFUL IMPERATIVE SENTENCE	Don't tip the bowl**!**

An interjection can be used with a comma or an exclamation mark. An exclamation mark increases the emphasis.

EXAMPLES	Wow**!** That was a great game**.**
	Oh**!** That was a great meal**.**
WITH A COMMA	Wow**,** that was a great game**.**

See Practice 11.1B

PRACTICE 11.1A > Using Periods Correctly in Sentences

Read each sentence. Then, rewrite each sentence, adding periods where they are needed.

EXAMPLE   I asked Dr Blake if he enjoyed reading my paper

ANSWER   *I asked Dr. Blake if he enjoyed reading my paper.*

1. Booker T Washington was born in Virginia in 1856

2. Meet me at 8:00 AM by the park bench

3. A A Milne wrote the *Winnie-the-Pooh* series

4. Mail this card to Ms Rachel A Smith on Wood Ave

5. Mt Everest is about 8,848 m tall

6. According to a NASA Web site, Earth rotates on its axis at approx 1,000 mph

7. The experiment requires 3 kg of copper sulfate

8. Saul asked us if we wanted to have Chinese food for dinner

9. The winner of the 100-m race is Grant Tidwell Jr

10. Every Saturday night, that show is SRO

PRACTICE 11.1B > Using Question Marks and Exclamation Marks Correctly in Sentences

Read the sentence. Then, write the correct end mark for each item.

EXAMPLE   Where are my keys

ANSWER   ?

11. How much money is left in the account

12. Where does she keep the tea

13. Don't peek

14. When is the next leap year

15. Quickly, turn on the lights

16. I've won

17. Do we have enough seats for everyone

18. Haven't I seen you somewhere before

19. Happy Birthday

20. Go, Rockets

SPEAKING APPLICATION

Take turns with a partner. Say declarative sentences, imperative sentences, and indirect questions. Your partner should listen for and identify each sentence type.

WRITING APPLICATION

Write two sentences that use question marks and two sentences that use exclamation marks.

11.2 Commas

A **comma** tells the reader to pause briefly before continuing a sentence. Commas may be used to separate elements in a sentence or to set off part of a sentence.

Commas are used more than any other internal punctuation mark. To check for correct comma use, read a sentence aloud and note where a pause helps you to group your ideas. Commas signal to readers that they should take a short breath.

Using Commas With Compound Sentences

A **compound sentence** consists of two or more main or independent clauses that are joined by a coordinating conjunction, such as *and, but, for, nor, or, so,* or *yet.*

> Use a **comma** before a conjunction to separate two or more independent or main clauses in a **compound sentence.**

Use a comma before a conjunction only when there are complete sentences on both sides of the conjunction. Do not use a comma if the conjunction joins a compound subject, a compound verb, prepositional phrases, or subordinate clauses.

EXAMPLE
Bill is leaving for duty **,** but I won't be able to see

independent clause   independent clause

him off.

In some compound sentences, the main or independent clauses are very brief, and the meaning is clear. When this occurs, the comma before the conjunction may be omitted.

EXAMPLES
Bill read carefully but he still didn't understand.

Brent would like to go in July but he doesn't have the time.

In other sentences, conjunctions are used to join compound subjects or verbs, prepositional phrases, or subordinate clauses. Because these sentences have only one independent clause, they do not take a comma before the conjunction.

CONJUNCTIONS WITHOUT COMMAS	
Compound Subject	Ben and Kate met for dinner on the river.
Compound Verb	The family laughed and reminisced while they ate.
Two Prepositional Phrases	My dog flew through the kitchen and out the door.
Two Subordinate Clauses	I enjoy trips only if they are relaxing and if my family comes with me.

A **nominative absolute** is a noun or pronoun followed by a participle or participial phrase that functions independently of the rest of the sentence.

RULE 11.2.2

> Use a comma after a **nominative absolute.**

The following example shows a comma with a nominative absolute.

EXAMPLE   Precious memories having been experienced, I decided to record them.

Avoiding Comma Splices

Remember to use both a comma and a coordinating conjunction in a compound sentence. Using only a comma can result in a **run-on sentence** or a **comma splice**. A **comma splice** occurs when two or more complete sentences have been joined with only a comma. Either punctuate separate sentences with an end mark or a semicolon, or find a way to join the sentences. (See Section 11.3 for more information on semicolons.)

RULE 11.2.3

> Avoid comma splices.

INCORRECT   The ice formed on the trees, many branches snapped under the weight.

CORRECT   The ice formed on the trees. Many branches snapped under the weight.

Using Commas in a Series

A **series** consists of three or more words, phrases, or subordinate clauses of a similar kind. A series can occur in any part of a sentence.

> **Use commas to separate three or more words, phrases, or clauses in a series.**

Notice that a comma follows each of the items except the last one in these series. The conjunction *and* or *or* is added after the last comma.

SERIES OF WORDS
The marine life included fish, crabs, coral, and dolphins.

SERIES OF PREPOSITIONAL PHRASES
The map directed them over the mountain, into the cave, and past the waterfall.

SUBORDINATE CLAUSES IN A SERIES
The magazine revealed that the game was perfect, the players were flawless, the refreshments were good, and the fans were excited.

If each item (except for the last one) in a series is followed by a conjunction, do not use commas.

EXAMPLE
I read novels and magazines and newspapers.

A second exception to this rule concerns items such as *salt and pepper*, which are paired so often that they are considered a single item.

EXAMPLES
During the holiday every table was set with a knife and fork, crystal and china, and salt and pepper.

Brett's favorite lunches are peanut butter and jelly, turkey and cheese, and soup and salad.

Using Commas Between Adjectives

Sometimes, two or more adjectives are placed before the noun they describe.

> **Use commas to separate coordinate adjectives,** also called **independent modifiers,** or adjectives of equal rank.

EXAMPLES   a fabulous, tasty meal

an excellent, lively, fun party

An adjective is equal in rank to another if the word *and* can be inserted between them without changing the meaning of the sentence. Another way to test whether or not adjectives are equal is to reverse their order. If the sentence still sounds correct, they are of equal rank. In the first example, *a tasty, fabulous meal* still makes sense.

If you cannot place the word *and* between adjectives or reverse their order without changing the meaning of the sentence, they are called **cumulative adjectives.**

> **Do not use a comma between cumulative adjectives.**

EXAMPLES   a new car cover
(*a car new cover* does not make sense)

many strange bugs
(*strange many bugs* does not make sense)

> **Do not use a comma to separate the last adjective in a series from the noun it modifies.**

INCORRECT   A big, strong, man lifted the weights.

CORRECT   A big, strong man lifted the weights.

See Practice 11.2A
See Practice 11.2B

PRACTICE 11.2A Using Commas Correctly in Sentences

Read each sentence. Then, rewrite each sentence, adding a comma or commas where they are needed.

EXAMPLE I drove by the house but he wasn't there.

ANSWER *I drove by the house, but he wasn't there.*

1. The gust of wind blew the stack of papers and they scattered everywhere.

2. Luke mowed the lawn clipped the hedges and watered the garden.

3. Sara must have fallen asleep or she would have called by now.

4. The tired disappointed soccer team walked slowly off the field.

5. The bulb had burned out but it was still hot.

6. My arm had that tingly fuzzy feeling.

7. Its hair blowing away from its face the sheep dog quickly ran down the street.

8. I like Italian Mexican and spicy hot Indian food.

9. We took chairs towels a cooler toys and magazines to the beach.

10. The restaurant offers ham and eggs peanut butter and jelly sandwiches and corned beef hash.

PRACTICE 11.2B Revising to Correct Errors in Comma Use

Read each sentence. Then, rewrite each sentence, adding or deleting commas as necessary.

EXAMPLE We collected, plastic bags, bits of paper and cans as we helped clean the park.

ANSWER *We collected plastic bags, bits of paper, and cans as we helped clean the park.*

11. I used my mitt, but left it, at baseball practice.

12. With the play, the concert and the magician this weekend, the auditorium is booked.

13. Cecily skipped, and sang on her way to school.

14. It's quiet in here yet I still can't hear you.

15. Bruce can't find his chemistry book his algebra homework or his three-page, French paper.

16. My cousin drove me to the airport, and gave me a thoughtful going-away present.

17. Her eyes twinkling she gave him the present.

18. Ian ate the last sandwich and then he drank the last of the lemonade.

19. The book cover was torn dirty, and smudged.

20. The ominous dark angry clouds gave way to a golden streak of sunshine.

SPEAKING APPLICATION

Take turns with a partner. Say compound sentences. Your partner should tell where a comma should go if your sentences were written.

WRITING APPLICATION

Write four sentences that use commas incorrectly. Exchange papers with a partner. Your partner should rewrite each sentence, adding or deleting commas as needed.

Using Commas After Introductory Material

Most material that introduces a sentence should be set off with a comma.

RULE 11.2.8 Use a comma after an introductory word, phrase, or clause.

KINDS OF INTRODUCTORY MATERIAL	
Introductory Words	Yes, we do expect to see them soon. No, there has been no offer. Well, I was definitely surprised by his answer.
Nouns of Direct Address	Marcus, will you go?
Introductory Adverbs	Hurriedly, they gathered up the supplies. Patiently, the teacher explained it to them again.
Participial Phrases	Thinking quickly, she averted a potential medical disaster. Standing next to each other in the line, we introduced ourselves and started to chat.
Prepositional Phrases	In the shade of the palm tree, a family sat on the beach. After the lengthy dance, we were all exhausted.
Infinitive Phrases	To choose the right gift, I consulted her parents and friends. To finish my project on time, I will have to cut some details.
Adverbial Clauses	When he asked for a driving permit, he was sure it would be denied. If you read books, you may be interested in this one.

Commas and Prepositional Phrases Only one comma should be used after two prepositional phrases or a compound participial or infinitive phrase.

EXAMPLES   In the back of the cab behind the coat, he found his wallet.

To find their way in the crowd and to avoid confusion, the tourists asked for help.

It is not necessary to set off short prepositional phrases. However, a comma can help avoid confusion.

CONFUSING   In the window sun bleached the fabric.

CLEAR   In the window, sun bleached the fabric.

Using Commas With Parenthetical Expressions

A **parenthetical expression** is a word or phrase that interrupts the flow of the sentence.

> **Use commas to set off parenthetical expressions from the rest of the sentence.**

11.2.9   RULE

Parenthetical expressions may come in the middle or at the end of a sentence. A parenthetical expression in the middle of a sentence needs two commas—one on each side; it needs only one comma if it appears at the end of a sentence.

KINDS OF PARENTHETICAL EXPRESSIONS	
Nouns of Direct Address	Will you have dinner with us, Meg? I wonder, Mrs. Taft, where they'll go for dinner.
Conjunctive Adverbs	Someone had already bought them plates, however. We could not, therefore, buy the set.
Common Expressions	I listened to Mara's story as carefully as everyone else did, I think.
Contrasting Expressions	Bea is sixteen, not seventeen. Adie's smile, not her beauty, won Alan's heart.

Using Commas With Nonessential Expressions

To determine when a phrase or clause should be set off with commas, decide whether the phrase or clause is *essential* or *nonessential* to the meaning of the sentence. The terms *restrictive* and *nonrestrictive* may also be used.

An **essential,** or **restrictive, phrase** or **clause** is necessary to the meaning of the sentence. **Nonessential,** or **nonrestrictive, expressions** can be left out without changing the meaning of the sentence. Although the nonessential material may be interesting, the sentence can be read without it and still make sense. Depending on their importance in a sentence, appositives, participial phrases, and adjectival clauses can be either essential or nonessential. Only nonessential expressions should be set off with commas.

NONESSENTIAL APPOSITIVE	The project was completed by Jane, the top student in the class.
NONESSENTIAL PARTICIPIAL PHRASE	The majestic bridge, built in the 1900s, crosses the largest river in the country.
NONESSENTIAL ADJECTIVAL CLAUSE	The river, which overflows in the spring, is popular with rafters in summer.

Do not use commas to set off essential expressions.

ESSENTIAL APPOSITIVE	The part was played by the famous actor Tom Hanks.
ESSENTIAL PARTICIPIAL PHRASE	The man carrying the hammer is my brother.
ESSENTIAL ADJECTIVAL CLAUSE	The kayaking trip that Bill suggested could change my opinion of kayaking.

See Practice 11.2C
See Practice 11.2D

PRACTICE 11.2C > Placing Commas Correctly in Sentences

Read each sentence. Then, rewrite each sentence, adding a comma where it is needed.

EXAMPLE   Yes we grew zinnias this year.

ANSWER   *Yes, we grew zinnias this year.*

1. No my birthday isn't in August.

2. With the mystery finally solved the detective closed the case.

3. Dad I mowed the lawn Tuesday night not Wednesday night.

4. When he's sleepy Martin yawns a lot to stay awake.

5. Really I thought she was very mature.

6. To match the paint color we took a sample to the store.

7. The local Boy Scout group cleaned the statue which commemorates veterans.

8. In a hurry Adelita gathered her things and left the room.

9. We enjoyed reading and studying Homer Dr. Shenk.

10. When the art supplies are getting low let me know.

PRACTICE 11.2D > Revising Sentences for Proper Comma Use

Read each sentence. Then, rewrite each sentence, adding or deleting commas as necessary.

EXAMPLE   The picture frame, made of wood holds a photograph, of my mother.

ANSWER   *The picture frame, made of wood, holds a photograph of my mother.*

11. The ocean my favorite place to swim, was at high tide an hour ago.

12. However the apples bruised, anyway.

13. That animal is an opossum not a raccoon!

14. Annoyingly the clock radio blared on and off as I tried to sleep.

15. On the red carpet, before the awards show the actor gave many interviews.

16. The pilot who was a Navy pilot landed the plane safely.

17. The stamp which was auctioned, on Saturday sold for $18,000!

18. Julia let me know when you want to go home.

19. This book is mine I think.

20. He will not, therefore seek reelection in that state.

SPEAKING APPLICATION

Discuss with a partner the difference between the necessity of a comma in sentence 3 and the necessity of a comma in sentence 4. Tell what the purpose of the comma is in both sentences.

WRITING APPLICATION

Write a fantasy short story about a strange place full of ironies and contrasts. Be sure to use correct punctuation marks, including comma placement in clauses, nonrestrictive phrases, contrasting expressions, introductory material, and parenthetical expressions.

Using Commas With Dates, Geographical Names, and Titles

Dates usually have several parts, including months, days, and years. Commas separate these elements for easier reading.

RULE 11.2.10

> **When a date is made up of two or more parts, use a comma after each item, except in the case of a month followed by a day.**

EXAMPLES
The show took place on January 12, 2001, and the actors arrived January 1, 2001.

The trip began on July 4 and ended three months later.
(no comma needed after the day of the month)

Commas are also used when the month and the day are used as an appositive to rename a day of the week.

EXAMPLES
Sunday, March 15, was the day of the picnic.

Mark will arrive on Friday, June 15, and will stay until Monday.

When a date contains only a month and a year, commas are unnecessary.

EXAMPLES
I will arrive in April 2012.

Bette will visit Australia in August 2010.

If the parts of a date have already been joined by prepositions, no comma is needed.

EXAMPLE
The city bus system ran its second test in May of 1909.

RULE 11.2.11

When a geographical name is made up of two or more parts, use a comma after each item.

EXAMPLES   My brother who works in Miami, Florida, is moving into a new house.

They're going to Toronto, Ontario, Canada, for their vacation.

See Practice 11.2E

RULE 11.2.12

When a name is followed by one or more titles, use a comma after the name and after each title.

EXAMPLE   I see that Bill Johnson, M.D., attended the show.

A similar rule applies with some business abbreviations.

EXAMPLE   Quality Printing, Inc., distributes novels.

Using Commas in Numbers

Commas make large numbers easier to read by grouping them.

RULE 11.2.13

With large numbers of more than three digits, use a comma after every third digit starting from the right.

EXAMPLES   2,350 cars, 103,200 pennies, 2,500,415 books

RULE 11.2.14

Do not use a comma in ZIP Codes, telephone numbers, page numbers, years, serial numbers, or house numbers.

ZIP CODE	04707	YEAR NUMBER	2011
TELEPHONE NUMBER	(973) 886-7701	SERIAL NUMBER	703-546-791
PAGE NUMBER	Page 1146	HOUSE NUMBER	2435 Frederick Court

See Practice 11.2F

PRACTICE 11.2E > Using Commas With Dates and Geographical Names

Read each sentence. Then, rewrite each sentence to show where to correctly place commas in dates and geographical names.

EXAMPLE   Our flight landed in Vancouver British Columbia Canada.

ANSWER   *Our flight landed in Vancouver, British Columbia, Canada.*

1. Where were you on March 9 2008?

2. We went to Tucson Arizona in July of 2004.

3. The Carsons will be out of town from Monday February 8 until Saturday February 13.

4. Monterey California and Miami Florida are coastal cities.

5. Our new teacher is from Swansea Wales United Kingdom.

6. Texas became an official part of the United States on December 29 1845.

7. Monday July 17 is my birthday.

8. I'm heading for San Juan Puerto Rico.

9. By Thursday January 2 we will arrive in Kuala Lumpur Malaysia.

10. Heather was born on February 12 2000 in Dallas Texas.

PRACTICE 11.2F > Editing Sentences for Proper Comma Usage

Read each sentence. Then, rewrite each sentence, deleting or adding commas where they are needed.

EXAMPLE   Next, Monday, April 3 I'll be in Sydney New South Wales Australia.

ANSWER   *Next Monday, April 3, I'll be in Sydney, New South Wales, Australia.*

11. Alan R. Wilson Ph.D. has reviewed 1142 cases allergic reactions to penicillin.

12. My flight has a layover in London England.

13. Exactly 2008 drummers performed at the 2,008 Summer Olympics opening ceremony.

14. Did you vacation in Athens Georgia, or Athens Greece?

15. Cole Egan Jr. was born on March 6 1990.

16. Millie lives at 1,452 Main Street in New Seabury Connecticut.

17. Istanbul Turkey has become an international hotspot since June, of 1995.

18. Average Investors Inc. is a new company that opened downtown.

19. I had never read much about Sierra Leone West Africa until I read the article.

20. Sunday February 1 2009 will be a day long remembered in Pittsburgh Pennsylvania.

SPEAKING APPLICATION

Take turns with a partner. Use sentences 1 and 2 as models to say similar sentences. Your partner should tell which sentence needs a comma in the date.

WRITING APPLICATION

Write four sentences that contain dates, geographical names, and large numbers, but omit all commas. Exchange papers with a partner. Your partner should add commas where necessary.

Using Commas With Addresses and in Letters

Commas are also used in addresses, salutations of friendly letters, and closings of friendly or business letters.

> **Use a comma after each item in an address made up of two or more parts.**

RULE 11.2.15

Commas are placed after the name, street, and city. No comma separates the state from the ZIP Code. Instead, insert an extra space between them.

EXAMPLE   I received a card from Bill Smith, 125 Mountain Road, Wayne, New Jersey 07470.

Fewer commas are needed when an address is written in a letter or on an envelope.

EXAMPLE   Mrs. Jack Collins

25 Gold Avenue

Miami, FL 32211

> **Use a comma after the salutation in a personal letter and after the closing in all letters.**

RULE 11.2.16

See Practice 11.2G

SALUTATIONS	Dear Aunt Jean,	Dear Wanda,
CLOSINGS	Your friend,	Yours forever,

Using Commas in Elliptical Sentences

In **elliptical sentences,** words that are understood are left out. Commas make these sentences easier to read.

> **Use a comma to indicate the words left out of an elliptical sentence.**

RULE 11.2.17

EXAMPLE Michael celebrates his promotion formally;

Spencer, casually.

The words *celebrates his promotion* have been omitted from the second clause of the sentence. The comma has been inserted in their place so the meaning is still clear. The sentence could be restated in this way: *Michael celebrates his promotion formally; Spencer celebrates his promotion casually.*

Using Commas With Direct Quotations

Commas are also used to indicate where **direct quotations** begin and end. (See Section 11.4 for more information on punctuating quotations.)

> **Use commas to set off a direct quotation from the rest of a sentence.**

EXAMPLES "You came home early," commented Ben's mother.

He said, "The rehearsal ended earlier than planned."

"I hope," Susan's mother said, "my sister doesn't forget her toothbrush."

Using Commas for Clarity

Commas help you group words that belong together.

> **Use a comma to prevent a sentence from being misunderstood.**

UNCLEAR Near the highway developers were building an apartment building.

CLEAR Near the highway, developers were building an apartment building.

Misuses of Commas

Because commas appear so frequently in writing, some people are tempted to use them where they are not needed. Before you insert a comma, think about how your ideas relate to one another.

MISUSED WITH AN ADJECTIVE AND A NOUN	After work, I enjoy a healthy, nutritious, meal.
CORRECT	After work, I enjoy a healthy, nutritious meal.
MISUSED WITH A COMPOUND SUBJECT	After our meeting, my colleague Bill, and his friend Kurt, were invited to the dinner.
CORRECT	After our meeting, my colleague Bill and his friend Kurt were invited to the dinner.
MISUSED WITH A COMPOUND VERB	He gazed into her eyes, and sang the song he had written.
CORRECT	He gazed into her eyes and sang the song he had written.
MISUSED WITH A COMPOUND OBJECT	She chose a coat with a hood, and a long sash.
CORRECT	She chose a coat with a hood and a long sash.
MISUSED WITH PHRASES	Checking the mail, and looking for a package, Debbie walked past us.
CORRECT	Checking the mail and looking for a package, Debbie walked past us.
MISUSED WITH CLAUSES	She discussed what elements are crucial for a successful meal, and which caterers are most reliable.
CORRECT	She discussed what elements are crucial for a successful meal and which caterers are most reliable.

See Practice 11.2H

PRACTICE 11.2G Adding Commas to Addresses and Letters

Read each item. Then, add commas where needed.

EXAMPLE   Main Street Montclair New Jersey

ANSWER   *Main Street, Montclair, New Jersey*

1. London Ontario Canada

2. Hugs and kisses
   Aunt Susan

3. 16 Maple Street
   Erie PA 16509

4. Dear Mom and Dad

5. Abilene Texas

6. 12 Jones Terrace Suite 1B

7. Greetings my good friend

8. Jill Davis Clover Road Centerport New York

9. Dear Margarita Susannah and Rosa

10. Doug Sargent
    #4 Harrington Road
    Beach Haven CT 04102

PRACTICE 11.2H Revising Sentences With Misused Commas

Read each sentence. Then, if a sentence contains a misused comma or commas, rewrite it. If the sentence is correct, write *correct*.

EXAMPLE   When I recall, my visit to Barcelona, Spain I think of all the art.

ANSWER   *When I recall my visit to Barcelona, Spain, I think of all the art.*

11. When Sheila goes hiking she takes her canteen, and compass.

12. Young Dylan looked left and right, and waited for the cars to stop.

13. This Tuesday, July 3, is my friend's party.

14. The teacher, said "Put away your books, and take out your pencils."

15. Melvin Cranford left his house that morning but, he forgot his laptop.

16. Apples, pears, bananas and, oranges are all great examples of healthy foods.

17. The trip started in, Lisbon Portugal, and ended in Madrid, Spain.

18. Before leaving, Anne, and her sister Jean, locked the doors.

19. Sitting on the grass, and drinking lemonade, Lizzy was enjoying the warm day.

20. Jack chose a blue jacket, and a blue tie.

SPEAKING APPLICATION

Discuss with a partner the necessity of placing commas in addresses. Propose an explanation as to why commas aren't used in zip codes.

WRITING APPLICATION

Write ten compound sentences with dates, lists, or multiple adjectives. Be sure to use commas properly.

11.3 Semicolons and Colons

The **semicolon (;)** is used to join related independent clauses. Semicolons can also help you avoid confusion in sentences with other internal punctuation. The **colon (:)** is used to introduce lists of items and in other special situations.

Using Semicolons to Join Independent Clauses

Semicolons establish relationships between two independent clauses that are closely connected in thought and structure. A semicolon can also be used to separate independent clauses or items in a series that already contain a number of commas.

> Use a semicolon to join related independent clauses that are not already joined by the conjunctions *and, but, for, nor, or, so,* or *yet*.

EXAMPLE   We explored the museum together; we were amazed at all the exhibits we found there.

Do not use a semicolon to join two unrelated independent clauses. If the clauses are not related, they should be written as separate sentences with a period or another end mark to separate them.

Note that when a sentence contains three or more related independent clauses, they may still be separated with semicolons.

EXAMPLE   The gate was open; the bone was gone; the puppy had disappeared.

Semicolons Join Clauses Separated by Conjunctive Adverbs or Transitional Expressions

Conjunctive adverbs are adverbs that are used as conjunctions to join independent clauses. **Transitional expressions** are expressions that connect one independent clause with another one.

> Use a semicolon to join independent clauses separated by either a **conjunctive adverb** or a **transitional expression**.

CONJUNCTIVE ADVERBS	*also, besides, consequently, first, furthermore, however, indeed, instead, moreover, nevertheless, otherwise, second, then, therefore, thus*
TRANSITIONAL EXPRESSIONS	*as a result, at this time, for instance, in fact, on the other hand, that is*

Place a semicolon *before* a conjunctive adverb or a transitional expression, and place a comma *after* a conjunctive adverb or transitional expression. The comma sets off the conjunctive adverb or transitional expression, which introduces the second clause.

EXAMPLE   She never lost her cool; in fact, she stayed completely calm.

Because words used as conjunctive adverbs and transitions can also interrupt one continuous sentence, use a semicolon only when there is an independent clause on each side of the conjunctive adverb or transitional expression.

EXAMPLES   We arrived yesterday ahead of schedule; therefore, we had time for a meal, a rest, and some sightseeing.

We were very impressed, however, by John's knowledge of leadership skills and his ability to motivate people.

Using Semicolons to Avoid Confusion

Sometimes, semicolons are used to separate items in a series.

RULE 11.3.3

Use semicolons to avoid confusion when independent clauses or items in a series already contain commas.

When the items in a series already contain several commas, semicolons can be used to group items that belong together. Semicolons are placed at the end of all but the last complete item in the series.

INDEPENDENT CLAUSES

The land, reportedly overflowing with flowers, was a myth; and the disappointed, tired visitors would only find it in storybooks.

ITEMS IN A SERIES

On our journey, many people greeted our cousins, who come from Palermo; my uncles, who live in Rome; and our grandparents, the Russos, who live in Venice.

Semicolons appear most commonly in a series that contains either nonessential appositives, participial phrases, or adjectival clauses. Commas should separate the nonessential material from the word or words they modify; semicolons should separate the complete items in the series.

APPOSITIVES

I sent invitations to Ms. Watts, my science teacher; Mr. Johnson, my principal; and Mrs. White, the librarian.

PARTICIPIAL PHRASES

I acquired a fascination with aquatic life from television, viewing science programs; from scuba diving, learning about oceanography; and from magazines, reading about fish.

ADJECTIVAL CLAUSES

The miniature train set that I bought has spare cars, which are brand new; a bridge, which opens and closes; and a tunnel, which has a light.

Using Colons

The **colon (:)** is used to introduce lists of items and in certain special situations.

RULE 11.3.4

> Use a colon after an independent clause to introduce a list of items. Use commas to separate three or more items.

Independent clauses that appear before a colon often include the words *the following, as follows, these,* or *those.*

EXAMPLES   For my interview, I had to speak with the following people: the president, the manager, and the director.

RULE 11.3.5

> Do not use a colon after a verb or a preposition.

INCORRECT   William always orders: steak, potatoes, salad, and fruit.

CORRECT   William always orders steak, potatoes, salad, and fruit.

RULE 11.3.6

> Use a colon to introduce a quotation that is formal or lengthy or a quotation that does not contain a "he said/she said" expression.

EXAMPLE   Oliver Wendell Holmes Jr. wrote this about freedom: "It is only through free debate and free exchange of ideas that government remains responsive to the will of the people and peaceful change is effected."

Even if it is lengthy, dialogue or a casual remark should be introduced by a comma. Use the colon if the quotation is formal or has no tagline.

A colon may also be used to introduce a sentence that explains the sentence that precedes it.

> **Use a colon to introduce a sentence that summarizes or explains the sentence before it.**

EXAMPLE   Her explanation for being late was believable **:**
She had gotten stopped by a police officer.

Notice that the complete sentence introduced by the colon starts with a capital letter.

> **Use a colon to introduce a formal appositive that follows an independent clause.**

EXAMPLE   I had finally decided on a career **:** teaching.

The colon is a stronger punctuation mark than a comma. Using the colon gives more emphasis to the appositive it introduces.

> **Use a colon in a number of special writing situations.**

SPECIAL SITUATIONS REQUIRING COLONS	
Numerals Giving the Time	5:30 A.M. 6:15 P.M.
References to Periodicals (Volume Number: Page Number)	*People* 74:12 *Sports Illustrated* 53:15
Biblical References (Chapter Number: Verse Number)	2 Timothy 1:9
Subtitles for Books and Magazines	*A Field Guide to Lions: African Lands and Wildlife*
Salutations in Business Letters	Dear Mrs. Glenstone: Dear Madam:
Labels Used to Signal Important Ideas	**Warning:** Private Property

See Practice 11.3A
See Practice 11.3B

PRACTICE 11.3A ▸ **Adding Semicolons and Colons to Sentences**

Read each sentence. Then, rewrite each sentence, inserting a semicolon or colon where needed.

EXAMPLE   I can see your point on the other hand, I can see her point, too.

ANSWER   *I can see your point; on the other hand, I can see her point, too.*

1. Sarah always says what she thinks she has a reputation for being honest.

2. There is only one item on the list nuts.

3. Abraham exercised and ate healthy foods therefore, he lived a long, healthy life.

4. Brett likes to take walks in the morning it gives him energy for the rest of the day.

5. I took a trip to see the oldest commissioned warship in the Navy the USS *Constitution*.

6. Nicholas is always doing something he never seems to get tired.

7. Tommy knows what he wants a puppy!

8. He takes a lot of computer courses as a result, he knows how to fix the program.

9. There can be only two outcomes in a football game win or lose.

10. The ship's captain has a very important rule Everyone must wear a life jacket.

PRACTICE 11.3B ▸ **Using Semicolons and Colons**

Read each item. Then, for each item, write a complete sentence, using the item, the punctuation indicated in parentheses, and additional words.

EXAMPLE   The class went on two field trips that year (colon)

ANSWER   *The class went on two field trips that year: one to the Washington Monument and the other to the Smithsonian Museum.*

11. chicken or fish (colon)

12. The night is so clear (semicolon)

13. Paul's dog knows three tricks (colon)

14. Mary's uncle lives in Rhode Island (colon)

15. He buried the treasure (semicolon)

16. Throughout the day (colon)

17. Jack liked the movie (semicolon)

18. Addie is reading her favorite book (semicolon)

19. The hostess had only one thing to say (colon)

20. consequently (semicolon)

SPEAKING APPLICATION

Discuss with a partner the similarities between your corrections for sentences 2, 7, and 9. Explain how the sentences would be different if commas were used instead.

WRITING APPLICATION

Write a paragraph about a family vacation. Then, combine some sentences with colons and semicolons. Your new sentences must make sense and be grammatically correct.

11.4 Quotation Marks, Underlining, and Italics

Quotation marks (" ") set off direct quotations, dialogue, and certain types of titles. Other titles are <u>underlined</u> or set in *italics*, a slanted type style.

Using Quotation Marks With Quotations

Quotation marks identify spoken or written words that you are including in your writing. A **direct quotation** represents a person's exact speech or thoughts. An **indirect quotation** reports the general meaning of what a person said or thought.

> A **direct quotation** is enclosed in quotation marks.

RULE 11.4.1

DIRECT QUOTATION
"When I learn to ride," said the boy, "I'll use the bike path every day."

> An **indirect quotation** does not require quotation marks.

RULE 11.4.2

INDIRECT QUOTATION
The boy said that when he learns to ride, he plans to use the bike path every day.

Both types of quotations are acceptable when you write. Direct quotations, however, generally result in a livelier writing style.

Using Direct Quotations With Introductory, Concluding, and Interrupting Expressions

A writer will generally identify a speaker by using words such as *he asked* or *she said* with a quotation. These expressions, called **conversational taglines** or **tags,** can introduce, conclude, or interrupt a quotation.

Direct Quotations With Introductory Expressions

Commas help you set off introductory information so that your reader understands who is speaking.

> **RULE 11.4.3**
>
> **Use a comma after short introductory expressions that precede direct quotations.**

EXAMPLE My sister warned**,** **"**If you borrow my cellphone, you'll be responsible for it.**"**

If the introductory conversational tagline is very long or formal in tone, set it off with a colon instead of a comma.

EXAMPLE At the end of the day**,** Tom spoke of his plans**:** **"**I plan to visit many countries to understand different cultures.**"**

Direct Quotations With Concluding Expressions

Conversational taglines may also act as concluding expressions.

> **RULE 11.4.4**
>
> **Use a comma, question mark, or exclamation mark after a direct quotation followed by a concluding expression.**

EXAMPLE **"**If you sign the contract**,** you'll be responsible for paying the rent**,** **"** the landlord warned**.**

Concluding expressions are not complete sentences; therefore, they do not begin with capital letters. Closing quotation marks are always placed outside the punctuation at the end of direct quotations. Concluding expressions generally end with a period.

Divided Quotations With Interrupting Expressions

You may use a conversational tagline to interrupt the words of a direct quotation, which is also called a **divided quotation.**

> Use a comma after the part of a quoted sentence followed by an interrupting conversational tagline. Use another comma after the tagline. Do not capitalize the first word of the rest of the sentence. Use quotation marks to enclose the quotation. End punctuation should be inside the last quotation mark.

 RULE 11.4.5

EXAMPLE   "If you sign the contract**,** " the landlord warned**,**
"you'll be responsible for paying the rent**.** "

> Use a comma, question mark, or exclamation mark after a quoted sentence that comes before an interrupting conversational tagline. Use a period after the tagline.

 RULE 11.4.6

EXAMPLE   "You signed the contract**,** " stated the landlord**.**
"You are responsible for paying the rent**.**"

Quotation Marks With Other Punctuation Marks

Quotation marks are used with commas, semicolons, colons, and all of the end marks. However, the location of the quotation marks in relation to the punctuation marks varies.

> Place a comma or a period *inside* the final quotation mark.
> Place a semicolon or colon *outside* the final quotation mark.

 RULE 11.4.7

EXAMPLES   "Kodie was the best dog**,** " sighed my mom.

EXAMPLES   We were recently informed about his
"groundbreaking novel **"** ; it was just published.

> Place a question mark or an exclamation mark inside the final quotation mark if the end mark is part of the quotation. Do not use an additional end mark.

RULE 11.4.8

EXAMPLE   Betty pondered**,** "How could I fail the test **?** "

RULE 11.4.9 Place a question mark or exclamation mark outside the final quotation mark if the end mark is part of the entire sentence, not part of the quotation.

EXAMPLE   We were appalled when he said, "No"!

Using Single Quotation Marks for Quotations Within Quotations

As you have learned, double quotation marks **(" ")** should enclose the main quotation in a sentence. The rules for using commas and end marks with double quotation marks also apply to **single quotation marks.**

RULE 11.4.10 Use **single quotation marks (' ')** to set off a quotation within a quotation.

EXAMPLES   "I remember John quoting Jane, 'If the day was longer we could do more work'" Bill said.

"The lawyer said, 'Great news!'" Alicia explained.

Punctuating Explanatory Material Within Quotations

Explanatory material within quotations should be placed in brackets. (See Section 11.7 for more information on brackets.)

RULE 11.4.11 Use brackets to enclose an explanation located within a quotation. The brackets show that the explanation is not part of the original quotation.

EXAMPLE   The president said, "This treaty is an agreement between two countries [France and Italy]."

See Practice 11.4A
See Practice 11.4B

PRACTICE 11.4A **Using Quotation Marks**

Read each sentence. Then, rewrite each sentence, inserting quotation marks where needed.

EXAMPLE   There is something wrong here, he said.

ANSWER   *"There is something wrong here," he said.*

1. Leonard asked, Who will be delivering the newspaper in the morning?

2. Throughout the play, the actor repeated the same line: Look into your heart.

3. Who borrowed my magazine? asked Dan.

4. I just heard a great song, remarked Jared.

5. You have to be careful, said his father, about walking the dog in the park.

6. Is that painting by Picasso? asked Susan.

7. Don't be late! Mom warned.

8. Ms. Kane replied, Plato once said, Science is nothing but perception.

9. Is it okay to say, See ya later?

10. The manager explained, The report should give details about the product [cellphones].

PRACTICE 11.4B **Revising for the Correct Use of Quotation Marks**

Read each sentence. Then, rewrite each sentence correcting the misuse of quotation marks.

EXAMPLE   "Beth told me to show up at eight o'clock, said Bill."

ANSWER   *"Beth told me to show up at eight o'clock," said Bill.*

11. "Who turned out all the lights"? asked Randy.

12. "I can see the sign, Pat informed us."

13. "Ralph just finished eating lunch, said Luther."

14. "Who, said Marcus, would not appreciate this music?"

15. "The word 'basically' is often overused" and can be unnecessary, said Tina.

16. Melissa asked "for my help," and I said Sure.

17. "Don't go down there", my mother told me, "you'll spoil the surprise."

18. "Ronald said, Not a chance!"

19. "The newest member of our team [Carrie] will play centerfield, said Coach Warren."

20. The story started with: 'Flopsy said to Flor' "I'm sleepy."

SPEAKING APPLICATION

Take turns with a partner. Say some sentences with direct quotes and other sentences with indirect quotes. Your partner should indicate which sentences would need quotation marks if they were written.

WRITING APPLICATION

Write five sentences with misused quotation marks. Exchange papers with a partner. Your partner should correct the misuse of the quotation marks.

Using Quotation Marks for Dialogue

A conversation between two or more people is called a **dialogue.**

> **When writing a dialogue, begin a new paragraph with each change of speaker.**

The sun slowly rose over the edge of the pink-sandy beach, as the waves lapped the shore.

Blake sat on the cool rock and talked with his sister about his plans.

"I'm going north," said Blake. "I think I'll like the weather better; you know I love to ski and snowboard."

"Have you started packing yet?" asked Kate. "Can I have your surfboard?"

"It's all yours," said Blake. "It is fine with me if I never use it again."

> **For quotations longer than a paragraph, put quotation marks at the beginning of each paragraph and at the end of the final paragraph.**

John McPhee wrote an essay about a canoe trip on the St. John River in northern Maine. He introduces his readers to the river in the following way:

"We have been out here four days now and rain has been falling three. The rain appears to be ending. Breaks of blue are opening in the sky. Sunlight is coming through, and a wind is rising.

"I was not prepared for the St. John River, did not anticipate its size. I saw it as a narrow trail flowing north, twisting through balsam and spruce—a small and intimate forest river, something like the Allagash . . . ."

Using Quotation Marks in Titles

Generally, quotation marks are used around the titles of shorter works.

> **Use quotation marks to enclose the titles of short written works.**

11.4.14 RULE

WRITTEN WORKS THAT USE QUOTATION MARKS	
Title of a Short Story	"The Raven" by Edgar Allen Poe "The Cask of Amontillado" by Edgar Allen Poe
Chapter From a Book	"Playing Pilgrims" in *Little Women* "The Laurence Boy" in *Little Women*
Title of a Short Poem	"The Road Not Taken" by Robert Frost
Essay Title	"Compensation" by Ralph Waldo Emerson
Title of an Article	"Collapse of the Bell Towers" by Barbie Nadeau

> **Use quotation marks around the titles of episodes in a television or radio series, songs, and parts of a long musical composition.**

11.4.15 RULE

ARTISTIC WORK TITLES THAT USE QUOTATION MARKS	
Episode	"Rendition" from *60 Minutes*
Song Title	"Born in the USA" by Bruce Springsteen
Part of a Long Musical Composition	"Spring" from The Four Seasons "E.T. Phone Home" from E.T. The Extra-Terrestrial soundtrack

> **Use quotation marks around the title of a work that is mentioned as part of a collection.**

11.4.16 RULE

The title *Plato* would normally be underlined or italicized. In the example below, however, the title is placed in quotation marks because it is cited as part of a larger work.

EXAMPLE   "Plato" from *Great Books of the Western World*

Using Underlining and Italics in Titles and Other Special Words

Underlining and **italics** help make titles and other special words and names stand out in your writing. Underlining is used only in handwritten or typewritten material. In printed material, italic (slanted) print is generally used instead of underlining.

RULE 11.4.17

> Underline or italicize the titles of long written works and the titles of publications that are published as a single work.

WRITTEN WORKS THAT ARE UNDERLINED OR ITALICIZED	
Title of a Book	*Little Women* *Oliver Twist*
Title of a Newspaper	*The Washington Post*
Title of a Play	*Macbeth* *Romeo and Juliet*
Title of a Long Poem	*Song on a May Morning*
Title of a Magazine	*The New Yorker*

The portion of a newspaper title that should be italicized or underlined will vary from newspaper to newspaper. *The New York Times* should always be fully capitalized and italicized or underlined. Other papers, however, can be treated in one of two ways: the *Los Angeles Times* or the Los Angeles *Times*. You may want to check the paper's Web site for correct formatting.

RULE 11.4.18

> Underline or italicize the titles of movies, television and radio series, long works of music, and works of art.

ARTISTIC WORKS THAT ARE UNDERLINED OR ITALICIZED	
Title of a Movie	*Gone with the Wind* *West Side Story*
Title of a Television Series	*M*A*S*H, I Love Lucy*
Title of a Long Work of Music	*Symphony No. 3 in E flat Major*
Title of an Album (on any media)	*Love Me Tender*
Title of a Painting	*The Last Supper, Woman*
Title of a Sculpture	*David, Venus De Milo*

RULE

Do not underline, italicize, or place in quotation marks the name of the Bible, its books and divisions, or other holy scriptures, such as the Torah and the Qu'ran.

11.4.19

EXAMPLE   Ben read from Psalms in the Old Testament.

Government documents should also not be underlined or enclosed in quotation marks.

RULE

Do not underline, italicize, or place in quotation marks the titles of government charters, alliances, treaties, acts, statutes, speeches, or reports.

11.4.20

EXAMPLE   The Taft-Hartley Labor Act was passed in 1947.

RULE

Underline or italicize the names of air, sea, and space craft.

11.4.21

EXAMPLE   We saw the *Apollo IX* module.

RULE

Underline or italicize words, letters, or numbers (figures) used as names for themselves.

11.4.22

EXAMPLES   Her *i's* and her *I's* look too much like *1's*.

Avoid sprinkling your speech with *like*.

RULE

Underline or italicize foreign words and phrases not yet accepted into English.

11.4.23

See Practice 11.4C
See Practice 11.4D

EXAMPLE   "*Buenos noches*," she said, meaning "goodnight" in Spanish.

PRACTICE 11.4C **Using Punctuation in Titles and Dialogue**

Read each sentence. Then, rewrite each sentence, adding correct punctuation where needed. If any words need to be italicized, underline those words.

EXAMPLE   Tanya said Please hurry!

ANSWER   *Tanya said, "Please hurry!"*

1. When does the first train depart? asked Vince.

2. "Tanya replied, In one hour."

3. "It's not exactly the Orient Express, is it? Vince commented."

4. Tanya said, We can read during the ride. I'm bringing To Kill a Mockingbird.

5. I'll bring Newsweek, Vince said.

6. All last month, said John, we read Macbeth in English class.

7. Tonight, Professor McCarthy gives his lecture How Humans Cure the Blues.

8. Ramond's CD More to Come is receiving excellent reviews.

9. "Carly said, My favorite painting is Monet's Waterlilies."

10. Abe replied, "I like classical music, like Debussy's Clair de Lune."

PRACTICE 11.4D **Revising Punctuation in Titles and Dialogue**

Read each sentence. Then, rewrite the sentence using correct punctuation. If any words need to be italicized, underline those words.

EXAMPLE   Lana said "My favorite book is Jane Eyre."

ANSWER   *Lana said, "My favorite book is Jane Eyre."*

11. I have a copy of van Gogh's painting Sunflowers, said Sam.

12. "I've heard the song Starry, Starry Night about Vincent Van Gogh, said Monica."

13. My favorite painting is Lucas by Chuck Close said Martha.

14. Have you seen Rodin's sculpture The Thinker? asked Juan.

15. Grant calls his sculpture The Athlete said Nina.

16. I received an A for that sculpture, Grant told us.

17. We're reading Romeo and Juliet in class, Drew informed everyone.

18. Toward the end of the movie The Usual Suspects Karl said, is when the plot starts to twist.

19. Did you see last night's episode of Galaxy Wars? asked Jim.

20. Monica informed us, "The last boat to leave the dock was the Sea Lion."

SPEAKING APPLICATION

Take turns with a partner. Say sentences that contain both dialogue and titles. For each sentence, your partner should indicate which words should be put in quotation marks and/or italicized.

WRITING APPLICATION

Write an essay that uses sarcasm or irony in the plot, the setting, or the main character(s). Include two uses of italics in your essay. Be sure to use correct punctuation, including quotation marks to indicate sarcasm or irony.

11.5 Hyphens

The **hyphen (-)** is used to combine words, spell some numbers and words, and show a connection between the syllables of words that are broken at the ends of lines.

Using Hyphens in Numbers

Hyphens are used to join compound numbers and fractions.

> **Use a hyphen when you spell out two-word numbers from twenty-one through ninety-nine.**

RULE 11.5.1

EXAMPLES   twenty-two centimeters   seventy-seven feet

> **Use a hyphen when you use a fraction as an adjective but not when you use a fraction as a noun.**

RULE 11.5.2

ADJECTIVE   The recipe calls for one-half cup of flour.

NOUN   Three quarters of the movie is already over.

> **Use a hyphen between a number and a word when they are combined as modifiers. Do not use a hyphen if the word in the modifier is possessive.**

RULE 11.5.3

EXAMPLES   The coach called a 15-minute timeout.

The editors put 12 months' work into the book.

> **If a series of consecutive, hyphenated modifiers ends with the same word, do not repeat the modified word each time. Instead, use a suspended hyphen (also called a dangling hyphen) and the modified word only at the end of the series.**

RULE 11.5.4

EXAMPLE   The ninth- and tenth-grade students came.

Using Hyphens With Prefixes and Suffixes

Hyphens help your reader easily see the parts of a long word.

RULE 11.5.5

> **Use a hyphen after a prefix that is followed by a proper noun or proper adjective.**

The following prefixes are often used before proper nouns: *ante-, anti-, mid-, post-, pre-, pro-,* and *un-.*

EXAMPLES   pre - World War II   mid - May

RULE 11.5.6

> **Use a hyphen in words with the prefixes *all-, ex-,* and *self-* and words with the suffix *-elect.***

EXAMPLES   ex - president   president - elect

Many words with common prefixes are no longer hyphenated. Check a dictionary if you are unsure whether to use a hyphen.

Using Hyphens With Compound Words

Hyphens help preserve the units of meaning in compound words.

RULE 11.5.7

> **Use a hyphen to connect two or more words that are used as one compound word, unless your dictionary gives a different spelling.**

EXAMPLES   editor - in - chief   re - election
            daughter - in - law   not - for - profit

RULE 11.5.8

> **Use a hyphen to connect a compound modifier that appears before a noun. The exceptions to this rule include adverbs ending in *-ly* and compound proper adjectives or compound proper nouns that are acting as an adjective.**

EXAMPLES WITH HYPHENS	EXAMPLES WITHOUT HYPHENS
a well-made pair of boots	widely distributed reports
the bright-eyed student	Native American children
an up-to-date report	a highly unlikely suspect

When compound modifiers follow a noun, they generally do not require the use of hyphens.

EXAMPLE   The boots were **well made.**

However, if a dictionary spells a word with a hyphen, the word must always be hyphenated, even when it follows a noun.

EXAMPLE   The score was up-to-date.

Using Hyphens for Clarity

Some words or group of words can be misread if a hyphen is not used.

> **Use a hyphen within a word when a combination of letters might otherwise be confusing.**

RULE **11.5.9**

EXAMPLES   worn-out, write-off, year-end

> **Use a hyphen between words to keep readers from combining them incorrectly.**

RULE **11.5.10**

See Practice 11.5A

See Practice 11.5B

INCORRECT   the mail delivery-carrier

CORRECT   the mail-delivery carrier

PRACTICE 11.5A > Using Hyphens Correctly

Read each sentence. Then, write the words that need hyphenation, adding hyphens where necessary.

EXAMPLE   Manuel lived in a high rise building.

ANSWER   *high-rise*

1. There is a clear cut reason that a life jacket is worn on a boat.

2. The free throw shot was a last ditch effort to win the game.

3. We bought our skiis at an offseason sale.

4. I had to add three quarters of a gallon of oil to my car.

5. The film crew took a 15 day hiatus.

6. My mother in law devised a good game plan.

7. The so called expert mishandled restoring the priceless portrait.

8. David told me one third of the school's computers have virusrelated problems.

9. The announcement will be made in mid July.

10. Tracy had a bird's eye view of the outfield.

PRACTICE 11.5B > Revising Sentences With Hyphens

Read each sentence. Then, rewrite the sentence correcting any error in the use of a hyphen. If the punctuation is correct, write *correct*.

EXAMPLE   Can you believe this scarf is hand-made?

ANSWER   *Can you believe this scarf is handmade?*

11. You need to make a U turn at the next intersection.

12. I had a short lived-career as a song-writer.

13. If Kyle wins one more time, he is in the semi-final of the tournament.

14. The teacher assigned extra credit homework to any interested student.

15. Richard was twenty six when he bought a dog.

16. This is our best-selling jukebox.

17. Attending the event is a once in a lifetime opportunity.

18. We need an all purpose cleanser for this house-work.

19. The mayor elect will walk in the parade.

20. The sound-effects at the movie theater come from top of the line speakers.

SPEAKING APPLICATION

Take turns with a partner. Use hyphenated words in sentences about your school. Your partner should listen for and identify which words need hyphens.

WRITING APPLICATION

Write a paragraph about what you may be doing seven years in the future. Use at least three hyphenated words not used in Practice 11.5B in your paragraph.

Using Hyphens at the Ends of Lines

Hyphens help you keep the lines in your paragraphs more even, making your work easier to read.

Dividing Words at the End of a Line

Although you should try to avoid dividing a word at the end of a line, if a word must be broken, use a hyphen to show the division.

> **If a word must be divided at the end of a line, always divide it between syllables.**

RULE 11.5.11

EXAMPLE   The brave soldiers had been sending letters to their families describing their base.

> **A hyphen used to divide a word should never be placed at the beginning of the second line. It must be placed at the end of the first line.**

RULE 11.5.12

INCORRECT   The workers and volunteers made a very de
-tailed plan for the search.

CORRECT   The workers and volunteers made a very detailed plan for the search.

Using Hyphens Correctly to Divide Words

One-syllable words cannot be divided.

> **Do not divide one-syllable words even if they seem long or sound like words with two syllables.**

RULE 11.5.13

INCORRECT   ri-dge   ho-use   lod-ge
CORRECT   ridge   house   lodge

RULE 11.5.14 Do not divide a word so that a single letter or the letters *-ed* stand alone.

| INCORRECT | a-dept | read-y | e-ject | abash-ed |
| CORRECT | adept | ready | eject | abashed |

RULE 11.5.15 Avoid dividing proper nouns and proper adjectives.

| INCORRECT | Hea-ther | Is-rael |
| CORRECT | Heather | Israel |

RULE 11.5.16 Divide a hyphenated word only after the hyphen.

| INCORRECT | We are planning a party with my sis-ter-in-law next week. |
| CORRECT | We are planning a party with my sister-in-law next week. |

RULE 11.5.17 Avoid dividing a word so that part of the word is on one page and the remainder is on the next page.

Often, chopping up a word in this way will confuse your readers or cause them to lose their train of thought. If this happens, rewrite the sentence or move the entire word to the next page.

See Practice 11.5C
See Practice 11.5D

PRACTICE 11.5C > Writing Correctly Divided Words

Read each group of divided words. Then, write the word in each group that is not correctly divided with the correct hyphenation, or write it as one word if it should not be divided.

EXAMPLE   per-son   fol-low   suburb-an

ANSWER   *subur-ban*

1. clo-ak   mys-tery   fol-low
2. embar-rass   fak-ed   em-balm
3. Donn-a   flow-er   mother-in-law
4. rain-y   peti-tion   shut-ter
5. bell-owed   char-acter   pat-ted
6. mar-shall   tap-ped   self-ser-vice
7. can-dle   ap-ple   o-ver
8. clum-sy   Ste-vens   offi-cer
9. comp-lete   mov-able   de-linquent
10. se-vere   no-tion   far-mer

PRACTICE 11.5D > Using Hyphens to Divide Words

Read each sentence. If the word at the end of the line has not been correctly hyphenated, then divide the word correctly, or write it as one word.

EXAMPLE   The congressional committee deb-ated all sides of the argument.

ANSWER   *de-bated*

11. My mother and father are celebra-ting their wedding anniversary.
12. Above the treetops, I could see the Olym-pic flag moving in the wind.
13. Aunt Mary offen sends souvenirs fr-om the countries she visits.
14. The name of the student who won is Ann-ette Chima.
15. My brother, sister, cousin, and I had a lov-ely time vacationing in Aruba last summer.
16. My favorite things to do outdoors are runn-ing, cycling, and swimming.
17. I have realized that it is necessary to e-valuate my options before making a decision.
18. The nervous girl looked down self-con-sciously and blushed.
19. Micah's brother is known to borrow man-y of Micah's things.
20. Even though I was on vacation, she call-ed me every day.

SPEAKING APPLICATION

Take turns with a partner. Say ten words not found in Practice 11.5C. Your partner should tell where each word can be divided.

WRITING APPLICATION

Write five sentences that include an incorrectly divided word at the end of a line. Exchange papers with a partner. Your partner should correct your sentences so that they are divided correctly.

11.6 Apostrophes

The **apostrophe (')** is used to form possessives, contractions, and a few special plurals.

Using Apostrophes to Form Possessive Nouns

Apostrophes are used with nouns to show ownership or possession.

RULE 11.6.1 **Add an apostrophe and -s to show the possessive case of most singular nouns.**

EXAMPLES   the tie of the man   the man**'**s tie

the tail of the dog   the dog**'**s tail

Even when a singular noun already ends in -*s,* you can usually add an apostrophe and -*s* to show possession. However, names that end in the *eez* sound get an apostrophe, but no -*s.*

EXAMPLE   The Ganges**'** source is in the Himalayas.

For classical references that end in -*s,* only an apostrophe is used.

EXAMPLES   Moses**'** brother   Zeus**'** thunderbolt

RULE 11.6.2 **Add an apostrophe to show the possessive case of plural nouns ending in -s or -es.**

EXAMPLE   the scent of the foxes   the foxes**'** scent

RULE 11.6.3 **Add an apostrophe and an -s to show the possessive case of plural nouns that do not end in -s or -es.**

EXAMPLE the songs of the choir

the choir's songs

> Add an apostrophe and *-s* (or just an apostrophe if the word is a plural ending in *-s*) to the last word of a compound noun to form the possessive.

RULE 11.6.4

APOSTROPHES THAT SHOW POSSESSION	
Names of Businesses and Organizations	the All-Sports Company's central office the Navy Officer's Club the Dean of Students' office
Titles of Rulers or Leaders	Catherine the Great's victories Louis XVI's palace the president of the college's decision
Hyphenated Compound Nouns Used to Describe People	my father-in-law's house the secretary-treasurer's notes the nurse-practitioner's manager

> To form possessives involving time, amounts, or the word *sake,* use an apostrophe and an *-s* or just an apostrophe if the possessive is plural.

RULE 11.6.5

APOSTROPHES WITH POSSESSIVES	
Time	a week's vacation four days' vacation an hour's time
Amount	one gallon's worth five cents' worth
Sake	for Benjamin's sake for goodness' sake

RULE 11.6.6

To show joint ownership, make the final noun possessive.
To show individual ownership, make each noun possessive.

JOINT
OWNERSHIP

I enjoyed Rita and Blane's movie.

INDIVIDUAL
OWNERSHIP

Rory's and Beth's shoes are sitting here.

Use the owner's complete name before the apostrophe to form the possessive case.

INCORRECT
SINGULAR

Kri's house

CORRECT
SINGULAR

Kris's house

INCORRECT
PLURAL

three girl's shoes

CORRECT
PLURAL

three girls' shoes

Using Apostrophes With Pronouns

Both indefinite and personal pronouns can show possession.

RULE 11.6.7

Use an apostrophe and -s with indefinite pronouns to show possession.

EXAMPLES

somebody's work boots

each other's addresses

RULE 11.6.8

Do not use an apostrophe with possessive personal pronouns; their form already shows ownership.

EXAMPLES

her albums	our car	her blue shoes
its windows	their house	whose house

Be careful not to confuse the contractions *who's, it's,* and *they're* with possessive pronouns. They are contractions for *who is, it is* or *it has,* and *they are.* Remember also that *whose, its,* and *their* show possession.

PRONOUNS	CONTRACTIONS
Whose homework is this?	*Who's* coming to dinner?
Its tires were all flat.	*It's* going to snow.
Their dinner is ready.	*They're* coming to dinner.

Using Apostrophes to Form Contractions

Contractions are used in informal speech and writing. You can often find contractions in the dialogue of stories and plays; they often create the sound of real speech.

> Use an apostrophe in a **contraction** to show the position of the missing letter or letters.

11.6.9 RULE

COMMON CONTRACTIONS			
Verb + *not*	cannot could not	can't couldn't	are not will not	aren't won't
Pronoun + *will*	he will you will she will	he'll you'll she'll	I will we will they will	I'll we'll they'll
Pronoun + *would*	she would he would you would	she'd he'd you'd	I would we would they would	I'd we'd they'd
Noun or Pronoun + *be*	you are she is they are	you're she's they're	I am Jane is dog is	I'm Jane's dog's

Still another type of contraction is found in poetry.

EXAMPLES   e'en *(even)*   o'er *(over)*

Other contractions represent the abbreviated form of *of the* and *the* as they are written in several different languages. These letters are most often combined with surnames.

EXAMPLES   O'Reilly

d'Martino

o'clock

l'Abbé

Using Contractions to Represent Speaking Styles
A final use of contractions is for representing individual speaking styles in dialogue. As noted previously, you will often want to use contractions with verbs in dialogue. You may also want to approximate a regional dialect or a foreign accent, which may include nonstandard pronunciations of words or omitted letters. However, you should avoid overusing contractions in dialogue. Overuse reduces the effectiveness of the apostrophe.

EXAMPLES   "Hey, ol' buddy. How you feelin'?"

"Don' you be foolin' me."

Using Apostrophes to Create Special Plurals

Apostrophes can help avoid confusion with special plurals.

> Use an apostrophe and *-s* to create the plural form of a letter, numeral, symbol, or a word that is used as a name for itself.

EXAMPLES   *A*'s and *an*'s cause confusion.

There are three *9*'s in that number.

I don't like to hear *if*'s or *maybe*'s.

Form groups of *3*'s or *4*'s.

You have three *?*'s in a row.

See Practice 11.6A
See Practice 11.6B

PRACTICE 11.6A Identifying the Use of Apostrophes

Read each sentence. Then, tell if each apostrophe is used to form a *possessive*, a *contraction*, a *speaking style*, or a *special plural*.

EXAMPLE Who is the party's candidate for mayor this year?

ANSWER *possessive*

1. I watched as the boy's hat blew away in the wind.

2. The man tipped his hat and said, "Good evening, Li'l Lady."

3. The towing company removed the owner's car from where it was illegally parked.

4. He'll be back tomorrow.

5. Queen Victoria's reign was supreme.

6. I received all *A*'s this semester.

7. Snow covered the houses' roofs on my block.

8. The dog's out in the yard.

9. The house address contains two *4*'s.

10. The wind told the naughty children, "Stop your fightin'."

PRACTICE 11.6B Revising to Add Apostrophes

Read each sentence. Then, rewrite each sentence, adding apostrophes as needed.

EXAMPLE Its been hectic, but Ive had fun playing in the school band this year.

ANSWER *It's been hectic, but I've had fun playing in the school band this year.*

11. Didnt he say what time he would arrive at Davids party?

12. Its such a beautiful day; well take a walk around the block.

13. She said the wallet Jim found was hers, but she couldnt describe what was inside it.

14. There are too many *ifs* and *ands* in her essay.

15. The dogs bark was worse than its bite.

16. The suns rays warmed my face.

17. Uncle John just returned from his only nieces recital.

18. We need to pick up Mr. ODonnell at OHare Airport at seven oclock.

19. Jacks car, a vintage model, is his most prized possession.

20. Why cant we stay up a little longer?

SPEAKING APPLICATION

Take turns with a partner. Say sentences with words that indicate possession, contractions, special plurals, or speaking styles. Your partner should identify how each word uses an apostrophe.

WRITING APPLICATION

Write five sentences that correctly use apostrophes to show possession, contractions, or plurals of letters or numbers.

11.7 Parentheses and Brackets

Parentheses enclose explanations or other information that may be omitted from the rest of the sentence without changing its basic meaning or construction. Using parentheses is a stronger, more noticeable way to set off a parenthetical expression than using commas. **Brackets** are used to enclose a word or phrase added by a writer to the words of another.

Parentheses

Parentheses help you group material within a sentence.

> **Use parentheses to set off information when the material is not essential or when it consists of one or more sentences.**

EXAMPLE   The challenge of climbing the mountain **(** as they learned from the other teams **)** was more difficult than they thought.

> **Use parentheses to set off numerical explanations such as dates of a person's birth and death and around numbers and letters marking a series.**

EXAMPLES   Jim McNash sailed around the world with the help of his friend, John L. Smith **(** 1950–2005 **)**.

Go to the store and pick up these items: **(** 1 **)** compass, **(** 2 **)** tent, **(** 3 **)** hiking boots.

Who painted the Sistine Chapel: **(** a **)** Michelangelo, **(** b **)** DaVinci, or **(** c **)** Monet?

Although material enclosed in parentheses is not essential to the meaning of the sentence, a writer indicates that the material is important and calls attention to it by using parentheses.

> **When a phrase or declarative sentence interrupts another sentence, do not use an initial capital letter or end mark inside the parentheses.**

EXAMPLE   Bill finally finished his project (we all watched from the beginning) at the end of the fair.

> **When a question or exclamation interrupts another sentence, use both an initial capital letter and an end mark inside the parentheses.**

EXAMPLE   Serena (She is a fantastic runner !) finished first.

> **When you place a sentence in parentheses between two other sentences, use both an initial capital letter and an end mark inside the parentheses.**

EXAMPLE   New York is known for its fabulous museums. (See the Museum of Natural History as an example .) History is interesting to learn about.

> **In a sentence that includes parentheses, place any punctuation belonging to the main sentence after the final parenthesis.**

EXAMPLE   The town council approved the stadium changes (after some debate) , and they explained where the new stadium would be built (with some doubts about how the changes will be received) .

Special Uses of Parentheses

Parentheses are also used to set off numerical explanations such as dates of a person's birth and death and numbers or letters marking a series.

EXAMPLES   Michelangelo **(**1475-1564**)** was a famous Italian painter.

Alan's phone number is **(**909**)** 963-9644.

Her study abroad will take her to **(**1**)** France, **(**2**)** Italy, and **(**3**)** England.

Brackets

Brackets are used to enclose a word or phrase added by a writer to the words of another writer.

> **Use brackets to enclose words you insert in quotations when quoting someone else.**

EXAMPLES   Cooper noted: "And with *[E.T.'s]* success, 'Phone home' is certain to become one of the most often repeated phrases of the year **[**1982**]**."

"The results of this vote **[**75–5**]** indicate overwhelming support for our new council person," he stated.

The Latin expression *sic* (meaning "thus") is sometimes enclosed in brackets to show that the author of the quoted material has misspelled or mispronounced a word or phrase.

EXAMPLE   Michaelson, citing Dorothy's signature line from *The Wizard of Oz,* wrote, "Theirs **[**sic**]** no place like home."

See Practice 11.7A
See Practice 11.7B

PRACTICE 11.7A > Using Parentheses and Brackets Correctly

Read each item. Then, rewrite each sentence, adding the items indicated in parentheses. The items can be placed in parentheses or brackets.

EXAMPLE   Your essay is on my desk.
           (all ten pages of it)

ANSWER   *Your essay (all ten pages of it)
           is on my desk.*

1. He finally answered the phone.
   (huffing and puffing)

2. The men in question deserve awards.
   (Jack White, Ted Inge, and Craig Erezuma)

3. "He was a nown celebrity in town." (sic)

4. Some writers don't use word processing programs. (including myself)

5. The statement was made by President Jimmy Carter. (former)

6. Jack bought the tickets. (who is a big football fan)

7. "The school is two miles from the hospital, and three from the police station." (miles)

8. "I'll call you tomorrow." (Friday)

9. I smiled when I saw the expression on his face. (and my heart skipped a beat)

10. She whispered the secret word. (joyful)

PRACTICE 11.7B > Revising to Add or Parentheses or Brackets

Read each sentence. Then, rewrite each sentence, adding parentheses or brackets where needed.

EXAMPLE   "The prize money $500 was donated."

ANSWER   *"The prize money [$500] was
           donated."*

11. Before it could reach the station, the old train a relic of frontier days broke down.

12. "The mayor Joe Roy attended the ceremony and gave a warm speech."

13. We saw it the ball and ducked.

14. Please read this information I enclosed it as Attachment A.

15. He is a former officer admiral in the Navy.

16. According to the law, the Holmes property that borders Crystal Lake belongs to a Native American tribe.

17. "The robber put the monie sic in the bag."

18. This contract promises that we will 1 deliver the refrigerator, 2 install the refrigerator, and 3 take away the old refrigerator.

19. The witness said, "I saw him the defendant coming out of the back door."

20. The movie a box-office hit was made with a shoe-string budget and no catering!.

SPEAKING APPLICATION

Discuss with a partner the difference between using parentheses and using brackets. What would the consequence be if they were used interchangeably?

WRITING APPLICATION

Write five sentences. Then, have a partner tell you some additional information to add to each sentence. Rewrite each sentence, including the additional information in brackets or parentheses.

11.8 Ellipses, Dashes, and Slashes

An **ellipsis** (. . .) shows where words have been omitted from a quoted passage. It can also mark a pause or interruption in dialogue. A **dash** (—) shows a strong, sudden break in thought or speech. A **slash** (/) separates numbers in dates and fractions, shows line breaks in quoted poetry, and represents *or*. A slash is also used to separate the parts of a Web address.

Using the Ellipsis

An **ellipsis** is three evenly spaced periods, or ellipsis points, in a row. Always include a space before the first ellipsis point, between ellipsis points, and after the last ellipsis point. (The plural of *ellipsis* is *ellipses*.)

RULE 11.8.1

> Use an **ellipsis** to show where words have been omitted from a quoted passage.

ELLIPSES IN QUOTATIONS	
The Entire Quotation	"The Black River, which cuts a winding course through southern Missouri's rugged Ozark highlands, lends its name to an area of great natural beauty. Within this expanse are old mines and quarries to explore, fast-running waters to canoe, and wooded trails to ride."—Suzanne Charle
At the Beginning	Suzanne Charle described the Black River area in Missouri as having " . . . old mines and quarries to explore, fast-running waters to canoe, and wooded trails to ride."
In the Middle	Suzanne Charle wrote, "The Black River . . . lends its name to an area of great natural beauty. Within this expanse are old mines and quarries to explore, fast-running waters to canoe, and wooded trails to ride."
At the End	Suzanne Charle wrote, "The Black River, which cuts a winding course through southern Missouri's rugged Ozark highlands, lends its name to an area of great natural beauty . . . "

11.8.2 RULE

Use an ellipsis to mark a pause in a dialogue or speech.

EXAMPLE   The director shouted, "Ready . . . and . . . action!"

Dashes

A **dash** signals a stronger, more sudden interruption in thought or speech than commas or parentheses. A dash may also take the place of certain words before an explanation. Overuse of the dash diminishes its effectiveness. Consider the proper use of the dash in the rule below.

Use **dashes** to indicate an abrupt change of thought, a dramatic interrupting idea, or a summary statement.

11.8.3 RULE

USING DASHES IN WRITING	
To indicate an abrupt change of thought	The book doesn't provide enough information on the Netherlands—by the way, where did you buy the book?
	I cannot believe how many answers my sister missed—she doesn't even want to talk about it.
To set off interrupting ideas dramatically	The palace was built—you may find this hard to believe—in one year.
	The palace was built—Where did they get the resources?—in one year.
To set off a summary statement	An excellent academic record and great test scores—if you have these, you may be able to get into an Ivy League college.
	To see her name printed in the program—this was her greatest dream.

Use **dashes** to set off a **nonessential appositive** or modifier
when it is long, when it is already punctuated, or when you
want to be dramatic.

APPOSITIVE   The cause of the damage to the screen and the
windows—a strong gust of wind—whipped
through the house.

MODIFIER   The sports writer—bored with writing about
overpaid athletes—quit the following week.

Dashes may be used to set off one other special type of sentence
interrupter—the parenthetical expression.

Use **dashes** to set off a **parenthetical expression** when it is
long, already punctuated, or especially dramatic.

EXAMPLE   Today, we visited an art museum—what a
fascinating place—set in the middle of a
large city.

Slashes

A **slash** is used to separate numbers in dates and fractions, lines
of quoted poetry, or options. Slashes are also used to separate
parts of a Web address.

Use slashes to separate the day, month, and year in dates
and to separate the numerator and denominator in numerical
fractions.

DATES   She listed her employment date as 9/01/09.

I left on my trip on 8/07/09.

FRACTIONS   4/5   2/3   1/2

Use slashes to indicate line breaks in up to three lines of quoted poetry in continuous text. Insert a space on each side of the slash.

EXAMPLE   I used a quote from William Blake, "Tyger! Tyger! burning bright. **/** In the forests of the night," to begin my paper.

Use slashes to separate choices or options and to represent the words *and* and *or*.

EXAMPLES   Choose your topping: apples **/** nuts **/** syrup.

Each owner should bring a leash and treats **/** food.

You can type and **/** or hand-write the last page of the essay.

Use slashes to separate parts of a Web address.

EXAMPLES   http: **//** www.fafsa.ed.gov **/**
(for financial aid for students)

http: **//** www.whitehouse.gov **/**
(the White House)

http: **//** www.si.edu **/**
(the Smithsonian Institution)

See Practice 11.8A
See Practice 11.8B

Read each sentence. Then, rewrite each sentence, adding dashes, slashes, or ellipses where appropriate.

EXAMPLE   The measurement must be within 1 8 of an inch.

ANSWER   *The measurement must be within 1/8 of an inch.*

1. "I was just wondering" Gia mused.

2. The pandas at the zoo they are so playful are the main attraction.

3. There is one thing actually several things that I need to tell you.

4. Sarah bought a new pet a guinea pig.

5. We only need 3 4 of a yard of that blue material.

6. I listened carefully as the teacher read Lincoln's inaugural address: "Four score and seven years ago."

7. You will need a pen pencil.

8. There was only one thing to do surrender.

9. The movie went on and on.

10. I ended my paper with a quote from a poem by Edgar Allan Poe, "All that we see or seem/ Is but a dream within a dream."

Read each sentence. Then, use the appropriate punctuation to add or delete the information in parentheses to or from each sentence.

EXAMPLE   Mr. Lewis is a kind, fair, and knowledgeable teacher. (Delete kind, fair, and.)

ANSWER   *Mr. Lewis is a . . . knowledgeable teacher.*

11. Jeff or Jim may return by train. (Add *and*.)

12. The new secretary must be prepared to do a great deal of work. (Add *Lisa*.)

13. The regulation states, "All agencies must document overtime or risk losing federal funds." (Delete *or risk losing federal funds*.)

14. My cousin Jeff is coming to visit. (Add *my favorite relative*.)

15. Many people will attend the Fourth of July festivities. (Add *Independence Day*.)

16. We will invite Susan to our party. (Add *she is the new girl next door*.)

17. Miss Jones is a special guest of my mother. (Add *former college roommate*.)

18. The hungry lion roared. (Delete *roared*.)

19. Grandfather remembers when bread cost a dime. (Add *but that was a long time ago*.)

20. All the presentations were excellent. (Add *speeches*.)

SPEAKING APPLICATION

Take turns with a partner. Say different sentences that would use ellipses, dashes, or slashes if they were written. Your partner should indicate which punctuation each of your sentences needs.

WRITING APPLICATION

Use sentences 11, 14, and 18 as models to write similar sentences. Exchange papers with a partner. Your partner should use the appropriate punctuation to add or delete information to or from your sentences.

Using Periods, Question Marks, and Exclamation Marks

Read each sentence. Rewrite each sentence, adding question marks, periods, and exclamation marks where needed.

1. What an incredible movie that was

2. Take out the garbage

3. How many classes are you taking this year

4. He asked if I knew anyone who could help out with the production

5. Mark Lucas, Sr, took the long way home after work

6. Listen when I am talking to you

7. School was canceled today Why

8. How nice it is that we can all get together this weekend

9. Is someone helping you prepare for the big meeting

10. Oh You scared me

PRACTICE 2 > **Using Commas Correctly**

Read each sentence. Rewrite each sentence, adding commas where needed. If a sentence is correct as is, write *correct*.

1. I went to the store but I forgot the list.

2. Sam and Erica met each other at the main gate of the stadium.

3. Losing little time he grabbed his cellphone and dialed 911.

4. The exam included multiple choice short answer and essay questions.

5. The show was a dazzling exciting event.

6. He yelled up the stairs "Mom are you coming down soon?"

7. The party started at 7 not at 8.

8. The Declaration of Independence was signed on July 4 1776.

9. "Her address is 27 Spring Street Lakeville Iowa 35675" Ron said.

10. I thought that happened in May 2003.

PRACTICE 3 > **Using Colons, Semicolons, and Quotation Marks**

Read each sentence. Rewrite each sentence, using colons, semicolons, and quotation marks where needed. If a sentence is correct as is, write *correct*.

1. I am not needed there tonight I am staying at home instead.

2. This radio station plays all kinds of music jazz, pop, country, and R&B.

3. My favorite poem, replied Connie, is Dream Deferred by Langston Hughes.

4. The students told us their favorite subjects Jane English Todd chemistry and Eric history.

5. Will had a great first day of work his new co-workers are really friendly.

6. He didn't need to say anything more I could read his expression from a mile away.

7. Please don't be late, my mother implored. The train leaves at exactly 356.

8. Maria was a little early however, she waited for everyone else to arrive.

9. Caution Falling rock zone ahead.

10. She told me how much she enjoyed my singing.

Continued on next page ▶

Cumulative Review Chapters 10–11

Using Apostrophes

Read each sentence. Rewrite each sentence, using apostrophes where needed. If a sentence is correct as is, write *correct*.

1. Caras aunt owns two large beauty salons on the south side of town.

2. Frost's poetry is read by many students today.

3. Artemis hunting tools are often depicted alongside the goddess.

4. My mother-in-laws house is always filled with people for the holidays.

5. Susie always adds her two cents to any discussion.

6. Whos in charge here because its not me.

7. He wouldnt dream of taking his sisters car without her permission.

8. I can't say for certain if he's coming to Chris's holiday party.

9. School starts promptly at 7 oclock every morning.

10. Its not that she doesnt want to be here; its that she hasnt got enough time to attend every meeting.

PRACTICE 5 **Using Underlining (or Italics), Hyphens, Dashes, Slashes, Parentheses, Brackets, and Ellipses**

Read each sentence. Rewrite each sentence, adding underlining (or italics), hyphens, dashes, slashes, brackets, parentheses, or ellipses. If a sentence is correct as is, write *correct*.

1. This May will be my grandparents' forty fifth wedding anniversary.

2. Arthur's essay describes how "it the Grand Canyon is the most amazing natural treasure in the United States."

3. Amelia's mother she came to the United States when she was a girl told us tales of her journey.

4. Did you ever see the film it's a classic Gone With the Wind?

5. Air Force One is the airplane used by the president.

6. I will see the show on 10 21 2009.

7. The cross country trip unbelievable as it may be only took them one week.

8. This novel is set during Reconstruction 1865–1877.

9. The Pledge of Allegiance is an oath that begins, "I pledge to the flag of the United States of America."

10. Her father a world-renowned author wrote many memorable novels.

PRACTICE 6 **Using Capital Letters Correctly**

Read each sentence. Rewrite each sentence, using capital letters where they are needed.

1. this tuesday i have an important meeting with the board of education.

2. he won the pulitzer prize last year for his article on the republican party, published in *the new york times*.

3. "is your mother english," stephanie asked, "or is she australian?"

4. "the directions say to go south, past interstate 95," Michael read, "and I think we'll drive by springfield."

5. this fall we are going to the pumpkin festival in vermont.

Modes
of Writing

Writing is a process that begins with the exploration of ideas and ends with the presentation of a final piece of writing. Often, the types of writing we do are grouped into modes according to their form and purpose.

Narration

Whenever writers tell any type of story, they are using narration. Most narratives share certain elements, such as characters, a setting, a sequence of events, and, often, a theme. The following are some types of narration:

● **Autobiographical Writing** Autobiographical writing tells a true story about an important period, experience, or relationship in the writer's life.

Effective autobiographical writing includes:

- *A series of events that involve the writer as the main character*
- *Details, thoughts, feelings, and insights from the writer's perspective*
- *A conflict or an event that affects the writer*
- *A logical organization that tells the story clearly*

Types of autobiographical writing include personal narratives, autobiographical sketches, reflective essays, eyewitness accounts, and memoirs.

● **Short Story** A short story is a brief, creative narrative.

Most short stories contain:

- *Details that establish the setting in time and place*
- *A main character who undergoes a change or learns something during the course of the story*
- *A conflict or a problem to be introduced, developed, and resolved*
- *A plot—the series of events that make up the action of the story*
- *A theme or message about life*

Types of short stories include realistic stories, fantasies, historical narratives, mysteries, thrillers, science fiction, and adventure stories.

Description

Descriptive writing is writing that creates a vivid picture of a person, place, thing, or event.

Most descriptive writing includes:
- *Sensory details—sights, sounds, smells, tastes, and physical sensations*
- *Vivid, precise language*
- *Figurative language or comparisons*
- *Adjectives and adverbs that help to paint a word picture*
- *An organization suited to the subject*

Types of descriptive writing include description of ideas, observations, travel brochures, physical descriptions, functional descriptions, remembrances, and character sketches.

Persuasion

Persuasion is writing or speaking that attempts to convince people to accept a position or take a desired action. The following are some types of persuasion:

● **Persuasive Essay**

A persuasive essay presents a position on an issue, urges readers to accept that position, and may encourage a specific action.

An effective persuasive essay:
- *Explores an issue of importance to the writer*
- *Addresses an arguable issue*
- *Is supported by facts, examples, statistics, or personal experiences*
- *Tries to influence the audience through appeals to the readers' knowledge, experiences, or emotions*
- *Uses clear organization to present a logical argument*

Forms of persuasion include editorials, position papers, persuasive speeches, grant proposals, advertisements, and debates.

● **Advertisements**

An advertisement is a planned communication that is meant to be seen, heard, or read. It attempts to persuade an audience to buy or use a product or service. Advertisements may appear in print or broadcast form.

An effective advertisement includes:
- *A concept, or central theme*
- *A device, such as a memorable slogan, that catches people's attention*
- *Language that conveys a certain view of a product or issue*

Common types of advertisements include public service announcements, billboards, merchandise ads, service ads, and public campaign literature.

Exposition

Exposition is writing that relies on facts to inform or explain. Effective expository writing reflects an organization that is well planned—one that includes a clear introduction, body, and conclusion. The following are some types of exposition:

- **Comparison-and-Contrast Essay**
  A comparison-and-contrast essay analyzes similarities and differences between or among two or more things.

  An effective comparison-and-contrast essay:
  - *Identifies a purpose for comparing and contrasting*
  - *Identifies similarities and differences between or among two or more things, people, places, or ideas*
  - *Gives factual details about the subjects*
  - *Uses an organizational plan suited to the topic and purpose*

- **Cause-and-Effect Essay** A cause-and-effect essay examines the relationship between events, explaining how one event or situation causes another.

  A successful cause-and-effect essay includes:
  - *A discussion of a cause, event, or condition that produces a specific result*
  - *An explanation of an effect or result*
  - *Evidence and examples to support the relationship between cause and effect*
  - *A logical organization that makes the relationship between events clear*

- **Problem-and-Solution Essay** A problem-and-solution essay describes a problem and offers one or more solutions. It describes a clear set of steps to achieve a result.

  An effective problem-and-solution essay includes:
  - *A clear statement of the problem, with its causes and effects summarized*
  - *A proposal of at least one realistic solution*
  - *Facts, statistics, data, or expert testimony to support the solution*
  - *A clear organization that makes the relationship between problem and solution obvious*

Research Writing

Research writing is based on information gathered from outside sources.

An effective research paper:
- *Focuses on a specific, narrow topic*
- *Presents relevant information from a variety of sources*
- *Is clearly organized and includes an introduction, body, and conclusion*
- *Includes a bibliography or works-cited list*

In addition to traditional research reports, types of research writing include statistical reports and experiment journals.

Response to Literature

When you write a response to literature, you can discover how a piece of writing affected you.

An effective response:
- *Reacts to a work of literature*
- *Analyzes the content of a literary work*
- *Focuses on a single aspect or gives a general overview*
- *Supports opinion with evidence from the text*

You might respond to a literary work in reader's response journals, literary letters, and literary analyses.

Writing for Assessment

Essays are commonly part of school tests.

An effective essay includes:
- *A clearly stated and well-supported thesis*
- *Specific information about the topic derived from your reading or from class discussion*
- *A clear organization with an introduction, body, and conclusion*

In addition to writing essays for tests, you might write essays to apply to schools or special programs, or to enter a contest.

Workplace Writing

Workplace writing communicates information in a structured format.

Effective workplace writing:
- *Communicates information concisely*
- *Includes details that provide necessary information and anticipate potential questions*

Common types of workplace writing include business letters, memorandums, résumés, forms, and applications.

Writing Effective
Paragraphs

A paragraph is a group of sentences that share a common topic or purpose. Most paragraphs have a main idea or thought.

Stating the Main Idea in a Topic Sentence

The main idea of a paragraph is directly stated in a single sentence called the topic sentence. The rest of the sentences in the paragraph support or explain the topic sentence, providing support through facts and details.

Sometimes the main idea of a paragraph is implied rather than stated. The sentences work together to present the details and facts that allow the reader to infer the main idea.

WRITING MODELS

from **The Secret Language of Snow**
Terry Tempest Williams and Ted Major

Many types of animal behavior are designed to reduce heat loss. Birds fluff their feathers, enlarging the "dead air" space around their bodies. Quails roost in compact circles, in the same manner as musk oxen, to keep warmth in and cold out. Grouse and ptarmigan dive into the snow, using it as an insulating blanket.

In this passage, the stated topic sentence is highlighted.

from **"The Old Demon"**
Pearl S. Buck

The baker's shop, like everything else, was in ruins. No one was there. At first she saw nothing but the mass of crumpled earthen walls. But then she remembered that the oven was just inside the door, and the door frame still stood erect, supporting one end of the roof. She stood in this frame, and, running her hands in underneath the fallen roof inside, she felt the wooden cover of the iron cauldron. Under this there might be steamed bread. She worked her arm delicately and carefully in. It took quite a long time, but even so, clouds of lime and dust almost choked her. Nevertheless she was right. She squeezed her hand under the cover and felt the first smooth skin of the big steamed bread rolls, and one by one she drew out four.

In this passage, all the sentences work together to illustrate the implied main idea of the paragraph: The woman searches persistently until she finds food.

Writing a Topic Sentence

When you outline a topic or plan an essay, you identify the main points you want to address. Each of these points can be written as a topic sentence—a statement of the main idea of a topical paragraph. You can organize your paragraph around the topic sentence.

A good topic sentence tells readers what the paragraph is about and the point the writer wants to make about the subject matter. Here are some tips for writing a strong topic sentence.

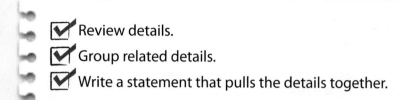

☑ Review details.

☑ Group related details.

☑ Write a statement that pulls the details together.

Writing Supporting Sentences

Whether your topic sentence is stated or implied, it guides the rest of the paragraph. The rest of the sentences in the paragraph will either develop, explain, or support that topic sentence.

You can support or develop the idea by using one or more of the following strategies:

Use Facts

Facts are statements that can be proved. They support your key idea by providing proof.

- **Topic Sentence:** Our football team is tough to beat.
- **Supporting Fact:** It wins almost all of its games.

Use Statistics

A statistic is a fact, usually stated using numbers.

- **Topic Sentence:** Our football team is tough to beat.
- **Supporting Statistic:** The football team's record is 10–1.

Use Examples, Illustrations, or Instances

An example, illustration, or instance is a specific thing, person, or event that demonstrates a point.

- **Topic Sentence:** Our football team is tough to beat.
- **Illustration:** Last week, the team beat the previously undefeated Tigers in an exciting upset game.

Use Details

Details are the specifics— the parts of the whole. They make your point or main idea clear by showing how all the pieces fit together.

- **Topic Sentence:** Our footbal team is tough to beat.
- **Detail:** There were only seconds left in last week's game, when the quarterback threw the winning pass.

Placing Your Topic Sentence

Frequently, the topic sentence appears at the beginning of a paragraph. Topic sentences can, however, be placed at the beginning, middle, or end of the paragraph. Place your topic sentence at the beginning of a paragraph to focus readers' attention. Place your topic sentence in the middle of a paragraph when you must lead into your main idea. Place your topic sentence at the end of a paragraph to emphasize your main idea.

Paragraph Patterns

Sentences in a paragraph can be arranged in several different patterns, depending on where you place your topic sentence. One common pattern is the TRI pattern (Topic, Restatement, Illustration).

- **T**opic sentence (State your main idea.)
- **R**estatement (Interpret your main idea; use different wording.)
- **I**llustration (Support your main idea with facts and examples.)

T	Participating in after-school clubs is one of the ways you can meet new people. Getting involved in extracurricular
R	activities brings you in contact with a wide range of individuals. The drama club, for example, brings together
I	students from several different grades.

Variations on the TRI pattern include sentence arrangements such as TIR, TII, IIT, or ITR.

I	This month alone the service club at our high school delivered meals to thirty shut-ins. In addition, members
I	beautified the neighborhood with new plantings. If any school-sponsored club deserves increased support, the
T	service club does.

Paragraphs
in Essays
and Other Compositions

To compose means "to put the parts together, to create." Most often, composing refers to the creation of a musical or literary work—a composition. You may not think of the reports, essays, and test answers you write as literary works, but they are compositions. To write an effective composition, you must understand the parts.

The Introduction

The introduction does what its name suggests. It introduces the topic of the composition. An effective introduction begins with a strong lead, a first sentence that captures readers' interest. The lead is followed by the thesis statement, the key point of the composition. Usually, the thesis statement is followed by a few sentences that outline how the writer will make the key point.

The Body

The body of a composition consists of several paragraphs that develop, explain, and support the key idea expressed in the thesis statement. The body of a composition should be unified and coherent. The paragraphs in a composition should work together to support the thesis statement. The topic of each paragraph should relate directly to the thesis statement and be arranged in a logical organization.

The Conclusion

The conclusion is the final paragraph of the composition. The conclusion restates the thesis and sums up the support. Often, the conclusion includes the writer's reflection or observation on the topic. An effective conclusion ends on a memorable note, for example, with a quotation or call to action.

Recognizing Types of Paragraphs

There are several types of paragraphs you can use in your writing.

Topical Paragraphs

A topical paragraph is a group of sentences that contain one key sentence or idea and several sentences that support or develop that key idea or topic sentence.

Functional Paragraphs

Functional paragraphs serve a specific purpose. They may not have a topic sentence, but they are unified and coherent because the sentences (if there is more than one) are clearly connected and follow a logical order. Functional paragraphs can be used for the following purposes:

- **To create emphasis** A very short paragraph of one or two sentences focuses the reader on what is being said because it breaks the reader's rhythm.

- **To indicate dialogue** One of the conventions of written dialogue is that a new paragraph begins each time the speaker changes.

- **To make a transition** A short paragraph can help readers move between the main ideas in two topical paragraphs.

WRITING MODEL

from **"The Hatchling Turtles"**

by Jean Craighead George

One morning each small turtle fought for freedom within its shell.

They hatched two feet down in the sand, all of them on the same day. As they broke out, their shells collapsed, leaving a small room of air for them to breathe. It wasn't much of a room, just big enough for them to wiggle in and move toward the sky. As they wiggled they pulled the sand down from the ceiling and crawled up on it. In this manner the buried room began to rise, slowly, inch by inch.

The highlighted functional paragraph emphasizes the struggle of the turtles to emerge from their shells.

Paragraph Blocks

Sometimes, you may have so much information to support or develop a main idea that it "outgrows" a single paragraph. When a topic sentence or main idea requires an extensive explanation or support, you can develop the idea in a paragraph block—several paragraphs that work together and function as a unit. Each paragraph in the block supports the key idea or topic sentence. By breaking the development of the idea into separate paragraphs, you make your ideas clearer.

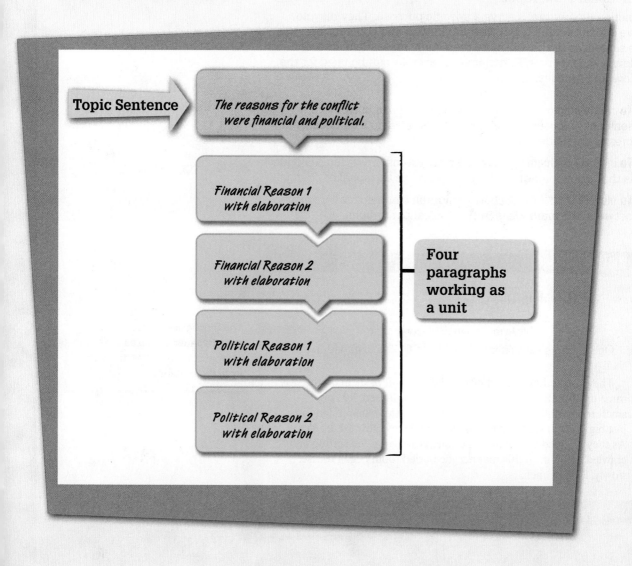

Topic Sentence

The reasons for the conflict were financial and political.

Financial Reason 1 with elaboration

Financial Reason 2 with elaboration

Political Reason 1 with elaboration

Political Reason 2 with elaboration

Four paragraphs working as a unit

Qualities
of Good Writing

The quality of your writing depends on how well you develop six important traits: ideas, organization, voice, word choice, sentence fluency, and conventions.

Organization

Organization refers to the way in which the ideas and details are arranged in a piece of writing. To enable readers to follow your ideas, choose an organization that makes sense for your topic, and stick with that organization throughout the piece of writing.

Ideas

Good writing begins with interesting ideas. Explore topics that you find interesting and that you think will interest others. Focus on presenting information that will be new and fresh to readers.

Voice

Just as you have a distinctive way of expressing yourself when you speak, you can develop a distinctive voice as a writer. Your voice consists of the topics you choose, the attitude you express toward those topics, the words you use, and the rhythm of your sentences. By developing your own voice, you let your personality come through in your writing.

Conventions

Conventions refer to the grammatical correctness of a piece of writing. Don't let errors in grammar, usage, mechanics, and spelling interfere with your message.

Word Choice

Words are the building blocks of a piece of writing. By choosing precise and vivid words, you will add strength to your writing and enable readers to follow your ideas and picture the things that you describe.

Sentence Fluency

In a piece of writing, it is important that sentences flow well from one to another. By using a variety of sentences—different lengths and different structures—and using transitions to connect them, you will create smooth rhythm in your writing.

Stages of the Writing Process

Writing is called a process because it goes through a series of changes or stages. These five stages are:

PREWRITING DRAFTING REVISING EDITING PUBLISHING

- In **prewriting**, you explore an idea by using various prewriting techniques, such as brainstorming and questioning.

- In **drafting**, you get your ideas down on paper or on the computer in roughly the format you intend.

- Once you finish your first draft, you decide on the changes, or **revisions**, you want to make.

- Finally, when you are happy with your work, you **edit** it, checking the accuracy of facts and for errors in spelling, grammar, usage, and mechanics.

- You then make a final copy and **publish** it, or share it with an audience.

You will not always progress through these stages in a straight line. You can backtrack to a previous stage, repeat a stage many times, or put the stages in a different sequence to fit your needs. To get an idea of what the writing process is like, study the following diagram. Notice that the arrows in the drafting and revising sections can lead you back to prewriting.

Prewriting
- Using prewriting techniques to gather ideas
- Choosing a purpose and an audience
- Ordering ideas

Drafting
- Putting ideas down on paper
- Exploring new ideas as you write

Publishing
- Producing a final polished copy of your writing
- Sharing your writing

Revising
- Consulting with peer readers
- Evaluating suggested changes
- Making revisions

Editing
- Checking the accuracy of facts
- Correcting errors in spelling, grammar, usage, and mechanics

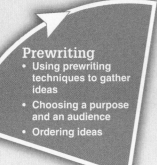

Prewriting
- Using prewriting techniques to gather ideas
- Choosing a purpose and an audience
- Ordering ideas

Prewriting

No matter what kind of writing assignment you are given, you can use prewriting techniques to find and develop a topic. Some prewriting techniques will work better than others for certain kinds of assignments.

Choosing a Topic

Try some of the following ways to find topics that fit your assignment.

● **Look Through Newspapers and Magazines** In the library or at home, flip through recent magazines or newspapers. Jot down each interesting person, place, event, or topic you come across. Review your notes and choose a topic that you find especially interesting and would like to learn more about.

● **Keep an Events Log** Every day you probably encounter many situations about which you have opinions. One way to remember these irksome issues is to keep an events log. For a set period of time—a day or a week—take a small notebook with you wherever you go. Whenever you come across something you feel strongly about, write it down. After the specified time period, review your journal and select a topic.

● **Create a Personal Experience Timeline** Choose a memorable period in your life and map out the events that occurred during that period. Create a timeline in which you enter events in the order they occurred. Then, review your timeline and choose the event or events that would make the most interesting topic.

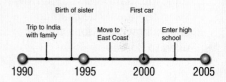

Narrowing Your Topic

Note that narrowing a topic is not an exact science. It is part of the creative process of writing, which involves experimentation and leads to discovery. Here are some specific techniques you can use.

● **Questioning** Asking questions often helps narrow your topic to fit the time and space you have available. Try asking some of the six questions that journalists use when writing news stories: *Who? What? When? Why? Where?* and *How?* Then, based on your answers, refocus on a narrow aspect of your topic.

● **Using Reference Materials** The reference materials you use to find information can also help you narrow a broad topic. Look up your subject in an encyclopedia, or find a book on it at the library. Scan the resource, looking for specific, narrow topics. Sometimes a resource will be divided into sections or chapters that each deal with a specific topic.

● **Using Graphic Devices** Another way to narrow a topic is to combine questioning with a graphic device, such as a cluster or inverted pyramid. Draw one in your notebook or journal, and write your broad topics across the top of the upside-down pyramid. Then, as the pyramid narrows to a point, break down your broad topic into narrower and narrower subcategories. The graphic shows how questions can be used to do this.

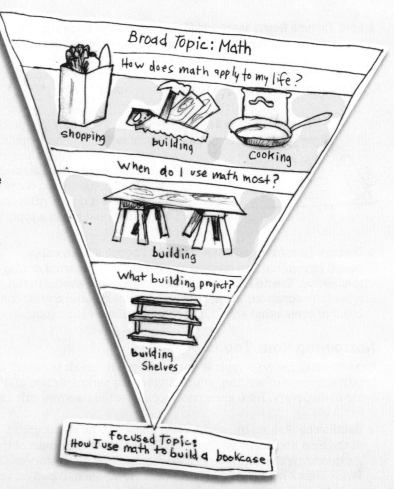

Broad Topic: Math

How does math apply to my life?

shopping   building   Cooking

When do I use math most?

building

What building project?

building Shelves

Focused Topic:
How I use math to build a bookcase

Purpose and Audience

Every piece of writing is written for an audience. Even when you write a secret in your journal, you are writing for an audience of one—yourself. To succeed in any writing task, you have to understand what your audience wants and needs to know.

Pinpointing your purpose is also essential when you write. Sometimes you write to fulfill an assignment; at other times you decide to whom you will write and why. For example, you might decide to write a letter to your sister about your bunkmates at camp. Your purpose might be to describe your bunkmates' looks and personalities. Another time you might write a letter to your principal about cellphones. Your purpose might be to convince her to ban cellphones inside your school.

● **Defining Your Purpose and Audience** Answering certain questions can help you define your purpose for writing and identify your audience.

- *What is my topic?*
- *What is my purpose for writing?*
- *Who is my audience?*
- *What does my audience already know about this topic?*
- *What does my audience need or want to know?*
- *What type of language will suit my audience and purpose?*

Gathering Details

After finding a topic to write about, you will want to explore and develop your ideas. You can do this on your own or with classmates. The following techniques may help you.

● **Interview a Classmate** Questioning a classmate can help both of you develop your topics. You can interview a friend who has a special skill. Find out how she or he developed that skill. You could also find an interview partner and question each other on an acceptable topic.

- **Fill In an Observation Chart** To come up with details to develop a piece of descriptive writing or to help you create the setting and characters for a narrative, you can fill in an observation chart. A writer created the chart that follows while wondering how to describe the school cafeteria at lunch time.

Once you have completed your own observation chart, circle the details you want to include in your piece of writing.

SUBJECT: *CAFETERIA AT LUNCHTIME*

See	Hear	Touch	Smell	Taste
swirl of motion	kids' voices	hot melted cheese	stuff they wash the floors with	tart juice
fluorescent lights	thuds and clunks of chairs and trays	wet plastic trays	delicious aroma of pizza	pepperoni
colors of plastic trays	scraping of chairs	cold, wet milk cartons	apple crisp baking	mild cheese

- **Do a Focused Freewriting** Freewriting can be used to either find or develop a topic. When it is used to develop a topic, it is called focused freewriting. Follow these four steps as you use focused freewriting to develop a topic:

1. Set a time limit. (Until you get used to freewriting, write for no more than five minutes at a time.)

2. Repeat to yourself the key words of your topic, and then write whatever comes to mind about them. Do not stop; do not read or correct what you write.

3. If you get stuck, repeat a word (even the word *stuck*), or write the last word you wrote until new ideas come. You can be sure they will.

4. When the time is up, read what you wrote. Underline parts that you like best. Decide which of these parts you will use in your piece of writing.

Drafting

Drafting
- Putting ideas down on paper
- Exploring new ideas as you write

In writing, an **organizational plan** is an outline or map that shows the key ideas and details that you want to include in the order that you want to include them. Following such a plan can help you structure your writing so that it makes a clearer and stronger impression on your audience.

Organizing Your Ideas

Often, a piece of writing lends itself to a particular order. For instance, if you are describing a scene so that readers can visualize it, spatial order may be your best option. However, if you are describing a person, you might compare and contrast the person with someone else you and your readers know, or you might reveal the person's character by describing a series of past incidents in chronological order.

ORGANIZATIONAL PLANS

Chronological Order	Events or details are arranged in the order in which they occur. Words showing **chronological order** include *first, next,* and *finally.*
Spatial Order	Details are given by location so that readers can visualize the scene, object, or person. Expressions showing **spatial order** include *to the right (or left), in the middle, nearby, in front of, on, beside, behind,* and *next to.*
Order of Importance	Events and details are arranged from the least to the most significant, or vice versa. Expressions showing **order of importance** include *most important, above all,* and *also.*
Logical Order	Each point that is made builds on previous information, and ideas are clearly linked. Expressions showing **logical order** include *it follows that, for example,* and *therefore.*

Introductions

The introduction to your paper should include a **thesis statement**, a sentence about your central purpose or what you plan to "show" in your paper. Here is a thesis statement for a paper on the ancient Kingdom of Ghana:

> Ghana was one of the strongest, richest kingdoms of its time.

An effective written introduction draws your readers into your paper and interests them in the subject. The way you introduce your paper depends on the goal you want to achieve and the type of writing you are doing. The following are some possibilities.

GOAL	TYPE OF INTRODUCTION	COULD BE USED FOR
Be clear and direct	a statement of the main point	• an informative paper • a research report • an editorial
Appeal to readers' senses	a vivid description	• a description of a scene • an observation report • a character sketch
Get readers' attention	a startling fact or statistic	• an informative paper • a persuasive essay • a research report
Lure readers into the story quickly	dialogue	• a story • a personal narrative
Make readers wonder	a question	• an informative paper • a persuasive essay • a research report
Give your writing authority	a quotation	• a persuasive essay • an informative paper • a research report • a book review or report

Elaboration

Sometimes what you write seems to be only the bare bones of a composition. In order to flesh out your work, you must add the right details. This process is called **elaboration**.

Certain types of elaboration are more effective for certain forms of writing, but there are no hard-and-fast rules about which type of elaboration to use. You can use facts and statistics in a poem if you want to! Some types of elaboration include the following:

Facts and Statistics	Facts are statements that can be proved true. Statistics are facts that you express as numbers.
Sensory Details	Sensory details are details that appeal to the five senses—sight, hearing, touch, smell, and taste.
Anecdotes	An anecdote is a short account of an interesting or funny incident.
Examples	An example is an instance of something.
Quotations	A quotation is someone's words—often those of an expert or public figure.
Personal Feelings	Personal feelings are thoughts and emotions that are yours alone.
Memories	Memories are recollections from the past.
Observations	Observations are things you have seen or noticed firsthand.
Reasons	Reasons are explanations of why something is true.

● **Uses of Elaboration** Here is a chart showing the types of elaboration you can use and what each is used for.

TYPE OF ELABORATION		USED FOR	
facts and statistics	▶	essays news stories feature articles business letters	advertisements reviews research reports
sensory details	▶	observations poems personal essays advertisements	stories plays descriptions
anecdotes	▶	journal entries personal letters news stories	personal essays feature articles
examples	▶	essays news stories business letters editorials advertisements poems	responses to literature book reports research reports feature articles reviews
quotations	▶	news stories feature articles essays	responses to literature book reports
personal feelings	▶	journal entries personal letters personal essays poems	editorials observations responses to literature persuasive essays
memories	▶	journal entries personal letters personal essays poems	descriptions observations stories
observations	▶	journal entries personal letters personal essays poems	reviews feature articles stories plays
reasons	▶	essays business letters reviews book reports news stories feature articles	editorials advertisements research reports responses to literature personal essays

Conclusions

The type of conclusion you will use depends on your subject and on your purpose. Here are some ways to end a paper effectively, with suggestions on what type of writing might best suit each type of conclusion.

- **Summarize Your Main Points** Review the most important ideas you have discussed and what you have said about them. Instead of just listing them, try to present them in a creative way. This will help you remember your key ideas.

  This is a great way to conclude the following types of writing:
  - *observation report*
  - *personal essay*
  - *research report*
  - *informative essay*
  - *comparison-and-contrast essay*

- **Resolve Conflicts and Problems** Bring your narrative to a close by addressing unanswered questions. Did the main character survive the battle? Did the enemies become friends?

  This is especially important when you are writing the following:
  - *personal narrative or autobiographical incident*
  - *story or fable*
  - *play*

- **Recommend an Action or Solution** You have presented your readers with an issue or problem. Now tell them what they can do about it. This will enable them to do something constructive after reading.

  This is a great way to conclude these writing pieces:
  - *persuasive essay*
  - *letter to the editor*
  - *problem-and-solution essay*

- **Offer a Final Comment or Ask a Question** Talk directly to your readers. You can do this by sharing your personal feelings, asking questions, or both. This will make your readers feel more involved.

  This is a great way to conclude the following:
  - *personal letter*
  - *persuasive essay*
  - *response to literature*
  - *review*

Revising

Revising
- Consulting with peer readers
- Evaluating suggested changes
- Making revisions

When you have included all your ideas and finished your first draft, you are ready to revise it. Few writers produce perfect drafts the first time around. You can almost always improve your paper by reworking it. Here are some hints to help you revise your work.

 Take a Break Do not begin to revise right after you finish a draft. In a few hours or days you will be better able to see the strengths and weaknesses of your work.

 Look It Over When you reread your draft, look for ways to improve it. Use a pencil to mark places where an idea is unclear or the writing is jumpy or disjointed. Also, remember to let yourself know when you have written an effective image or provided a wonderful example. Write Good! next to the parts that work well.

 Read Aloud Your ear is a wonderful editor. Read your work aloud and listen for dull, unnecessary, or awkward parts that you did not notice when you read your work silently. Are there any passages that you stumble over as you read aloud? Try different wordings and then read them aloud with expression, emphasizing certain words. Listen and identify which wording sounds best.

 Share Your Work Your friends or family members can help you by telling you how your work affects them. Ask them whether your ideas are clear. What is interesting? What is boring?

When it is time to revise a draft, many writers are tempted to just correct a few spelling mistakes and combine a sentence or two. Eliminating surface errors, however, is only a small part of revising. After all, what good is a neat and perfectly spelled paper if it does not make sense or prove a point? The word *revise* means "to see again" or "to see from a new perspective." In order to revise your work, you need to rethink your basic ideas.

Revising by Rethinking

Taking a close look at the ideas in your draft is the most important part of revising. Usually, you will spot some "idea" problems. When you do, it is time to get to work. Here are some strategies to help you rethink your draft.

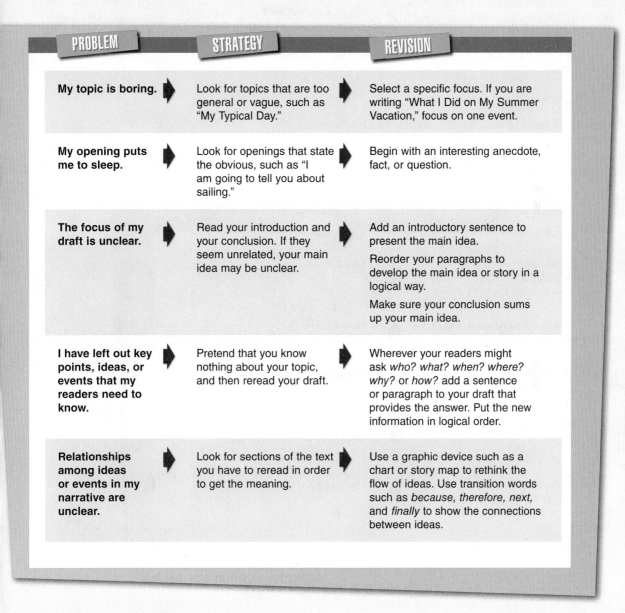

PROBLEM	STRATEGY	REVISION
My topic is boring.	Look for topics that are too general or vague, such as "My Typical Day."	Select a specific focus. If you are writing "What I Did on My Summer Vacation," focus on one event.
My opening puts me to sleep.	Look for openings that state the obvious, such as "I am going to tell you about sailing."	Begin with an interesting anecdote, fact, or question.
The focus of my draft is unclear.	Read your introduction and your conclusion. If they seem unrelated, your main idea may be unclear.	Add an introductory sentence to present the main idea. Reorder your paragraphs to develop the main idea or story in a logical way. Make sure your conclusion sums up your main idea.
I have left out key points, ideas, or events that my readers need to know.	Pretend that you know nothing about your topic, and then reread your draft.	Wherever your readers might ask *who? what? when? where? why?* or *how?* add a sentence or paragraph to your draft that provides the answer. Put the new information in logical order.
Relationships among ideas or events in my narrative are unclear.	Look for sections of the text you have to reread in order to get the meaning.	Use a graphic device such as a chart or story map to rethink the flow of ideas. Use transition words such as *because, therefore, next,* and *finally* to show the connections between ideas.

Revising by Elaborating

When you are sure your ideas are clear and in order, it is time to judge whether you have provided enough appropriate details. Remember, elaborating means developing and expanding on ideas by adding the right details. These details will help develop your ideas in clear and interesting ways.

You might choose any of the following types of details explained on page 327:

- *facts and statistics*
- *sensory details*
- *anecdotes*
- *examples*
- *quotations*
- *personal feelings*
- *memories*
- *observations*
- *reasons*

Revising by Reducing

Just as you need to add specific details when you revise your draft, you sometimes need to get rid of material that is unnecessary. Following are some ways you can solve revision problems by removing unneeded words.

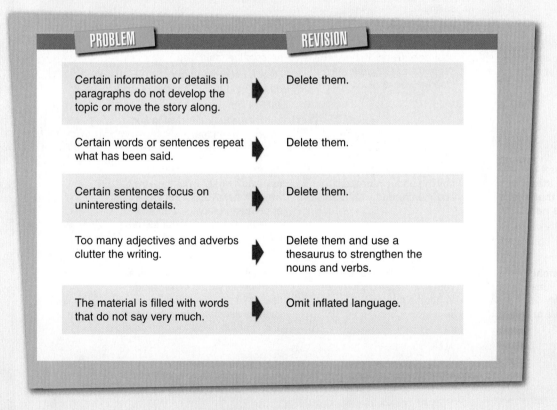

PROBLEM	REVISION
Certain information or details in paragraphs do not develop the topic or move the story along.	Delete them.
Certain words or sentences repeat what has been said.	Delete them.
Certain sentences focus on uninteresting details.	Delete them.
Too many adjectives and adverbs clutter the writing.	Delete them and use a thesaurus to strengthen the nouns and verbs.
The material is filled with words that do not say very much.	Omit inflated language.

Revising by Rewording

Choosing the right words is essential to good writing. As a final step in revising, improve your choice of words. At times, a better word will spring to mind. At other times, use a thesaurus to find words. As you rework your draft, you will reveal your own style.

The following chart can help you find the right word.

PROBLEM

Have I used the most effective word possible?

REVISION ACTIVITIES:

Choose specific nouns.
General: I wish I had some food.
Specific: I wish I had some pizza.

Choose active, colorful verbs.
General: The sick man walked to his bed.
Specific: The sick man hobbled to his bed.

Avoid the word *be*.
General: My horse is a good jumper.
Specific: My horse easily jumps four feet.

Choose the active voice.
General: Chocolate should never be fed to dogs.
Specific: Never feed dogs chocolate.

Editing

Editing is the process of finding and correcting errors in grammar, usage, and mechanics. When you have finished drafting and revising your paper, here is how to edit your work.

General Tips

- Look first for mistakes that you typically make.
- Proofread your paper for one type of error at a time.
- Read your work aloud word for word.
- When in doubt, use reference sources to help you.

Here are some specific editing strategies that may help you.

SPECIFIC TASKS

STRATEGY

Check Your Grammar

Have you written any run-on sentences or fragments?

Do your subjects and verbs agree?

 Check that each sentence has a subject and verb. Use a comma and conjunction to connect main clauses.

Make sure that singular subjects have singular verbs and plural subjects have plural verbs.

Check Your Usage

Have you used the past forms of irregular verbs correctly?

Have you used subject and object pronouns correctly?

Watch out for irregular verb forms such as *seen, done, gone,* and *taken.*

Check that the pronouns *me, him, her, us,* and *them* are used only after verbs or prepositions.

Check Your Punctuation

Does each sentence have the correct end mark?

Have you used apostrophes in nouns, but not in pronouns, to show possession?

Have you used quotation marks around words from another source?

Look for inverted word order that may signal a question.

Use a phrase with *of* to check for possession.

Avoid plagiarism by checking your notecards to be sure.

Check Your Capitalization

Did you begin each sentence or direct quotation with a capital letter?

Have you capitalized proper nouns?

Look for an end mark and then check the next letter.

Look for the name of specific people and places.

Check Your Spelling

Did you correctly spell all words?

Use a dictionary. Look for your common errors.

Publishing

Publishing
- Producing a final polished copy of your writing
- Sharing your writing

Once you have made a final, clean copy of a piece of writing that pleases you, you may want to share it with others. What you have to say might be important or meaningful to someone else. Here are some ways you can publish your writing—that is, bring it to the public eye.

- Submit your work to a school newspaper or magazine.

- Have a public reading of your work. Perform it in one of the following ways:
  - Over the school P.A. or radio system
  - In a school assembly or talent show
  - In a group in which members take turns reading their work
  - At your local library or community center

- If your work is a play or skit, have a group of classmates or the drama club present it.

- Work with classmates to put together a class collection of written work. You can have it copied and bound at a copy shop.

- Submit your piece to a local or national writing contest.

- Send your writing to a local newspaper or area magazine.

- Publish your own work and the writings of classmates by using a computer with a desktop publishing program.

Reflecting

Your writing can help you learn about your subject or the writing process—or even yourself. Once you have completed a writing assignment, sit back and think about the experience for a few minutes.

Ask yourself questions such as the following:

- What did I learn about my subject through my writing?

- Did I experiment with writing techniques and forms? If so, were my experiments successful? If not, what held me back?

- Am I pleased with what I wrote? Why or why not?

- Did I have difficulty with any part of the writing process? If so, which part gave me trouble? What strategies did I use to overcome my difficulties?

This resource section contains tips on writing in English and information on grammar topics that are sometimes challenging for English learners.

The numbered arrows in the side margins also appear on other pages of the Grammar Handbook that provide information on writing or instruction in these same grammar topics.

EL1

Understand the Demands of Writing in a Second Language

Talk with other writers.

When you write in an unfamiliar situation, it may be helpful to find a few examples of the type of writing you are trying to produce. For example, if you are writing a letter of application to accompany a résumé, ask your friends to share similar letters of application with you and look for the various ways your friends presented themselves in writing in that situation.

Use your native language as a resource.

You can also use your native language to develop your texts. Many people, when they cannot find an appropriate word in English, write down a word, a phrase, or even a sentence in their native language and consult a dictionary later. Incorporating key terms from your native language is also a possible strategy.

A Japanese term adds perspective to this sentence.

"Some political leaders need to have *wakimae*—a realistic idea of one's own place in the world."

Use dictionaries.

Bilingual dictionaries are especially useful when you want to check your understanding of an English word or find equivalent words for culture-specific concepts and technical terms. Some bilingual dictionaries also provide sample sentences.

Learner's dictionaries, such as the *Longman Dictionary of American English,* include information about count/non-count nouns and transitive/intransitive verbs. Many of them also provide sample sentences.

Understand English idioms.

Some English idioms function like proverbs. In the United States, for example, if someone has to "eat crow," they have been forced to admit they were wrong about something. But simpler examples of idiomatic usage—word order, word choice, and combinations that don't follow any obvious set of rules—are common in even the plainest English. If you are unsure about idioms, use Google or another search engine to find out how to use them.

INCORRECT IDIOM	Here is the answer **of** your question.
ACCEPTED IDIOM	Here is the answer **to** your question.
INCORRECT IDIOM	I had jet **legs** after flying across the Pacific.
ACCEPTED IDIOM	I had jet **lag** after flying across the Pacific.

Understand Nouns in English

Perhaps the most troublesome conventions for nonnative speakers are those that guide usage of the common articles *the, a,* and *an.* To understand how articles work in English, you must first understand how the language uses **nouns.**

Proper nouns and common nouns

EL2

There are two basic kinds of nouns. A **proper noun** begins with a capital letter and names a unique person, place, or thing: *Elvis Presley, Russia, Eiffel Tower.*

The other basic kind of noun is called a **common noun**. Common nouns such as *man, country* and *tower,* do not name a unique person, place, or thing. Common nouns are not names and are not capitalized unless they are the first word in a sentence.

PROPER NOUNS
Beethoven   Michael Jordan   Honda
South Korea   Africa
Empire State Building

COMMON NOUNS
composer   athlete   vehicle   country
continent   building

Count and non-count nouns

EL3

Common nouns can be classified as either **count** or **non-count**. Count nouns can be made plural, usually by adding the letter *s (finger, fingers)* or by using their plural forms (*person, people; datum, data*).

Non-count nouns cannot be counted directly and cannot take the plural form (*information,* but not *informations; garbage,* but not *garbages*). Some nouns can be either count or non-count, depending on how they are used. *Hair* can refer to either a strand of hair, when it serves as a count noun, or a mass of hair, when it becomes a non-count noun.

Count nouns usually take both singular and plural forms, while non-count nouns usually do not take plural forms and are not counted directly. A count noun can have a number before it (as in *two books, three oranges*) and can be qualified with adjectives such as *many* (as in *many books*), *some* (as in *some schools*), and *few* (as in *few people volunteered*).

Non-count nouns can be counted or quantified in only two ways: either by general adjectives that treat the noun as a mass (*much* information, *some* news) or by placing another noun between the quantifying word and the non-count noun (two *kinds* of information, a *piece* of news).

CORRECT USE OF HAIR AS A COUNT NOUN
Three blonde hairs were in the sink.

CORRECT USE OF HAIR AS A NON-COUNT NOUN
My roommate spent an hour combing his hair.

INCORRECT	five horse many accident
CORRECT	five horses many accidents
INCORRECT	three breads I would like a mustard on my hot dog.
CORRECT	three loaves of bread I would like some mustard on my hot dog.

Understand Articles in English

EL4

Articles indicate that a noun is about to appear, and they clarify what the noun refers to. There are only two kinds of articles in English, definite and indefinite.

1. **the:** *The* is a **definite article,** meaning that it refers to (1) a specific object already known to the reader, (2) one about to be made known to the reader, or (3) a unique object.

2. **a, an:** The **indefinite articles** *a* and *an* refer to an object whose specific identity is not known to the reader. The only difference between *a* and *an* is that *a* is used before a consonant sound (*a man, a friend, a yellow toy*), while *an* is used before a vowel sound (*an orange, an old shoe*).

Look at these sentences, which are identical except for their articles, and imagine that each is taken from a different newspaper story.

Rescue workers lifted **the** man to safety.

Rescue workers lifted **a** man to safety.

By using the definite article *the*, the first sentence indicates that the reader already knows something about the identity of this man. The news story has already referred to him.

The indefinite article *a* in the second sentence indicates that the reader does not know anything about this man. Either this is the first time the news story has referred to him, or there are other men in need of rescue.

RULES FOR USING ARTICLES

1. *A* or *an* is not used with non-count nouns.

   INCORRECT The crowd hummed with **an** excitement.
   CORRECT The crowd hummed with excitement.

2. *A* or *an* is used with singular count nouns whose identity is unknown to the reader or writer.

   INCORRECT Detective Johnson was reading book.
   CORRECT Detective Johnson was reading **a** book.

3. *The* is used with most count and non-count nouns whose particular identity is known to readers.

   CORRECT I bought a book yesterday. **The** book is about kayaking.

4. *The* is used when the noun is accompanied by a superlative form of a modifier: for example, *best, worst, highest, lowest, most expensive, least interesting.*

   CORRECT **The** most interesting book about climbing Mount Everest is Jon Krakauer's *Into Thin Air.*

Understand Verbs and Modifiers in English

Verbs, verb phrases, and helping verbs

EL5

Verbs in English can be divided between one-word verbs like *run, speak,* and *look,* and verb phrases like *may have run, have spoken,* and *will be looking.* The words that appear before the main verbs—*may, have, will, do,* and *be*—are called **auxiliary (or helping) verbs.** Auxiliary verbs help express something about the action of main verbs: for example, when the action occurs, whether the subject acted or was acted upon, or whether or not an action occurred.

Indicating tense with *be* verbs

EL6

Like the auxiliary verbs *have* and *do, be* changes form to signal tense. In addition to *be* itself, the **be verbs** are *is, am, are, was, were,* and *been.*

To show ongoing action, *be* verbs are followed by the present participle, which is a verb ending in *-ing.*

INCORRECT	I **am think** of all the things I'd rather **be do**.
CORRECT	I **am thinking** of all the things I'd rather **be doing**.

To show that an action is being done to the subject rather than by the subject, follow *be* verbs with the past participle (a verb usually ending in *-ed, -en,* or *-t*).

INCORRECT	The movie **was direct** by John Woo.
CORRECT	The movie **was directed** by John Woo.

Auxiliary verbs that express certain conditions

EL7

The auxiliary verbs *will, would, can, could, may, might, shall, must,* and *should* express conditions like possibility, permission, speculation, expectation, and necessity. Unlike the auxiliary verbs *be, have,* and *do,* the auxiliary verbs listed above do not change form based on the grammatical subject of the sentence (*I, you, she, he, it, we, they*).

Two basic rules apply to all uses of these auxiliary verbs. First, these auxiliary verbs are always followed by the simple form of the verb. The simple form is the verb by itself, in the present tense, such as *talk* but not *talked, talking,* or *to talk.*

INCORRECT	She **should studies** harder to pass the exam.
CORRECT	She **should study** harder to pass the exam.

The second rule is that you should not use these auxiliary verbs consecutively.

INCORRECT	If you work harder at writing, you **might could** improve.
CORRECT	If you work harder at writing, you **might** improve.

1. **Speculation:** If you had flown, you **would** have arrived yesterday.

2. **Ability:** She **can** run faster than Jennifer.

3. **Necessity:** You **must** know what you want to do.

4. **Intention:** He **will** wash his own clothes.

5. **Permission:** You **may** leave now.

6. **Advice:** You **should** wash behind your ears.

7. **Possibility:** It **might** be possible to go home early.

8. **Assumption:** You **must** have stayed up late last night.

9. **Expectation:** You **should** enjoy the movie.

10. **Order:** You **must** leave the building.

Placement of Modifiers

EL8

Modifiers will be unclear if your reader can't connect them to the words to which they refer. How close a modifier is to the noun or verb it modifies provides an important clue to their relationship.

Clarity should be your first goal when using a modifier.

UNCLEAR	Many pedestrians are killed each year by motorists **not using sidewalks**.
CLEAR	Many pedestrians **not using sidewalks** are killed each year by motorists.

An **adverb**—a word or group of words that modifies a verb, adjective, or another adverb—should not come between a verb and its direct object.

AWKWARD	The hurricane destroyed **completely** the city's tallest building.
BETTER	The hurricane **completely** destroyed the city's tallest building.

Try to avoid placing an adverb between *to* and its verb. This construction is called a **split infinitive**.

AWKWARD	The water level was predicted **to not rise**.
BETTER	The water level was predicted **not to rise**.

Understand English Sentence Structure

Words derive much of their meaning from how they function in a sentence.

With the exception of **imperatives** (commands such as *Watch out!*), sentences in English usually contain a *subject* and a *predicate*. A subject names who or what the sentence is about; the predicate tells what the subject is or does.

The Lion	is asleep.
subject	predicate

A predicate consists of at least one main verb. If the verb is **intransitive,** like *exist,* it does not take a direct object. Some verbs are **transitive,** which means they require a **direct object** to complete their meaning.

INCORRECT	The bird saw.
CORRECT	The bird saw a cat.

Some verbs (*write, learn, read,* and others) can be both transitive and intransitive, depending on how they are used.

INTRANSITIVE	Pilots fly.
TRANSITIVE	Pilots fly airplanes.

Formal written English requires that each sentence includes a subject and a verb, even when the meaning of the sentence would be clear without it. In some cases you must supply an expletive, such as *it* and *there*.

INCORRECT	Is snowing in Alaska.
CORRECT	It is snowing in Alaska.